The Archetypal Sunnī Scholar

The Archetypal Sunnī Scholar

Law, Theology, and Mysticism in the Synthesis of al-Bājūrī

Aaron Spevack

SUNY PRESS

Published by State University of New York Press, Albany

Printed in the United States of America

For information, contact State University of New York Press, Albany, NY
www.sunypress.edu

Production by Diane Ganeles
Marketing by Michael Campochiaro

Library of Congress Cataloging-in-Publication Data

Spevack, Aaron.
The archetypal Sunni scholar : law, theology, and mysticism in the synthesis of al-Bajuri / Aaron Spevack.
pages cm
Includes bibliographical references and index.
ISBN 978-1-4384-5371-2 (hardcover : alk. paper)
ISBN 978-1-4384-5370-5 (pbk. : alk. paper)
1. Bajuri, Ibrahim ibn Muhammad, 1783 or 1784–1860. 2. Muslim scholars—Egypt—Biography. I. Title.

BP80.B23515S74 2014
[B] 2014001946

10 9 8 7 6 5 4 3 2 1

Contents

Acknowledgments

The subject of this work, Ibrāhīm al-Bājūrī, begins each of his commentaries by discussing the tradition of starting one's works with the name of Allah, followed by praising Him, and then sending peace and blessings on the Prophet Muhammad. In keeping with al-Bājūrī's tradition, I too begin this work as such.

This work has undergone a number of transformations since it began as a dissertation proposal at Boston University. I am very grateful for the masterful guidance of my dissertation advisers, Professors Herbert Mason, Merlin Swartz, and Diana Lobel, whose careful and patient advice led to the first incarnation of this work. Support for research and writing the dissertation was made possible through the generosity of Boston University's University Professors Program. Some of the English translations of various Arabic passages in the dissertation, most of which remain in the current book, benefited tremendously from the careful readings and suggestions of Professor Shakir Mustafa. Prior to my graduate work at Boston University, Robert Wisnovsky's instruction, advice, and inspiration, along with that of the many other wonderful professors in Harvard University's Extension Division, were invaluable to my research trajectory.

I have been fortunate to have a number of mentors throughout my academic career, whose patient advising has been a tremendous source of guidance. These include Himmet Taskomur, Ahmad Atif Ahmad, Peri Bearman, Sait Ozervarli, Hikmet Yaman, Steve Yao, and a number of others from whose guidance I have greatly benefited. I have also found profound benefit in my private studies of classical Islamic legal and theological texts with Shaykhs Imadudin Abu Hijleh, Suheil Laher, Faraz Rabbani, Hamza Karamali, Taha Abdul-Basser, and Shaykha Najah Nady, to name but a few. To the latter I am also indebted for her help in procuring a number of scans of manuscripts of al-Bājūrī's unpublished works. My knowledge of Sufism has also benefited tremendously from the many live and recorded lectures of Shaykh Nuh Keller that I have had the honor of hearing.

This work has benefited tremendously from my time spent as a visiting research fellow at the Harvard Islamic Legal Studies Program, with the guidance and support of Baber Johansen, Peri Bearman, Nazim Ali, Ceallaigh Reddy, and the many fellows I met over the several summers spent there. Additionally, a very productive month of research at McGill University's Institute for Islamic Studies in July 2009 contributed to the first major revision of the dissertation in preparation for its submission to SUNY Press.

During a two-year Mellon Foundation post-doctoral fellowship at Hamilton College, I had the great privilege of working with a number of very supportive colleagues under the circumstances that were very conducive to research and writing. I also benefited from the support of my colleagues at Loyola University New Orleans during the two wonderful years spent among them. My colleagues at Colgate University have already provided so much support and advice in my first year with them.

For her tireless editorial wisdom, I am deeply appreciative of Valerie Turner, who has offered a great deal of assistance at several stages of this work's development. Peri Bearman and Jawad Qureshi also offered beneficial editorial insight in the final stages. In the eleventh hour, Carl Sharif El-Tobgui, Najah Nadi, and Muhammad Eissa gave much needed interpretive advice regarding the translation of al-Sayyid Muḥammad Shihāb al-Dīn's poem in praise of Ibrāhīm al-Bājūrī.

A portion of an earlier draft of Chapter 4 was excerpted and revised to produce my article "Apples and Oranges: The Logic of the Early and Later Logicians" in *Islamic Law and Society* 17, no. 2 (2010). Some of these substantially edited and revised portions have been reworked into the present work with the kind permission of Brill.

Finally, no words seem sufficient to thank my family without whose support and advice this work would never have come to fruition: My parents and sister for their support throughout it all, my wife for patiently supporting me during my transition from musician to academic, and my daughter for not pressing too many keys while I tried to type and cradle her simultaneously when she was just a few months old.

Introduction

When a young Egyptian man named Ibrāhīm al-Bājūrī left his father's home in hopes of studying the traditional sciences of Islam in late eighteenth-century Cairo, he began a traditional course of study that had dominated for centuries. He entered al-Azhar University and studied from a curriculum that consisted of commentaries and super-commentaries on texts written, in most cases, in previous generations; cases that covered the gamut of legal, theological, philosophical, and mystical[1] thought, as it had developed over the previous millennium. His teachers had studied in this tradition, and possibly contributed to it with their own commentaries or treatises. Many, though not all, of the students and teachers had a similar disposition, a disposition that corresponded to the way in which the sciences of Islam were taught and interpreted. They were what I call "archetypal scholars." Al-Bājūrī was one such archetypal scholar of the late pre-modern Sunnī tradition.

Al-Bājūrī was a scholar of Islamic jurisprudence of the school of Muḥammad, b. Idrīs al-Shāfiʿī (d. 204/820); a theologian in the tradition of Abū l-Ḥasan al-Ashʿarī (d. 324/935); a logician in the method of Fakhr al-Dīn al-Rāzī (d. 606/1209); a scholar of the Arabic language; and a Sufi of the Naqshbandī order.[2] He completed at least twenty works on a variety of topics including Ashʿarī creed, Shāfiʿī jurisprudence, and syllogistic logic, as well as linguistic sciences. He wrote only a few original epistles, most of his works were commentaries (*sharḥ/shurūḥ*) or super-commentaries (*ḥāshiya/ḥawāshī*), some on those of his own teacher Muḥammad al-Faḍālī (d. 1821), others on the works of scholars who had died centuries earlier.

Al-Bājūrī's education and career followed that of the many scholars who had preceded him. He did not break any molds, nor did he call for reformation and change. Yet he did offer his own opinion on various legal, theological, historical, philosophical, and mystical matters, and he interpreted the body of teachings that he inherited from his forefathers. He was, despite his deep knowledge of multiple subjects, committed to the tradition of scholarship that had preceded him and endured for many centuries, at least since the time of Abū Ḥāmid al-Ghazālī (d. 505/1111), and arguably prior to that. Al-Bājūrī's scholarship was based on a pattern that stressed the mastery of the three core sciences of law, theology, and mysticism, as well as various related sciences.

Al-Bājūrī was therefore a scholar who fit the mold of a certain archetype. I make use of this term, not necessarily in a strictly Jungian sense, but rather to indicate a model of scholarship that was a result of an inner and innate inclination, as well as one that was dictated by the primary texts of Islam itself (i.e., the Gabriel *ḥadīth*, discussed below). The term archetype also implies a model or pattern; scholars of the three core sciences could be found across the Muslim world throughout the many centuries of Islam's existence.

I present the archetypal scholar as one motivated by three innate drives:

- The need for authenticity and authority in belief and practice
- The need for harmony between intellect and revelation
- The need for a spiritual experience of faith achieved and explained in accordance with the law and creed.

These three innate drives correspond to the three dimensions of Islam—*islām*, *īmān*, and *iḥsān*—that were mentioned in the primary texts. Given that the primary texts associated with each dimension were either absolutely authentic or probabilistically authentic, and because the meanings of the texts, regardless of the degree of authenticity, were either completely clear or open to different interpretations, there necessarily resulted a range of consensus and disagreement. From the differing methodological approaches to and interpretations of the sources there arose multiple schools of thought in each of the three core sciences associated with the three dimensions of Islam.

I believe that the archetypal scholars, the sciences they studied, the methodologies they applied, and their means of authenticating knowledge were normative throughout the vast history of Sunnī Islam (and similarly in Shiʿī Islam, though not discussed here). Arguing the normativity of this model may seem unnecessary due to its widespread acceptance by pre-modern Muslims and by many early orientalists, however, a number of challenges to this view of Islamic intellectual history from multiple angles, both within the Islamic tradition and from the Western academy, have become part of a popular narrative that posits orthodoxy, normativity, and authenticity with what is in reality a limited and misinterpreted phenomenon within Sunnī Islam (that is, the so-called anti-rationalist traditionalists). Contrary to some popular narratives, I argue that the impetus of the archetypal scholar to study law within a *madhhab* (school or method of law and legal derivation), and to study theology according to one of the three traditional schools of theology which embraced, in varying degrees, the rational sciences and the mystical tradition of Sufism, was, in reality, the normative model of scholarship and the best approximation of what defined, and still defines "orthodoxy" and "orthopraxy" in Sunnī Islam. By declaring something to be normative, I do not mean that it is definitive, in that there are other models and approaches that exist and are accepted in varying degrees; rather, what I declare to be normative I believe to be the ideal for a majority of pre-modern scholars of Sunnī Islam.

The study of al-Bājūrī as a particular example of the archetypal scholar not only supports the above mentioned thesis, but also brings to light a second overarching argument made in this work, namely the falsity of the popular grand-narrative of "decline." In modern times, figures such as al-Bājūrī are almost entirely neglected, or at minimum dismissed as being purely derivative and of little importance. This stems, to my mind, from the pernicious and popular assumption that, due to the supposed decline in Islamic thought and culture beginning around the third/ninth century, the only figures worthy of study in the nineteenth century are those who were engaged in so-called reform, revival, and engaging the challenges of European thought and culture.[3]

The reasons for the popularity of this theory of decline are many. In matters related to law, early orientalists such as Christiaan Snouck Hurgronje and his student Joseph Schacht popularized the theory that the "gates" of *ijtihād* were closed, which they argued brought about the subsequent cessation of all original and independent legal reasoning. This problematic interpretation of the pre-modern discussion of *ijtihād* will be discussed in Chapter 4 of this work.

Popular assumptions of decline and stagnation in the realm of philosophy stem from the assumption that al-Ghazālī wrought a death blow to all philosophical reasoning with his widely accepted book "The Refutation of the Philosophers" in which he challenged a number of premises in the theories of the Muslim philosophers.[4]

Further, it assumes the uncritical acceptance of Muslim doxographers' categorization of scholars as *mutakallim* (theologian) or *faylasūf* (philosopher) and posits that these categories did not change or merge over time. And, it views Islamic intellectual history through the lens of Western thought, which separated "philosophy" and "theology" into two distinct categories "as a result of the institutional separation between faculties of arts and faculties of divinity in medieval European universities."[5] Given the falsity of these assumptions and the strength of Robert Wisnovsky's theory that "post-Avecennian *kalām* is truly Islamic Philosophy," we must put aside generations of uncritical acceptance of intellectual decline in the rational and legal sciences and undertake a greater investigation of later theologians' and jurists' works. The preliminary investigation of al-Bājūrī's writings on theology and logic offered here is, perhaps, a crucial and much needed contribution to the endeavor to better understand the efforts and impact of later Islamic thinkers.

The neglect of thirteenth/nineteenth-century scholarship, in addition to being informed by the theory of decline, may be a result of a lack of insight into the subtlety of the discourse[6] and an inability to comprehend some of the more complex theological and theoretical legal texts, due, in part, to the unavailability of many texts to early Orientalists.[7] Later pre-modern scholars such as al-Bājūrī may also have been neglected for being insufficiently "Greek" in their philosophy, or not European enough in law or the empirical sciences, and therefore viewed as backward and antiquated. Scholars such as al-Bājūrī believed in a spiritual world of talismans, marriages between humans and beings in the spiritual realm (i.e., *jinn*), and may have spoken of matters in the physical world that betrayed their ignorance of, or lack of concern for the empirical observations of Western scientists. But these matters ought not exclude such scholars from being important players and thinkers in other fields, with much to offer our investigations of the early and classical eras of Islam.

We may explain the relative lack of interest in late pre-modern scholars in other terms: they may not have been sufficiently controversial in personality, like Ibn Taymiyya or Ibn Sīnā (Avicenna), nor did they tend to write in their own voice as directly as Ibn Taymiyya, al-Ghazālī, or the early founders of the legal schools (*madhhabs*). Indeed it was rare for al-Bājūrī to use the first person personal pronoun; rather he tended to be busy describing, narrating, or commanding the reader to review a particular issue.

Al-Bājūrī received some attention in the late nineteenth and early twentieth centuries, as discussed in greater detail in Chapter 5, perhaps due to the importance colonial powers and the academics working in their service attached to understanding the practice on the ground in the Muslim lands under their control. From the early twentieth century onward, after reform movements and modernization swept the Muslim world, and the changing tides of social and political currents in the West changed the priorities and perspectives of Westerners, scholars such as al-Bājūrī seem to have diminished in importance.

A renewed interest in post ninth/fifteenth-century scholars is crucial for our understanding of the various stages of development in the Islamic tradition, as well as the multiple currents in the Islamic world today, including traditionalist, Salafī, Wahhābī, modernist, and others. In addition to arguing the normativity of the Gabrielian paradigm, with its emphasis on a balanced interrelation of law, theology, and Sufism, and an accepted range of consensus and scholarly disagreement in each science, this work further explores the normativity and popularity of the rational sciences (syllogistic logic and *kalām* in particular) in law and theology between the seventh/thirteenth and thirteenth/nineteenth centuries. In particular, the role of the Ashʿarī school in the *madrasa* (Islamic colleges) and the *madhhab*s (schools of law) will be explored in order to address the still popular theory that "rationalist" theologians were viewed as heterodox by the majority of Sunnī jurists. Furthermore, I pay significant attention to the normativity and centrality of Sufism in the life and studies of pre-modern Muslim scholars.

In short, there are two main theses supported by this study of the life and thought of al-Bājūrī, namely the normativity of the Gabrielian paradigm, with its wide road and diverse manifestations that resist oversimplification and monolithic analysis, and the falsity of many of the premises of the argument that Islamic thought and society declined due to the closure of the gates of independent juridical reasoning in the third/ninth century, and the death blow to and subsequent marginalization of philosophy in the sixth/twelfth century. Beyond these two overarching theses, this work also illuminates some of the contours of pre-reform thought and culture at al-Azhar, in and of itself a worthy investigation.

At times, attention is given to matters which are of interest and importance within both academic and intra-Islamic discourse, though perhaps in varying degrees. This is appropriate, to my mind, because both discourses impact the other and are not mutually exclusive, not merely because of the existence of Muslims in academia and academics amongst Muslims, but rather, because both camps recognize the value of the other's contributions, despite the existence of mutual criticism and differing motivations, methods, assumptions, and goals.

1

Al-Bājūrī's Life and Scholarship

Burhān al-Dīn Ibrāhīm al-Bājūrī b. al-Shaykh Muḥammad al-Jayzāwī b. Aḥmad was born in 1198/1783–4.[1] His education began with the study of the Qur᾽ān and its recitation (*tajwīd*) under his father's tutelage in his hometown of Bājūr, a village in the province of Manūfiyya in Lower Egypt. Writing about 100 years after al-Bājūrī's birth, nineteenth-century Egyptian cabinet minister ʿAlī Mubārak (d. 1893) describes the village of Bājūr as containing five mosques, each housing a tomb of the deceased namesake of the mosque.[2] They include Jāmiʿ al-Arbaʿīn, Jāmiʿ Ṣalāḥ al-Dīn, Jāmiʿ Shihāb al-Dīn, Jāmiʿ Sayydī Mazrūʿ, and Jāmiʿ Yūnus. It also contained one *zāwiyya* (Sufi lodge) called Zāwiyya ʿAjūr, indicating a strong Sufi presence in the village. Attached to the *zāwiyya* was a poultry farm, eleven small gardens that produced various types of fruit, one of which was bequeathed for the descendants of a certain Rustum Bayk who was buried there, and the rest being for some of the residents of the area. At the time of Mubārak's writing, the population totaled 1,998 people, all of whom were Muslim. The people of Bājūr were famous for making a licorice root drink and for growing cotton. The village itself was well known for the luminaries it produced, in particular al-Bājūrī.[3]

At the age of fourteen, al-Bājūrī entered al-Azhar—an institution of which he would later become rector—in order to study the traditional sciences of Islam. At the time, a typical day of study would have begun after the morning prayers with the study of the Qur᾽ān, followed by *ḥadīth*.[4] Then studies of the Qur᾽ānic sciences, such as its proper pronunciation (*tajwīd*) or its variant readings (*qira᾽āt*) commenced. This was followed by the study of various *ḥadīth* sciences, theological studies (*uṣūl al-dīn*)—which necessarily entailed the study of logic (*manṭiq*), as discussed later in this work—followed by the foundational sources of Islamic law (*uṣūl al-fiqh*) and its derived rulings (*furūʿ al-fiqh*). After the evening prayers, a time associated with spiritual contemplation and worship, the study of Sufism—Islamic mysticism—was undertaken.[5]

By al-Bājūrī's time, the Islamic sciences were often studied from condensed summary texts, with commentaries—sometimes word by word—and super-commentaries. There was an emphasis on oral and aural transmission of knowledge and the memorization of didactic poems or condensed texts on various sciences, from music to logic, Qur'ānic recitation to law. Such emphases also lent themselves well to educating the visually impaired, as there was a college for the blind at al-Azhar.[6]

After a year of studying the Islamic sciences, his studies were interrupted by the invasion of the French. In 1798, al-Bājūrī left al-Azhar and went to Giza (al-Jīza),[7] where he remained until 1801; he then returned to al-Azhar to complete his education. He excelled in his studies and began to teach and write on a variety of topics. In 1807, at the age of twenty-four, he completed his first book, a commentary on the work of one of his most important teachers, Muḥammad al-Faḍālī (d. 1821). He studied with al-Faḍālī until the latter's death; thus his studies as a student under the guidance of a master continued at least until then, though he had begun teaching and writing. Like al-Suyūṭī (d. 911/1505) before him, who began writing prior to being granted a full license to teach,[8] al-Bājūrī's writing and teaching at this stage were arguably part of the pedagogy. It should be noted, however, that even when one is promoted to the level of *shaykh* and teacher, the practice of studying texts and disciplines under the tutelage of another master often continues; one is always a student.

Al-Bājūrī's Teachers and Students

Al-Bājūrī studied with some of the most important scholars of his day. Listed among his prominent teachers are:

1. Muḥammad al-Amīr al-Kabīr al-Mālikī (d. 1817)
2. ʿAbdallāh al-Sharqāwī l-Shāfiʿī, Shaykh al-Azhar [1793–1812], (d. 1812)
3. Dāwūd al-Qalʿāwī (d. uncertain)
4. Muḥammad al-Faḍālī[9] (d. 1821)
5. Ḥasan al-Quwaysnī, Shaykh al-Azhar [1834–1838], (d. 1838)
6. Abū Ḥurayba al-Shintināwī l-Naqshbandī [Sufi shaykh], (d. 1852)[10]

Those who list al-Bājūrī as a teacher include Salīm al-Bishrī (d. 1916), who was Shaykh al-Azhar (1900–4, 1909–16), and Shams al-Dīn Muḥammad al-Inbābī (d. 1895), who also served as Shaykh al-Azhar in 1882 and again from 1886 to 1895. Another prominent student of al-Bājūrī was Rifāʿa al-Ṭahṭāwī (d. 1873), translator of French works of geography, author of a popular travelogue recording his experiences in Paris,[11] and considered by many a sort of proto-reformer. Although al-Bājūrī's and al-Ṭahṭāwī's professional lives overlapped and they both studied under al-Sharqāwī, al-Bājūrī appears to have had no inclination toward the reformist leanings of al-Ṭahṭāwī. It is reported that ʿAbbās I (d. 1854), the grandson of Muḥammad ʿAlī Pasha, and khedive of Egypt from 1849 to 1854, attended some of al-Bājūrī's lectures,[12] indicating, perhaps, that it was a period of better relations between al-Azhar and the government, as compared with the somewhat strained relations of Muḥammad ʿAlī Pasha's reign.

Scholars of diverse disciplines and *madhhab* affiliations studied with al-Bājūrī, coming from within and outside of Egypt. Interestingly, al-Bājūrī also had students who were the grandson and great-grandson of Muḥammad b. ʿAbd al-Wahhāb, namely ʿAbd al-Raḥmān b. Ḥasan b. Muḥammad (b. ʿAbd al-Wahhāb) Āl al-Shaykh (d. 1869) and ʿAbd al-Laṭīf b. ʿAbd al-Raḥmān b. Ḥassan Āl al-Shaykh (d. 1876), both of whom served as head of the religious estate at various times when the Saudi/Wahhabi alliance ruled parts of the Arabian penninsula.[13] ʿAbd al-Raḥmān had studied under his grandfather Muḥammad b. ʿAbd al-Wahhāb until the age of thirteen, when the latter died.

When Muḥammad ʿAlī Pasha put down the Wahhābī revolt of 1818, ʿAbd al-Raḥmān and his son ʿAbd al-Laṭīf moved to Egypt with their families. There they studied with scholars of al-Azhar for eight years, including some of the most prominent jurist-theologian-Sufis of the day, including al-Bājūrī's teacher al-Quwaysnī, the Mālikī jurist and Khalwatī Sufi Aḥmad al-Ṣāwī (d. 1825–6), and al-Bājūrī himself. ʿAbd al-Raḥmān studied *Sharḥ al-Khulāṣah* with al-Bājūrī, being al-Ashmūnī's (d. 900/1494–5) commentary on the thousand-line didactic grammar poem known as *Alfiyat ibn Mālik*.[14] Despite the political circumstances that may have brought ʿAbd al-Raḥmān and his son to Egypt, and their involvement in the conflict between the Ottomans and Saudis before and after residing in Egypt, their studying with top Azharī scholars indicates that the political animosity between Ashʿarīs and Wahhābī/Atharīs may not have been as clear-cut or far-reaching as some modern proponents of each school might assume. Indeed, Gilbert Delanoue mentions that refutations of and reactions to Wahhābī ideology did not surface in Egypt until the late nineteenth and early twentieth centuries, indicating the continued strength and influence of al-Bājūrī's and his predecessors' views.[15]

Al-Bājūrī wrote a number of *ijāza*s for various scholars; these can be found in Dār al-Kutub library in Cairo. They include an *ijāza* for Shaykh ʿAbd al-Munʿim b. Muḥammad al-Suyūṭī l-Jurjāwī l-Ṣaʿīdī l-Mālikī (d. 1326/1908). Al-Bājūrī grants him permission to narrate all that al-Bājūrī has narrated of *ḥadīth* (*al-marwiyyāt*), that for which al-Bājūrī has a chain of narration and permission (*sanad*), and in particular, those chains in which Shaykh Muḥammad b. Muḥammad al-Amīr al-Kabīr is found. A similar *ijāza* exists for Shaykh Aḥmad b. Muḥammad al-Jarjāwī (d. c. 1267/1851). A third exists for a Ḥanafī scholar, possibly of Turkish origin, named Ḥusnayn Aḥmad Jalbī, known as al-Malṭ al-Būtījī l-Ḥanafī. Another exists for a Ḥanbalī scholar named ʿAbd al-Sallam b. ʿAbd al-Raḥmān al-Shaṭī l-Dimashqī l-Ḥanbalī. A fifth *ijāza* exists for ʿAlī b. ʿAwḍ al-Bardīsī l-Jarjāwī (d. 1280/1864).[16] It is important to note that al-Bājūrī had students from all four Sunnī *madhhab*s (schools of law), as it indicates that, despite sometimes vehement disagreements between the schools, each was seen as valid and legitimate in al-Bājūrī's day (and prior), as discussed later in this work.

In addition to future rectors and scholars of law, theology, and history, some of al-Bājūrī's students were also prominent in Sufi movements, such as Muḥammad b. Khalīl al-Ḥifnāwī l-Hajrasī (d. 1910), an important figure in the development of the Rashīdī Idrīsī tradition and an initiate of the Khalwatiyya Sufi order.[17]

A student of some of al-Azhar's luminaries, and later a popular teacher of future scholars and leaders, al-Bājūrī appears to have risen above the general masses of students and professors. While there is little in the historical record to indicate how or why, it is probable that his rise through the scholarly ranks was a combination of academic acumen, personal connection to important scholars, and unquantifiable good fortune. Given some of his administrative decisions as rector of al-Azhar, discussed below, it is also probable that he had an assertive personality that may have attracted the attention and respect of his contemporaries.

A Traditional Shaykh al-Azhar in an Era of Attempted Reform

Al-Bājūrī taught at al-Azhar, and in 1847, at the age of sixty-four, became its rector (Shaykh al-Azhar), a position that he held until the end of his life. Little is known about his life prior to being appointed as the Shaykh al-Azhar. It is likely that his time before the appointment was spent teaching and writing, since all of his completed works were written before he assumed this well-respected and influential position. Upon his appointment, a certain al-Sayyid Muḥammad Shihāb al-Dīn (d. 1857–8) delivered twenty lines of poetry in praise of al-Bājūrī, which are reproduced in ʿAbd al-Razzaq al-Bayṭār's (d. 1917) *Ḥilyat al-bashar fī tārīkh al-qarn al-thālith ʿashar*. They are offered below in translation:

> Do you see the clouds scattered with its pearls ornamenting
> the gardens of roses and gillyflowers
> Or the heralds of morning that breathed and covered the
> gloom of darkness with its rays
> Like the rejoicing nightingales manifesting the ascending
> star, the era enjoying the graces of its abundant fortune
> He is an elucidating star, the resplendence of its light dispensing with need of lamp and illumination
> The dynasty of his grandeur raised the banner of glory, and
> attacked by the drawn sword of his famed merit.[18]
> How noble a scholar and gallant leader, a destination to
> which people traverse quickly across the barren wasteland for his sweeping knowledge
> He made the ascendant stars appear in the rising places of
> his glory; at the way stations he travels on with ease
> His commentaries processed (like a beautiful bride), delicate
> and fine, gleaming with the beautiful qualities of being
> inked and penned
> He is a land of merits and an ocean of virtues; pure, the
> impurities of turbidity passed him by
> I repeated the praise of his ornamented qualities for he is
> sugar, the sweetness of which was intensified by refining.
> He is a garden of gnosis manifesting low-hanging fruit
> (from the two gardens of Paradise), a sheath unbuttoned
> (like a blossoming bud).
> No wonder the times became delightful by his goodness
> and his sweet fragrance perfumed the entire universe.
> Oh fate, give the bow to him who knows how to shape it
> (i.e. al-Bājūrī), for you have been excessive in what came
> before and what followed.[19]
> This is the winner of the racetrack's prize, who won the
> glory by his praiseworthy endeavor

He is the master of the time, aid of his era, glory of his
age, facilitator of difficult matters
The world rejoiced at him, and by him its face shone with
the cheer of a happy person.
The cosmos is resplendent because of him, and it said
"make things ample and easy for him; the most luminous Imam is Shaykh al-Bājūrī."
Oh friend, speak of what has been narrated of him (i.e.
great deeds) and say "the transmission of my hadith is
authentic"
Blessed is he who by the Station of Ibrahim has performed
the obligation of his accepted pilgrimage
And walked (between the hillocks Safa and Marwa) and
circumambulated the Ka'ba of beneficence and power, he
who completes his religious rites without deficiency
So enjoy the bliss of drawing near, and make up what was
missed from avowed superogatory works
And to him I give the daughter of thought (i.e. this poem),
unveiled in the shyness of her parted eyelids.
The goals of that which she hopes is the breaking of her
seal,[20] that has ended with the utmost reverence.

Al-Bājūrī had to agree to some conditions of his appointment, namely that he would not oversee the officially recognized Sufi orders, which may have been the responsibility of previous rectors, and to consult other scholars before making major institutional decisions.[21] Prior to and during his tenure as Shaykh al-Azhar, he had a heavy teaching load. It is mentioned that he taught al-Rāzī's *Tafsīr* (exegesis) on the Qur'ān, a multivolume work which is said to contain so many digressive discussions into theology and other matters that it "contains everything except exegesis."[22] Those who attended were not merely young students aspiring to scholarship, but also many of the great scholars of al-Azhar. However, al-Bājūrī was apparently too "weak" to complete the voluminous exegesis; an incomplete commentary, presumed to be his lecture notes on al-Rāzī's *tafsīr*, is listed among his uncompleted works.[23]

Teaching long days most of his professional life may have been partially a result of the political dynamic between al-Azhar and the khedive. Muḥammad ʿAlī Pasha (d. 1849)[24] was often in conflict with the scholars of al-Azhar and had severely cut their funding, partially by appropriating the endowments of teaching mosques.[25] Muḥammad ʿAlī Pasha, an Albanian appointed as governor of Egypt under the Ottomans, sought to centralize and expand his power over Egypt and the surrounding areas in the Sudan. Influenced by British and French models of education and government, as well as his own perceptions of political rule, which derived, according to Gran, from his Albanian heritage,[26] he began a project of military, commercial, agricultural, educational, scientific, and political "reform."

The term "reform" is problematic in this era, as the popular implications of the term often suggest the import of "advanced" foreign ideas and technology that must be absorbed by the followers of the "old ways," and that these ideas either replace or transform what was previously prevalant.[27] While Muḥammad ʿAlī's reform efforts did involve many European components, there were other elements from within Egypt and the broader Islamic lands.[28] Muḥammad ʿAlī and his supporters among the *ʿulamāʾ* (religious scholars) such as Shaykh al-Azhar Ḥasan al-ʿAṭṭār (d. 1835) were interested in the study of Western medicine from an empirical perspective. However, those particular theological or legal matters on the agendas of later reformists, as well as matters of secularization, became more prominent in the years after al-Bājūrī's death, and appear to have played a minimal role in comparison to the economic, military, and political changes attempted by Muḥammad ʿAlī.

Al-Bājūrī, along with many other scholars of al-Azhar, opposed the reform program of Muḥammad ʿAlī Pasha, even during the term of the pro-government Shaykh al-Azhar Ḥasan al-ʿAṭṭār (1830–35).[29] The end of al-ʿAṭṭār's term also marks a more pronounced turn away from Muḥammad ʿAlī's reform attempts, and a return to al-Azhar's majority view of religion and government. Historical sources[30] inform us of the resistance of al-Bājūrī and his contemporaries to Muḥammad ʿAlī's reform efforts, though explicit reference to them in his works is not easily found.

One possible reference to the early reformist or proto-reformist discourse is al-Bājūrī's discussion of *waḍʿī ilāhī* and *waḍʿī bashrī* knowledge, the former being that which is based on divine revelation—directly and apodictically or through probabilistic deduction via principles and methods drawn from divine revelation—and the latter being knowledge that stems solely from human speculation on matters which cannot be known through direct empirical observation or purely rational sources. More specifically, al-Bājūrī identifies an example of *waḍʿī bashrī* knowledge as *siyāsat al-ḥukamāʾ*, which might be best translated as political philosophy, from which kings derive principles of leadership and rule.[31]

This may be an implicit reference to discussions of *siyāsa*, a term covering everything from policing, hygiene, schooling, and other social issues, "all of which was taken up—on the whole from 1860 onward—as the responsibility of government."[32] Rifāʿa al-Ṭahṭāwī (d. 1873), a younger contemporary and student of al-Bājūrī, and proto-reformer, wrote of *siyāsa* thus: "Islamic countries, however, have neglected to teach the rudiments of the science of sovereign government and its application."[33] Al-Bājūrī may not have seen this matter as one of sacred relevance, and thus may have been seeking to downplay its importance, without rejecting it outright. Indeed, he recognizes that Allah is the source of all things, but emphasizes the fact that *waḍʿī bashrī* knowledge is acquired by humans through reflection and investigation, and related to matters in which the *Sharīʿa* is apparently silent. Despite al-Bājūrī's recognition of the study and application of various forms of *siyāsa* by the rulers in his day, and proto-reformers such as al-Ṭahṭāwī's greater emphasis on the subject after al-Bājūrī's death, discussion of such matters was not restricted to the nineteenth century, and such a statement by al-Bājūrī could easily have been written hundreds of years prior. Therefore, al-Bājūrī's mention of it is not necessarily a reference to discussions of Western and secular reform.

Another possible implicit reference to the discussions of modernization around al-Bājūrī is his assessment of the theory of cloud formation and rainfall, found in his discussion on water that is suitable for ritual ablutions, wherein he distinguishes between the "proper" interpretation of the origins of rain, and the "incorrect" interpretation attributed to the Muʿtazilīs, who were presumably long gone by al-Bājūrī's time. Discussing the various forms of water that are found bubbling from the ground and falling from the sky, al-Bājūrī says that "All water descends from the sky. Allah says in the Qurʾān 'Have you not seen that Allah sends down water from the sky . . .' [Zumar: 21]. Mujāhid [d. 104/722] said: 'There is not water on the earth except that it is from the sky . . .'"

Al-Bājūrī further narrates from Mujāhid the possibility that there could be water on earth that is left over from the creation of the world, though he implicitly rejects the Muʿtazilī view, which he introduces with the passive past tense verb qīla ("it is said"), thus indicating that what follows is a weaker opinion. Al-Bājūrī says

> It has been said that that which descends from the skies, its source is from the ocean. Allah most high raises it, ejecting it by his kindness (luṭf) and perfects its amount until it is made pleasant by that raising, then He causes it to descend to the earth in order that it is utilized. . . .[34]

This, like the discussion of siyāsa mentioned above, might appear to be a subtle reference to "Western" scientific discussions of his day, however, it is in fact based on al-Barmāwī's assessment of the subject, written two centuries prior.[35] Therefore, in the absence of specific reference to issues of his day, attributing such discussions to al-Bājūrī's assessment of modernization is speculative at best. Despite al-Bājūrī's awkward denial of empirical fact based on a supernatural interpretation, the very fact that al-Bājūrī, by way of al-Barmāwī, was aware of an empirical interpretation of the workings of the natural world indicates that we should approach popular notions of "modernization" and "reform" with caution. This is especially true with regard to what knowledge pre-modern societies may have possessed before coming into contact with modern Western thought.

In al-Bājūrī's day, the benefits of reform and modernity tended to benefit Ottoman-Egyptian elites "involved in the army and the new industries,"[36] rather than those outside this sphere, such as the rural masses, or quite often, the *ʿulamāʾ*. Scholars at al-Azhar with heavy teaching loads and shrinking endowments not surprisingly may have comprised a large number of people who objected to Muḥammad ʿAlī's reforms, not merely on conservative religious grounds, but also because they perceived such reformation and modernization to be irrelevant in their spheres of concern.

Al-Bājūrī lived in a time in which reforms attempted by Muḥammad ʿAlī were partially undone by Abbas I; the full impact of the impetus toward modernization on a wide-scale cultural level really began after his death. My initial assessment, which remains after sustained investigation, is that al-Bājūrī's life seems to have been unaffected by the political projects of his country's leaders,[37] and his works do not appear to be significantly impacted by modern circumstances; legal and theological controversies related to relations with Europe or modernization are ambiguous if not wholly absent. This is especially notable in comparison to his younger contemporary al-Ṭahṭāwī, whose work, especially after al-Bājūrī's death, helped modernization take root.

Despite the apparently minimal impact of modern politics on his thought, al-Bājūrī's administrative life was certainly affected by the politics of his day. Snouck Hurgronje reports of al-Bājūrī's tenure as Shaykh al-Azhar:[38]

> Ibrâhīm al-Bâjûrî was Shaykh al-Azhar from 1263/1847 up to his death, Dhûl-ḳaʿdah 1277 (June 1861).[39] In his last years, however, he was really no longer capable of fulfilling his official duties due to his old age. The government therefore gave him in Muḥarram 1275/August 1858 four "deputies" (*wukalâʾ*) to assist with the official duties. These were:

> Shaykh Aḥmad Kabûh al-ʿIdwî l-Mâlikî, Shaykh Ismâʿîl al-Ḥalabî l-Ḥanafî, Shaykh Khalîfah al-Fashnî l-Shâfiʿî, Shaykh Muṣṭafâ l-Ṣâwî l-Shâfiʿî. After Bâjûrî's death, his office remained vacant, and the official duties were carried out by the two remaining "deputies": Shaykh Kabûh and Shaykh Khalîfah al-Fashnî, until the year 1281 (1864–65).[40]

The official duties referred to above included dealing with a number of administrative and institutional crises, including the event that led to the appointment of four deputies mentioned by Snouck Hurgronje. One such incident in 1270/1853 required al-Bājūrī to call in soldiers to search the quarters of the Maghribī students, after a group of students attacked al-Bājūrī over an issue of daily rations. The ringleaders of this attack were deported, though they testified that they had not intended any harm to al-Bājūrī.[41]

Muḥammad ʿAlī's policy of conscription also affected the daily functions of al-Azhar. The policy, designed to support his military campaigns, brought harm and suffering to many across Egypt.[42] Conscripts, usually from rural or impoverished urban backgrounds, faced protracted and trying military service in lands far from their homes—service that frequently resulted in their deaths.[43] Draft evasion was not uncommon and often involved self-maiming, absconsion, bribery, pleading, violence, and trickery.[44] During the Crimean War (1853–1856), al-Azhar became a haven for young men evading conscription into the army.[45] Each village had quotas and the village headmen (shaykhs) were responsible for managing the conscription of those eligible in their villages; failure to do so could result in caning, whipping, or imprisonment. In one instance, a group of village headmen searching for draft-evaders sought permission from al-Bājūrī to apprehend them. At the time, al-Bājūrī was sitting in his chair (kursī) teaching; he ordered the students present to forcibly eject the village headmen from the premises. The students attacked the headmen, beating them with "sandels, fists, and canes." In the process, one of the village headmen was killed, but it was not known who had struck him, so his death apparently went unpunished.[46]

Muḥammad ʿAlī had used al-Bājūrī's predecessor, Shaykh al-Azhar al-ʿAṭṭār and other ʿulamāʾ to enforce the draft; however, under al-Bājūrī the autonomy of the ʿulamāʾ was revived, giving them more power in relation to the government.[47] Al-Bājūrī's bold order to eject the village headmen may reveal a multifaceted intent; in part, it may have been a display of his concern for his students, but it may also have been a form of political resistance. Al-Bājūrī does not appear to have had any reservations about acting according to his beliefs or speaking his mind, even when it was in opposition to proposed or actual state policy. For example, when the Khedive Saʿīd wanted to forcibly relocate the Coptic Christians from Egypt to the Sudan, he sought a fatwā (legal edict) from al-Bājūrī regarding its permissibility, to which al-Bājūrī is reported to have responded:

> If you mean by your project the people of the Covenant who are the dwellers of the land and its owners, then grace be to Allah, no change has occurred to the Islamic Covenant and no breach thereof to incur their victimization and they must be left under the Covenant to the day of doom.[48]

The event that led to the appointment of four deputies to assist al-Bājūrī in his administrative duties, which also may have allowed him to focus on teaching and scholarship, was a clash between Syrian and Egyptian students which required police and army intervention and resulted in the arrest of more than thirty of the Egyptian students. Thus, by 1858, al-Bājūrī's ability to oversee the often unruly students of al-Azhar was clearly at issue, and it appears he was ultimately relieved of such administrative duties, though he retained the most important aspects of his position as Shaykh al-Azhar—namely teaching, scholarship, and probably religious consultation with the government. This arrangement lasted until al-Bājūrī's death, after which the position of Shaykh al-Azhar went unfilled until 1864–65, when Shaykh al-Arūsī (d. 1293/1876) was appointed. During this interim the administrative duties associated with the position were performed by Shaykh Kabūh and Shaykh Khalīfa al-Fashnī, as mentioned previously.

Al-Bājūrī's Character

The chronicles relate that al-Bājūrī was a deeply pious man devoted to seeking knowledge and its benefits, as well as to educating others and benefiting them thereby. He is described as one whose tongue was always "wet with praise" of Allah and the recitation of the Qurʾān, which he would complete in a day and a night, or nearly so. His love for the family of the Prophet is noted, and it is said that he would visit them often. Whether this refers to visiting the Prophet's descendants who were alive in his time, or the tombs of his famous descendants buried in Egypt is unclear, but the latter is probable.[49]

I have not seen any written documentation on al-Bājūrī's personal life, however, there are oral reports among Azharīs about his well-known difficult relationship with his wife, to whom he apparently stayed married despite their hardships, in order to protect her from the pains a future husband might cause her, and to protect any future husband from her![50]

Al-Bājūrī's administrative life, as mentioned earlier, appears to have involved him in some difficult worldly matters, such as the incident with the village *shaykhs* seeking draft-evaders. In his final years, he likely devoted himself to teaching and worship, having been removed from official duties and replaced by four deputies. Toward the end of his life, al-Bājūrī fell ill and was confined to bed. He died on Thursday, 28 Dhūl Qaʿda 1276/17 June 1860. Snouck Hurgronje and others have said that it was in the year 1277/1861, while still others have placed his death as late as 1281/1865, although this is incorrect. Al-Bājūrī was laid to rest in a graveyard called *turba al-mujāwirīn*, where other scholars of al-Azhar had been buried, including the prolific Azharī commentator Muḥammad al-Dasūqī (d. 1230/1815). [51]

Al-Bājūrī's Works

In his biographical notice on al-Bājūrī, Shaykh ʿAlī Jumʿa—former Grand Mufti[52] of Egypt—lists twenty completed works attributed to al-Bājūrī.[53] The first batch of works deals mostly with *kalām, manṭiq*, and the linguistic sciences. Al-Suyūṭī also began his voluminous writing career with the same subjects,[54] a clear indication that the trivium/quadrivium method had been firmly rooted in the Islamic curriculum for many centuries. Once he had sufficiently covered the trivium, al-Bājūrī ventured into the realm of law, though he did return to author some works on theology. His final work, perhaps his magnum opus, *Ḥāshiya ʿalā sharḥ b. al-Qāsim al-Ghazzī ʿalā matn Abī Shujāʿ fī fiqh al-Shāfiʿiyya* [A gloss on Ibn al-Qāsim al-Ghazzī's commentary on Abū Shujāʿ's manual of Shāfiʿī *fiqh*] was completed some twenty years after his initial prolific production of works, with only the *Mawāhib al-laduniyya sharḥ al-shamāʾil al-Muḥammadiyya* breaking the apparent silence in 1835. He did, however, leave at least six unfinished works that address a host of topics ranging from *uṣūl al-fiqh* to *kalām*, as well as two works on *tafsīr*. Perhaps these works, his heavy teaching load, and, in the latter part of his life, his official administrative duties, slowed the publication of additional works.

Sufism is treated in al-Bājūrī's theological and legal works, especially in his *Tuḥfat al-murīd*. This list of his works includes his commentary on the *Burda*—a poem covering the biography (*sīra*) of the Prophet from a decidedly Sufi perspective—and commentaries on Ibn Ḥajar al-Haytamī's (d. 974/1566–67) and Aḥmad al-Dardīr's (d. 1201/1786) works on the birthday (*mawlid*) of the Prophet. The latter is really a subject of jurisprudence, but is also tied to Sufism, as the Sufis are often the most active proponents of *mawlid* celebrations.

Chronological List of al-Bājūrī's Completed Works[55]

- 1222/1807: *Ḥāshiya ʿalā risālat al-Faḍālī fī qawl "lā illah illa-Llāh"* [A gloss on al-Faḍālī's Epistle on the saying "there is no god but Allah"]. This text covers many possible grammatical and theological interpretations and implications of the testimony of faith, "there is no god but Allah."
- 1223/1808: *Ḥāshiya taḥqīq al-maqām ʿalā risālat kifāyatu al-ʿawām fī mā yajibu ʿalayhim fī ʿilm al-kalām li-l-Faḍālī* [Verification of the station: A gloss on al-Faḍālī's Sufficiency of the common folk regarding that which is obligatory upon them of the science of *kalām*]. This work, following al-Sanūsī, is a statement of creed which outlines the core points of later Ashʿarī thought, namely that which is necessary (*wājib*), impossible (*mustaḥīl*), and possible (*jāʾiz*) with regard to Allah and His messengers. Additional information about the Prophet's genealogy, definitions of core terms, and discussions of intra-Ashʿarī disagreements, like those found in *Tuḥfat al-murīd* and *Ḥāshiya ʿalā muqaddimat al-Sanūsī* are also included.
- 1224/1809: *Fatḥ al-qarīb al-majīd sharḥ bidāyat al-murīd fī l-tawḥīd li-l-Shaykh al-Sibāʿī* [Openings from the close and majestic: A commentary on al-Sibāʿī's "The seeker's introduction to *tawḥīd*"].
- 1225/1810: *Ḥāshiya ʿalā mawlid al-Muṣṭafā li Ibn Ḥajar al-Haytamī* [A gloss on Ibn Ḥajar al-Haytamī's "The birthday of the chosen one (the Prophet Muḥammad)"]. A text discussing the proofs, merits, and history of celebrating the Prophet Muḥammad's birthday.

- 1225/1810: *Ḥāshiya ʿalā mukhtaṣar al-Sanūsī fī l-manṭiq* [A gloss on the abridgment of al-Sanūsī on the science of logic].
- 1226/1811: *Ḥāshiya ʿalā matn al-sullam li-l-Akhḍarī fī ʿilm al-manṭiq* [A gloss on al-Akhḍarī's text: The staircase of the science of logic]. Another commentary on a popular work of *manṭiq*, with a useful discussion of the types of *manṭiq* and the various opinions regarding its permissibility.
- 1226/1811: *Ḥāshiya ʿalā matn al-Samarqandiyya fī fann al-bayān* [A gloss on Samarqandī's text on the science of rhetoric].
- 1227/1812: *Fatḥ al-khabīr al-laṭīf sharḥ naẓm al-taṣrīf fī fann al-taṣrīf li-l-Shaykh ʿAbd al-Raḥmān b. ʿĪsā* [The opening of subtle knowledge: A commentary on the poem of conjugation regarding the science of conjugation].
- 1227/1812: *Ḥāshiya ʿalā matn al-Sanūsiyya fī ʿilm al-tawḥīd* [A commentary on al-Sanūsī's text on the science of *tawḥīd*]. A short text covering the details of *tawḥīd* according to the later Ashʿarī school. The *matn* is terse and packed with statements needing further clarification, thus al-Sanūsī himself produced a commentary on the text. This text is also the source of al-Faḍālī's work mentioned above, as well as numerous other texts including *Matn Ibn ʿĀshir* and al-Bājūrī's *Risāla* listed below. The impact of this text on Ashʿarī thought cannot be understated, and indeed is an area of important future research.
- 1227/1812: *Ḥāshiya ʿalā mawlid al-Muṣṭafā li-l-Shaykh al-Dardīr* [A commentary on Shaykh al-Dardīr's birthday of the chosen]. Another text discussing the topic of celebrating the Prophet's birthday.
- 1229/1813: *Fatḥ rabb al-bariyya sharḥ al-durra al-bahiyya fī naẓm al-ājurūmiyya li-l-ʿAllāma al-ʿImrīṭī* [The opening of creation: A commentary on al-ʿAllāma al-ʿImrīṭī's "The radiant pearl regarding Ibn al-Ājurūm's poem"]. A work discussing the popular didactic text on Arabic grammar by Ibn al-Ājurūm.
- 1229/1813: *Ḥāshiya ʿalā al-Burda al-sharīfa li-l-Būṣīrī* [A gloss on al-Būṣīrī's "The Poem of the cloak"]. Another

text commonly studied and commented upon in the *ḥāshiya* tradition, al-Būṣīrī's *Burda* [*The Poem of the Cloak*] is hugely popular around the world today and has been for centuries. Al-Bājūrī's lengthy commentary covers basic explanations of intended meaning, grammatical analysis, and historical background, as well as more detailed issues such as the debate over whether the Prophet had been given knowledge of the Pen (*qalam*) and Preserved Tablet (*al-lawḥ al-maḥfūẓ*).

- 1234/1818: *Ḥāshiya al-is ʿād ʿalā Bānat Su ʿād* [The commentary of happiness on the poem entitled "Bānat Suʿād"]. A commentary on an early Islamic poem by the Companion Kaʿb b. Zuhayr (d. 24/644–5), also sometimes called *Qasīdat al-burda* [*The Poem of the Cloak*], as the Prophet gave his cloak to Ibn Zuhayr in appreciation of his poem. The same occurred to al-Būṣīrī in a dream, which is why his work is also referred to as the *Burda* [*The Poem of the Cloak*].
- 1234/1818: *Tuḥfat al-murīd sharḥ Jawharat al-tawḥīd li-l-laqqānī* [The gift of the aspirant: A commentary on the gem of divine unity]. A commentary on al-Laqānī's didactic poem (in *rajz* meter) summarizing the basic creed and methodology of Sunnī Islam according to the later Ashʿarīs. While it is a one-volume text under 400 pages (in the edition used for this work) it may in fact be al-Bājūrī's most important work, as its popularity spread beyond the Shāfiʿī school. In it, al-Bājūrī lays out his three-dimensional conception of Islam, focusing mainly on *ʿaqīda* (as the original poem does); yet also discussing his views on *ijtihād;* the necessity of following *madhhabs*; the role, importance, and methods of Sufism; the errors of the philosophers; and a host of other issues.
- 1234/1818: *Fatḥ al-fatāḥ ʿalā ḍawʿ al-miṣbāḥ fī aḥkām al-nikāḥ* [The opening of the opener on the light of the lamp regarding the rulings of marriage]. A treatise on the subject of marriage.
- 1236/1820: *al-Tuḥfat al-khayriyya ʿalā al-fawāʾid al-Shanshūriyya sharḥ al-manẓūma al-raḥbiyya fī l-mawārīth* [The beneficent gift regarding al-Shanshūrī's useful benefits: A commentary on the poem al-*Raḥbiyya* regarding inheritance].

- 1238/1822: *al-Durar al-ḥisān ʿalā fatḥ al-Raḥmān fī mā yaḥṣīlu bihi al-islām wa-l-īmān li-l-Zubaydī* [The splendid pearls, a commentary on al-Zubaydī's book, "The opening of the Merciful in that which is attained by *islām* and *īmān*"]. A commentary on a short work discussing some essential aspects of faith and practice.

- 1238/1822: *Risālat al-Bājūriyya fī fann al-kalām*, or *Risāla fī ʿilm al-tawḥīd* [al-Bājūrī's "Epistle on the science of *kalām*" or "Epistle on the science of *tawḥīd*"].[56] A short epistle on the subject of *tawḥīd*. Essentially an abridgment of al-Faḍālī's *Risālat kifāyat al-ʿawām fī mā yajibu ʿalayhim fī ʿilm al-kalām* (discussed above). A concise summary of the main points of Ashʿarī *ʿaqīda* designed for the lay person.

- 1251/1835: *Mawāhib al-laduniyya sharḥ al-shamāʾil al-Muḥammadiyya* [The mystically imparted gifts: A commentary on al-Tirmidhī's work on the characteristics of Muḥammad].[57] A commentary on al-Tirmidhī's collection of *ḥadīth*s describing various aspects of the Prophet's life, manners, appearance, and interactions. Interpretations and explanations of the *ḥadīth*s are given.

- 1258/1842: *Ḥāshiya ʿalā sharḥ Ibn al-Qāsim al-Ghazzī ʿalā matn Abī Shujāʿ fī fiqh al-Shāfiʿiyya* [A gloss on Ibn al-Qāsim al-Ghazzī's "Commentary on Abū Shujāʿ's manual of Shāfiʿī *fiqh*"]. A large two-volume *ḥāshiya* on Ibn al-Qāsim al-Ghazzī's *sharḥ* on Abū Shujāʿ's *Manual of Shāfiʿī fiqh* (known as *Matn Abī Shujāʿ*). The short *matn* is arranged according to the traditional chapters (*abwāb*) of standard *fiqh* books. The *sharḥ*, being a terse commentary, is expounded on by al-Bājūrī's gloss, which goes much deeper than the original *matn* or *sharḥ*. The *matn* also does not always conform to the later relied upon (*muʿtamad*) positions in the *madhhab*, thus on its own it would not be considered a sufficient text from which to learn *fiqh*. Rather, it seems to be a tradition to honor the *matn* by expounding on its contents while also offering what were later deemed to be the more correct views on various matters.

- *al-Musalsalāt* [A collection of chains of authorization]. A collection of a type of *ḥadīth*s called *al-tasalsal*, which al-Bājūrī describes as

> a class of narrations, the apparent meaning of which is that there is no dust on them, either with regard to the attribute of what has been narrated, or with regard to the narrator, or his state, or with regard to the time in which it was narrated.[58]

In this work, al-Bājūrī narrates a number of *ḥadīth*, in which each link in the chain of narration has a similar circumstance, such as being narrated on a given day, at a holiday prayer, while the narrator holds the hand of the one he narrates from, or while holding a set of prayer beads.

Unfinished Works

- *Ḥāshiya ʿalā jamʿ al-jawāmiʿ fī uṣūl al-fiqh li Tāj al-Subkī* [A gloss on Tāj al-Subkī's "Collection of collections regarding *uṣūl al-fiqh*"].[59]
- *Ḥāshiya ʿalā sharḥ al-Saʿd li ʿaqāʾid al-Nasafī* [A gloss on Saʿd [al-Taftazānī's] commentary on al-Nasafī's creed].[60]
- *Ḥāshiya ʿalā matn al-manhaj fī fiqh al-Shāfiʿiyya li Shaykh al-Islām Zakariyya al-Anṣārī* [A gloss on Shaykh al-Islām Zakariyya al-Anṣārī's text: "The method regarding Shāfiʿī *fiqh*"].[61]
- *Sharḥ manẓūma al-Shaykh al-Bukhārī fī l-tawḥīd* [A commentary on the didactic poem of Shaykh al-Bukhārī regarding *tawḥīd*].
- *Ḥāshiya ʿalā tafsīr al-Rāzī* [A gloss on Fakhr al-Dīn al-Rāzī's exegesis on the Qurʾān].
- *Taʿlīq ʿalā tafsīr al-kashāf li-l-Zamakhsharī* [A commentary on al-Zamakhsharī's exegesis: "The discoverer of revealed truths"].
- *Ḥāshiya ʿalā sharḥ al-Talkhīṣ* [A gloss on al-Taftazānī's commentary on al-Khaṭīb al-Qazwīnī's (d. 739/1339) popular rhetoric text: "Epitome of the key regarding the science of meanings and clarification."][62]

Al-Bājūrī's literary output further illuminates the contours and textures of the archetypal scholar. He wrote on the core sciences—*fiqh*, *uṣūl al-dīn*, and *taṣawwūf*—as well as their ancillary and supporting sciences. His *fiqh* writings were based on the Shāfiʿī school, in a lineage that stretches back to al-Ghazālī, via al-Nawawī (d. 676/ 1277), Ibn Ḥajar, and al-Ramlī (d. 1004/1596). His theological writings were deeply entrenched in al-Sanūsī's thought, along with other later Ashʿarīs such as al-Taftazānī (c. 792/1390) and al-Rāzī. His Sufism is imbued with Ghazālian, Naqshbandī, and a great deal of Shādhilī thought, as demonstrated by the many references to Shādhilī scholars such as al-Būṣīrī, al-Shādhilī's forefather Abū Madyan (d. 594/1198), and others.[63]

I became interested in al-Bājūrī's works with the notion that to understand al-Bājūrī's thought is to understand an important and widespread conception of Sunnī Islam as it was taught in the pre-modern world, especially in al-Azhar and similar centers of learning. Prior to the changes made to al-Azhar's curriculum in the twentieth century, a student at al-Azhar would customarily study most of the texts found in a compendium called *Majmuʿat al-mutūn*.[64] Study would consist of reading commentaries and glosses on these core texts (*mutūn*), followed by the opportunity to write commentaries.[65] While many of al-Bājūrī's contemporaries wrote similar commentaries, sometimes on the same works, it is unclear why al-Bājūrī's became the standard even after his time, especially in Shāfiʿī law and Ashʿarī theology.

I have endeavored to ask this question of some of my associates who have studied at al-Azhar or under Shāfiʿī scholars, and have yet to hear any conclusive reasons for al-Bājūrī's fame. A common explanation for such things among Azharīs is "ḥuẓūẓ al-kutub min ḥuẓūẓ kātibīhā," that is, the fortune of books is according to the fortune of their authors. In every generation, scholars of equal caliber produce books; for unquantifiable reasons, some become more famous than others. Perhaps the answer may be found in the activities of al-Bājūrī's students and their positions in society, as some of them became Shaykh al-Azhar after his death. Gran mentions that al-Bājūrī taught many hours each day for most of his professional life,[66] interacting with many students and teachers as both a teacher and an administrator, thereby likely ensuring that a significant number of people were affected by his thought and influence. Additionally, since al-Bājūrī held the title Shaykh al-Azhar under Muḥammad ʿAlī Pasha and his successors, this position of influence may have affected the popularity of his books. Sachau, however, believed that the quality of al-Bājūrī's works warranted their popularity, so power may not be the deciding factor.

Al-Bājūrī does not explain in great detail his reasons for writing the commentaries that he did, other than the fact that a group of students, colleagues, or people in general (*khalq*), would ask him to do so, sometimes multiple times. Or, in some cases with regard to his earlier works, it came to his mind to write one and his teacher gave him permission (*ijāza*) to do so. In the case of his *Ḥāshiya ʿalā sharḥ Ibn al-Qāsim al-Ghazzī ʿalā matn Abī Shujāʿ fī fiqh al-Shāfiʿiyya*, he admits that there is great merit in the *Sharḥ* and in other glosses (*ḥawāshī*) such as that of al-Barmāwī, but that some of the passages are difficult and thus must be clarified and written in simpler terms.[67] Likewise in the introduction to his *Tuḥfat al-murīd*, being a *ḥāshiya* on al-Laqānī's *Jawharat al-tawḥīd*, he states that he was asked to write a gloss that would "unveil the ambiguous passages that contain allusions and secrets."[68] In doing so, he refers to previous commentaries, especially that of al-Laqānī's son, ʿAbd al-Salām.

In the case of a commentary on his teacher's books, it is clear that such undertakings may have been motivated by a desire to sharpen his knowledge of the subject, serve other students by explaining the text, serve his teacher's legacy, and perhaps begin building a corpus of published and peer-reviewed texts for professional advancement. In the case of al-Bājūrī's commentaries on texts such as those by Ibn al-Qāsim al-Ghazzī or al-Laqānī, one may wonder why, after centuries of popularity, other commentators' works were eclipsed by al-Bājūrī's.

Al-Bājūrī's Commentaries and Their Predecessors

I have endeavored to compare three of al-Bājūrī's commentaries with their popular predecessors. I have compared Ḥāshiya ʿalā sharḥ Ibn al-Qāsim al-Ghazzī ʿalā matn Abī Shujāʿ fī fiqh al-Shāfiʿiyya with al-Barmāwī's commentary on the famed Shāfiʿī text; Tuḥfat al-murīd with ʿAbd al-Salām al-Laqānī's commentary; and al-Bājūrī's commentary on al-Akhḍarī's Sullam with his teacher al-Quwaysnī's commentary. Although there are aspects of al-Bājūrī's commentaries that appear to be derivative from previous commentaries, even those which his commentaries came to replace (especially al-Barmāwī's), they nonetheless evidence al-Bājūrī's navigation of the tradition and offer his own insight.

Al-Bājūrī's *Tuḥfat al-murīd* is one of his most popular works, being a commentary on the popular didactic poem *Jawharat al-tawḥīd* on Islamic theology. Al-Bājūrī's commentary is still studied today around the world, with multiple critical editions by various contemporary scholars. ʿAbd al-Salām al-Laqānī's commentary on his father's poem was a standard commentary for centuries. Though substantial in its depth, it is far shorter than al-Bājūrī's *Tuḥfat al-murīd*. Its length and depth indicate that it might ideally be an introductory commentary, worth studying before reading al-Bājūrī's *Tuḥfat al-murīd*.

Issues that al-Laqānī treats in a sentence or two warrant paragraphs or even pages in al-Bājūrī's commentary. In discussing Allah's attribute of existence (*wujūd*), al-Laqānī makes no mention of the controversial issue *waḥdat al-wujūd* (the unity of existence). In contrast, al-Bājūrī, as well as his contemporary al-Ṣāwī,[69] go into considerably more depth. At times al-Bājūrī and al-Ṣāwī overlap in their depth (and wording, perhaps indicating borrowing or exposure to a common source), but al-Bājūrī often goes a bit further. Also, whereas al-Ṣāwī seems to offer more of an apologetic explanation of the term, al-Bājūrī is forgiving of its use, but pushes readers away from the topic. They make a similar statement about the common folk who say "Allah is existent in every place." Al-Bājūrī, however, rejects this, stating that it is impermissible, since it gives the mistaken impression of indwelling and incarnation, whereas al-Ṣāwī accepts and supports it when interpreted as "He is with every existent thing, that is, he is not absent from anything." Despite this overlap, al-Bājūrī additionally cites *shaṭḥ* statements (ecstatic utterances), Junayd's ruling on al-Ḥallāj's execution, and treats the subject from his own perspective.

Al-Bājūrī's discussion of the verse of al-Laqānī's poem on the matter of Allah preferring some angels and prophets over others provides further evidence that al-Bājūrī's commentary is more than a derivative summary, rather it is an expression of his views on the subject of theology. He examines such questions as: Are the angels better than all prophets, except Muḥammad? Are other prophets better than angels? Are some humans better than some angels, while other angels may be better than them? Is there a decisive statement on the matter? Should one refrain from even discussing the issue?

Interestingly, al-Bājūrī prefers the Māturīdī opinion over the dominant Ashʿarī opinion, and argues that some humans (prophets) are better than all angels, some humans (including some of the Prophet Muḥammad's Companions) are better than some but not all angels, some angels are better than some humans, and some are lower in rank than some humans but better than others. Regarding the Māturīdī position expressed in al-Laqānī's poem, al-Bājūrī says: "And this is the preponderant way," that is, the more reliable position.[70] Al-Ṣāwī holds the same opinion and both al-Bājūrī and al-Ṣāwī express their conclusion using the same language (again indicating either borrowing, or a shared source), while ʿAbd al-Salām al-Laqānī opines that all angels are better than all humans, except prophets, in disagreement with al-Bājūrī and al-Ṣāwī who hold that Abū Bakr, ʿUmar, ʿUthman, and ʿAlī are superior to the generality of angels other than Gabriel, Isrāfil, Mikāʾīl, and ʿIzrāʾīl. Al-Bājūrī and al-Ṣāwī's opinions overlap in the matter of their disagreement with ʿAbd al-Salām al-Laqānī, while in the matter of the unity of existence, al-Bājūrī and al-Ṣāwī disagree and ʿAbd al-Salām al-Laqānī is silent. It appears from this brief comparison, and a more comprehensive reading and investigation, that al-Bājūrī was using the genre of commentary to express his own views. Sometimes this was done by citing one opinion with which he agrees, from multiple conflicting opinions; at other times he states his opinion without citing a previous source (though often one exists). Presenting various precedents is a form of expressing one's opinions, and the fact that al-Bājūrī includes topics absent from other commentaries, or opinions in contradiction to other commentaries, indicates that he exercised some degree of autonomy, as discussed in greater detail in Chapters 3 and 4.[71]

Regarding al-Bājūrī's commentary and its relation to al-Barmāwī's commentary on al-Ghazzī's commentary on *Matn* Abī Shujāʿ, the derivative nature of some passages of al-Bājūrī's commentary is more apparent. It is clear that he did not seek to contradict and do away with al-Barmāwī's view, as his introduction indicates, but it is also clear that he went far beyond merely clarifying some passages that were unclear in al-Barmāwī's work.

For example, al-Barmāwī's commentary is shorter and more focused than al-Bājūrī's. At times, it appears that al-Bājūrī is speaking in his own voice, where in fact he is echoing al-Barmāwī, as when he says "this issue has come to be called 'the matter of the Pashas' with the people of these times (*ahl ʿaṣr*)" which is a verbatim quote from al-Barmāwī; although written centuries earlier it may still have been relevent.[72] However, al-Bājūrī's deeper discussions delve into side matters not mentioned by al-Barmāwī, thus indicating that al-Bājūrī did not view his commentary as a mere restatement or updated version of al-Barmāwī's.

When Abū Shujāʿ says "[I was asked] to write a short work on *fiqh* according to the *madhhab* of Imam Shāfiʿī,"[73] al-Bājūrī uses al-Ghazzī's two additional adjectives "al-Aʿẓam al-Mujtahid" (the great *mujtahid*) as an opportunity to discuss the issue of *ijtihād*.[74] Basing himself on al-Barmāwī, he covers similar ground, but explains some concepts in greater detail than al-Barmāwī, and also adds discussions not found in al-Barmāwī, such as the question of whether or not Ibn Ḥajar and al-Ramlī were capable of comparing and preferring an opinion of one *mujtahid* over another (*tarjīḥ*).[75]

Regarding the inclusion of the *basmalah* (the statement "In the name of Allah") at the beginning of the book, al-Barmāwī says little on the subject, whereas al-Bājūrī unpacks its *ḥadīth* sources and mentions five possible rulings regarding reciting it.[76] A comparison of the chapter on *ʿaqīqa*[77] by al-Barmāwī and al-Bājūrī clearly indicates that al-Bājūrī kept much of al-Barmāwī's text, though he added to it substantially. Each passage of the original text upon which they are commenting (that is al-Ghazzī's commentary on *Matn* Abī Shujaʿ) yields al-Barmāwī's main points in al-Bājūrī's text, sometimes word for word or paraphrased, followed by significant additional commentary by al-Bājūrī. Al-Bājūrī adds grammatical explanations and/or proofs from *ḥadīths* for the various components of the *ʿaqīqa*, along with comments on the *ḥadīths*' authenticity and implications. He further comments on the subject at hand with regard to what he feels should be explained in more detail.

By way of example, both mention the practice of rubbing the head of the newborn with the blood of the animal sacrificed on the occasion of the child's birth (*al-ʿaqīqa*). Al-Barmāwī declares it *makrūh*, while acknowledging a report from Ḥasan al-Basrī, who declared this practice recommended (*mandūb*). "Rubbing the head [i.e., the newborn's] with its blood [i.e., the sacrificed animal's] is disliked [*makrūh*], in opposition to the opinion of al-Ḥasan al-Basrī—may Allah be pleased with him—who considered it recommended (*mandūb*)."[78] Al-Bājūrī calls it an act from the times of pre-Islamic ignorance (*al-jāhiliyya*), saying it is not from the Prophet's recommended actions (*sunna*) despite al-Nawawī reporting a rigorously authenticated (*ṣaḥīḥ*) report from the Prophet.

> It is not recommended (*lā yasunnu*) to rub his [i.e., the newborn's head] with the blood of the sacrificed animal, because it is from an action of the era of pre-Islamic ignorance. However, the rigorously authenticated report (*al-khabar al-ṣaḥīḥ*) as found in [al-Nawawī's] *al-Majmūʿ* [states], is that he [i.e., the Prophet] said: "For the boy is his sacrifice, so spill its blood upon him and remove from him harm." With that, al-Ḥasan [al-Basrī] and Qatāda considered it highly meritorious (*mustaḥab*) to rub his head with blood and then wash it away.[79]

Here both give a similar ruling, but al-Bājūrī seems harsher in his condemnation, and apparently rejects the *ḥadīth* based on the principle that a practice associated with a pre-Islamic practice is impermissible (at least in the sense of being *makrūh*). He adds a number of details not found in al-Barmāwī's text, namely the association of the practice with pre-Islamic custom, al-Baṣrī's proof for his differing ruling being a rigorously authenticated *ḥadīth*, the location and text of this *ḥadīth*, and al-Qatāda's (d. 118/736) further support of al-Baṣrī (d. 110/728).

The third set of commentaries that I compared were al-Bājūrī's commentary on al-Akhḍarī's *al-Sullam* (an introductory text on syllogistic logic (*manṭiq*)), the commentary of al-Bājūrī's teacher al-Quwaysnī, and that of al-Dasūqī (d. 1230/1815). Al-Quwaysnī's is the shortest of the three, and ostensibly the most basic. All three cover similar ground, although, like the previous sets of commentaries, al-Bājūrī's tends to be more comprehensive and goes into greater depth. By way of example, both al-Dasūqī and al-Bājūrī comment similarly on the matter of the three different opinions regarding the permissibility of logic (whether it is forbidden, necessary, or permissible for one firmly grounded in the faith), perhaps indicating a common source. Al-Quwaysnī however, treats the subject more tersely, but like al-Bājūrī and al-Dasūqī, clearly states that the subject of debate is only the logic of the early logicians; the logic of the later logicians being agreed upon in its permissibility.[80] The editor of the text also acknowledges that the disagreement regards the earlier forms of logic. Al-Quwaysnī's text is shorter, perhaps intended as an introductory text to be expounded on by the teacher. Al-Bājūrī, however, appears to feel impelled to cover more ground. While this may be, in part, intended to assist the student, it may also be that al-Bājūrī saw these commentaries as a platform from which to express his opinions, perhaps in a way that teaching did not allow, or in a way that teaching alone would not preserve. It may be that he had something to say, to which he felt future generations should be privy.

Al-Bājūrī's Literary Sources and the Commentary Tradition

It is apparent from the comparison of these texts that they tend to draw from common sources, at times from previous commentaries, but each expounds on (or condenses) the topic in its own way. In each case, al-Bājūrī's commentaries tend to exceed the others in examples, related and tangential discussions, proofs, and grammar. There are likely other commentaries which exceed his attention to detail, though I have not cited them here.

In each case, al-Bājūrī indicates to the reader that he is familiar with previous commentaries, which he praises, and he states that he is offering his own clarifications in order to further elucidate the original texts. It is clear that al-Bājūrī relies heavily on past commentaries, as well as post seventh/thirteenth-century texts, however, it is not yet clear to me whether or not he had access to all of the pre-Mamlūk texts that he cites, such as al-Shāfiʿī's texts, or al-Muzanī's (d. 264/877), or other foundational texts. After studying al-Bājūrī's *Tuḥfat al-murīd*, Delanoue concludes:

> We can effectively conclude from reading this manual, that Baguri has almost no direct contact with religious literature of the classical age. The works he uses, indeed those he has at his disposal, are attributable to authors from the Mamluk and Ottoman eras; these authors are mostly—but not exclusively—Egyptians and Maghrebins; some were teachers, or teachers of teachers.[81]

That al-Bājūrī was teaching from and producing a commentary on Fakhr al-Dīn al-Rāzī's exegesis of the Qurʾān indicates that he had access to at least one pre-Mamlūk text. Likewise, he was working on a commentary on the exegesis of the Muʿtazilī scholar al-Zamakhsharī (d. 538/1144), bringing us to two important pre-Mamlūk texts at his disposal. As discussed later, it is likely that al-Bājūrī read al-Shīrāzī, albeit potentially accompanied by the commentaries of al-Nawawī or other Mamlūk-era scholars. Whether he read al-Ashʿarī, al-Baqillānī, or other scholars of the "Classical Age" remains to be seen, yet it seems fair to question the extent to which Delanoue's comment holds true.

In any case, there is no doubt that al-Bājūrī relied heavily on previous commentaries, as well as what was transmitted from his teachers, but he certainly referenced earlier works, regardless of whether or not he had direct access to them in their entirety. That he and his contemporaries relied on later recensions and discussions is often viewed as evidence of decline, though, ironically, this reliance was often a result of later works being deemed more dependable, because they had been processed and refined over many generations.

We see al-Bājūrī functioning within a connected tradition whose pedagogy dictates that one study and be firmly rooted in the tradition, yet also offer a service to his contemporaries by clarifying, or in some cases, challenging,[82] the works of previous authors. Shaykh ʿAlī Jumʿa's views in explanation and defense of the tradition of writing commentaries support this sentiment. Al-Bājūrī, he explains, was one of the last great commentators in a tradition of commentary that evolved in stages, beginning with al-Nawawī, whose *al-Minhāj* is an explanation of al-Rāfiʿī's *al-Muḥarrar*, moving then to the time of al-Taftazānī (c. 792/1390) and al-Jurjānī (c. 816/1413), both of whom wrote commentaries on an *uṣūl al-fiqh* text by Ibn al-Ḥājib.[83] After this time, Shaykh Sulaymān al-Jamal (c. 1204/1790) wrote commentaries on al-Suyūṭī's works; al-Suyūṭī was a prolific commentator in his day—his commentary on al-Nawawī's *Taqrīb* is still an important work in the field of *ḥadīth*. Jumʿa states that the commentary tradition spread after this time, and that the twelfth/eighteenth century began a phase of commentary that lasted until 1350/1931.

After this brief historical outline of the commentary tradition, Jumʿa offers his view as to why it occurred: from al-Shāfiʿī's time until that of al-Nawawī, the Arabic language was stable and secure and the culture was largely oral. Thus, one gathers from his explanation that people understood the texts because of their closeness to the language; they could discuss their meanings in greater detail with their teachers. When, in al-Nawawī's time, Baghdad was sacked by the Tartārs (Mongols), its books were burned, and its scholars killed. These events ushered in the era of commentary literature, the goal of which was to preserve the knowledge of religion and transmit it accurately to future generations.

Thus, it was not, according to Jumʿa, a matter of decline, but rather the necessity of explaining the texts to later generations in the language of their time. It might, however, be argued that this was in fact the decline—that is, all efforts went into interpretation and transmission—however, this does not mean that all independent legal reasoning (*ijtihād)* came to an end, rather, as discussed below, certain types of *ijtihād* continued. Additionally, there may have been motivations other than just the impetus toward preservation, specifically, professional advancement: writing commentaries may have been a means of establishing one's professional credentials.[84]

Jumʿa also states that the endeavor was a communal effort and a conversation across the lands and generations of Islam. While it is true that many foundational matters had been decided, the fact that in each generation a number of scholars wrote commentaries on similar works, discussing a shared set of topics, and offering their own opinions on them, is proof that the situation was not, as is often presented, one of mindless regurgitation of past authors' thoughts. Furthermore, a host of issues not discussed in the times of the early founders of the *madhhabs* became an almost mandatory subject matter, thus increasing the quantity of data with which each generation dealt. Furthermore, *ijtihād*, Ibn Sīnā's metaphysics, or a particular literary format rather than another are not the sole measure of intellectual vibrancy or critical thinking within an Islamic society; therefore, the notion of decline is probably an oversimplification of the matter based on the arbitrary assignment of value to certain discussions over others.[85]

Al-Bājūrī's life and works were certainly influenced, in varying degrees, by the intellectual, cultural, and political milieu in which he lived, yet he and his intellectual career are representative of a broad model of scholarship and a method of education that was normative for centuries before his time, within and outside of Egypt. The following chapter discusses al-Bājūrī's view of religion, religious history and method, and the nature of the tradition which he inherited, embraced, and transmitted.

2

Al-Bājūrī's View of Religion and Method in the Egyptian Milieu

The Archetype and Method

Al-Bājūrī and most of his contemporaries and predecessors were what I call archetypal scholars. While he did not use this term, his view of normative scholarship would have conformed to the description of the archetypal scholar given below. The archetypal scholar was a jurist, a theologian, and a mystic. He was the ideal, the authority, the representative of Sunnī teachings in the pre-modern Muslim world, the scholar (*ʿālim*). While numerous scholars focused mainly on ancillary or supporting sciences—such as belles-lettres, grammar, *ḥadīth* memorization and transmission, and *tajwīd*[1]—the archetypal scholars were often the super-scholars who became rectors of major universities, and given titles such as Shaykh al-Islam, and the likes.

Authority and Authenticity: *Ijāza*, *Idhn*, *Isnād*, and *Ijtihād*

Such super-scholars felt the need for authenticity and authority in legal rulings, theological doctrines, and mystical practices; they adhered to a system of authority that qualified a student in a given subject based on his confirmed understanding of core texts. This understanding was confirmed by teachers, whose understandings were confirmed by their teachers, in a successive chain of confirmation reaching back to the Prophet or the person considered to be the founder of a given discipline. The archetypal scholar's understanding was formally confirmed by an ijāza, which could generally be called a license to teach.[2]

Some of al-Bājūrī's early works are commentaries on his teacher al-Faḍālī's theological works, namely *Kifāyat al-ʿawām* and *Risālat fī Lā ilāha illa-Llāh*. In the introductions to both books he mentions that al-Faḍālī gave him permission (*idhn*) to write these commentaries, indicating that he relied on al-Faḍālī's confirmation of his mastery of the texts, and was likely still in the process of becoming a fully recognized scholar in his own right.[3]

As mentioned in the previous chapter, al-Bājūrī granted *ijāzas* to a number of people, including students from each of the four *madhhabs*. In one *ijāza*, written for a Shaykh ʿAlī l-Jurjāwī, al-Bājūrī says, after the traditional praises of Allah and salutations on the Prophet, and other introductory matters:

> . . . My brother, the great scholar and sea of understanding, Shaykh ʿAlī l-Jurjāwī b. Shaykh ʿAwaḍ al-Bardīsī asked that I grant him an *ijāza*, so I granted him permission in that in which I had been granted permission, in narration of *ḥadīths*, Qurʾānic exegesis (*tafsīr*), and other than that such as the *kutub al-maʿqūl* (books on the rational sciences). . . .[4]

With the *ijāza* tradition, a scholar could name his intellectual forefathers, that is, state his *isnād* (chain of transmission) for a given text or discipline. If not explicitly stated in the *ijāza*, the chain of transmission might be deduced by determining from whom one's teacher received *ijāzas*, and then the same would be done for his teachers, on back through the chain to the founder of the discipline, author of the text, or narrator of the *ḥadīth*, respectively. The validity of such a claim could be determined in much the same way that the validity of a *ḥadīth* can be determined, by examining the overall character and qualification of the people mentioned in the chain, as well as through other historiographical means.

An example of an explicitly stated *isnād* can be found in al-Bājūrī's *al-Musalsalāt*, in which al-Bājūrī narrates a *ḥadīth* about the merits of fasting the 10th day of the Islamic month of Muḥarram—known as the day of *ʿāshūrā*. He narrates the *ḥadīth* from his teacher al-Amīr al-Kabīr, who narrates from his father (from whom al-Bājūrī also narrates), who lists his *isnād* back to the Prophet. The *isnād* itself tells us something about the scholars through whom al-Bājūrī's knowledge passed, as it includes people from different lands and affiliations, including a Mālikī follower of the Shādhilī order from the city of Fez, as well as ʿAbd al-Salām al-Laqānī who narrates from his father, Ibrāhīm al-Laqānī on whose work *Jawharat al-tawḥīd* both ʿAbd al-Salām, and, a few centuries later, al-Bājūrī both wrote commentaries.

Al-Bājūrī mentions that his teacher Muḥammad b. al-Imām al-Amīr took the *ḥadīth* of *ʿāshūrā* from his father, on the day of

ʿāshūrā, many times in the presence of notables and scholars, and then gave al-Bājūrī an *ijāza* (also on the day of *ʿāshūrā*), permitting him to narrate it to others, just as al-Amīr's father had done for his son and all those present. He also indicates that al-Amīr had heard it narrated by his father, as well as narrated it back to his father, indicating two important means of transmitting and verifying knowledge, that is, listening to and absorbing from a teacher or narrating to one's teacher to verify proper recitation, memorization, or understanding.[5]

The archetypal scholar also recognized that authority in some matters requires mastery of multiple disciplines of which only a few scholars were capable, and thus he adhered to the system of following a *mujtahid*—one capable of *ijtihād*—if he himself had not yet reached the same level of *ijtihād*.[6] This was the view of al-Bājūrī and indeed was the standard view throughout much of Sunnī history. Al-Bājūrī, some of his contemporaries such as Shaykh Muḥammad ʿIlīsh, as well as earlier scholars such as al-Suyūṭī, held that about 300 years after the death of the Prophet the first level *ijtihād* of the founders of the Sunnī schools of law (*madhāhib*) came to an end.[7] However, as discussed below, this did not entail that all *ijtihād* came to an end, or that those who did not declare *ijtihād* for themselves did not exercise juridical autonomy, that is, state their own legal opinions.

The Harmony of Reason and Revelation

The archetypal scholar is also a theologian who, in addition to requiring authenticity and authority in transmission and judgment, expects a harmony between reason and revelation such that theological beliefs do not lead to excess in metaphorical or anthropomorphic interpretation.

The archetypal scholar falls into two main categories with regard to theology. The first category includes those scholars who have a thorough knowledge of the rational sciences, including rational proofs (*kalām*) and sometimes syllogistic logic (*manṭiq*); these sciences enable them to buttress the tenets of faith with rational proofs. Some from this category, though not all, also use the interpretive method of *taʾwīl* (metaphorical interpretation) to interpret primary texts that ostensibly contain contradictions between the intellect and revelation. A classic example is Allah's declared dissimilarity from creation and the relation between this dissimilarity and, for example, His use of the term *yad* (hand) or the likes with regard to Himself. Other scholars in this first category include those who engage in the discussion of creedal matters using rational proofs (*kalām*), yet do not utilize metaphorical interpretation (*ta'wīl*), rather they left such problematic texts uninterpreted, believing that the reality of their meaning should be left to the one who said them (Allah or the Prophet Muḥammad). This method is called *tafwīḍ* (lit., entrustment or consignment).

Al-Bājūrī was an archetypal scholar of this first category of theologians who, as discussed later in this work, was an Ashʿarī who considered *kalām* to be a communal obligation. He considered logic (*manṭiq*)," as a supporting science of *kalām*, to be a communal obligation as well. He opined that one had a choice between *ta'wīl* and *tafwīḍ*, though he appeared to prefer *ta'wīl*. Although he adhered to the Ashʿarī school overall, since uncritical acceptance (*taqlīd*) was, in his opinion, impermissible in matters of faith, he did not blindly adopt all Ashʿarī views, and even held opinions associated with the Māturīdī school that were in opposition to the Ashʿarī school.

The second category of theologians, who are referred to as Atharīs throughout this work, includes those scholars who refrain from entering into discussions of creed that rely on rational proofs and *ta'wīl*; they claim that in matters of theology reliance need only be on texts transmitted from Allah or the Prophet, that is, the Qur'ān or the *Ḥadīth*. This second category includes two subcategories of scholars, namely those who engage in *tafwīḍ*, and those who do not. Those who do not engage in *tafwīḍ*, and also avoid rational proofs and *ta'wīl*, rely on an interpretive method that appears to be excessively literalistic, at least outwardly, though closer examination reveals that they utilize a complex method of justification, which may just as well be termed *kalām*. These scholars accept problematic terms literally, rather than metaphorically, yet they also redefine the literal definition according to the textual context.[8] The success of the scholars of this second category at avoiding the use of rational proofs is a subject of debate that will be discussed throughout this work.

Al-Bājūrī does not pay much attention to the theological opinions of this second category of theologians, regardless of their views on *tafwīḍ*, as their theological influence had little impact on al-Bājūrī and his colleagues, despite the revival of their thought among the followers of Muḥammad b. ʿAbd al-Wahhāb. Like many Ashʿarīs, al-Bājūrī dismissed those scholars who are against *kalām*, *ta'wīl*, and *tafwīḍ*, as a minority of anthropomorphists whose views appear unworthy of consideration. In many ways, however, when viewed from a different perspective, the views of the Atharīs are not as radically different from the Ashʿarīs. Though not without controversy and explanation, many such Atharīs are also, arguably, included in the category of archetypal scholars.

Sharīʿa Compliant Spirituality

The archetypal scholar is also a mystic who feels the need for a spiritual[9] (*ruḥānī*) experience of faith that can be achieved and explained without contradicting his or her juristic and theological views. He affirms the goals, realities, and states of *taṣawwūf* (the science of Islamic mysticism or Sufism), particularly the unitive experience (though with varying interpretations and explanations), and applies certain methodological teachings—in concordance with his understanding of the *Sharīʿa*—in order to achieve them. While there may be some realities and states that are debated, as well as disagreement about the means of achieving the goals of Sufism, the archetypal scholar sees *taṣawwūf* as being necessarily linked to *fiqh* (jurisprudence) and *uṣūl al-dīn* (lit., the foundations of religion, more generally meaning theology).

Like the study of the legal and theological sciences, Sufism must be transmitted from legitimate teachers whose mastery of the discipline was necessarily confirmed by their teachers, themselves confirmed and qualified by an authentic chain of authority. A fully realized Sufi could trace his spiritual genealogy via a connected chain of authorities called a *silsila*, just as a narrator of *ḥadīth* could mention his *isnād*.

Al-Bājūrī considered Sufism to be a fruit of all the Islamic sciences, despite it having its own technical terminology and specialists. Others considered Sufism its own science, though necessarily connected to law and theology. Many rectors and professors of al-Azhar, including al-Bājūrī, had Sufi affiliations, and it was taught in varying degrees in many institutions of higher learning, including al-Azhar. According to some previously mentioned accounts, a student at al-Azhar in the nineteenth century began his day with the study of the Qurʾān, just after the morning prayers, followed by *ḥadīth*, Qurʾānic sciences (exegesis, *tajwīd*, etc.), *ḥadīth* sciences (biography of narrators, etc.), theology, legal methodology, jurisprudence, and eventually closing his daily studies with Sufism after the evening prayer.[10] While purely speculative, I assume that Sufism was saved until the end of the day, as a reminder that those ruinous traits that may have arisen in disagreements on matters of law and interpretation must be removed from one's heart. In addition, the spiritual fulfillment students hoped to attain from the study and application of Sufi principles was likely sought as night, a time of reflection and additional prayer, fell. In any case, Sufism in al-Bājūrī's day was an accepted norm though it was studied and practiced with differing approaches and emphases depending on the individual. In al-Bājūrī's time, the archetypal scholar had ample opportunity to tread the Sufi path, seeking a spiritual experience of faith that was in harmony with his legal and theological opinions.

The Gabrielian Paradigm: Al-Bājūrī's View of the Three Dimensions of Islam

The innate drive of the archetypal scholar for authentic and qualified legal scholarship, harmonious rational and revelation-based theology, and spiritually meaningful experiences of faith and practice within the boundaries of the orthodox legal and theological teachings corresponds to the primary emphases of his religion. There are three core dimensions to the archetypal scholar—legal, theological, and spiritual—each related to one of the three core sciences of Sunnī Islam, respectively. Sunnī Islam was traditionally considered to consist of three main elements: *islām*, *īmān*, and *iḥsān*—that is, law, belief, and mysticism. This tripartite division of Islam's key constituents can be found in the *ḥadīth* literature, as well as in the chapter headings of a good number of pre-modern works that were intended to be comprehensive treatments of Islam, either in the form of basic manuals for the average person, or more specialized texts on topics such as comparative jurisprudence.[11]

I call the tripartite division of Islam's core dimensions the Gabrielian paradigm. The narrator of the famed "Gabriel *Ḥadīth*" found in the *ḥadīth* collection of Muslim b. Ḥajjāj (d. 261/875) recounts an event in which the angel Gabriel came to the Prophet and his Companions in human form and posed a series of questions to the Prophet, and affirmed their answers. The questions led to an explanation of the religion of Islam as consisting of three interrelated parts: *islām*, *īmān*, and *iḥsān*. Al-Bājūrī narrates and comments on this *ḥadīth* in his book *al-Durar al-ḥisān ʿalā fatḥ al-Raḥmān fī mā yaḥṣīlu bihi al-islām wa-l-īmān li-l-Zubaydī* [The splendid pearls: A commentary on al-Zubaydī's book, The opening of the Merciful in that which is attained by *islām* and *īmān*]. Although al-Zubaydī's text focuses only on *islām* and *īmān*, al-Bājūrī narrates the entire *ḥadīth*, including the discussion of *iḥsān*. The three dimensions of the religion of Islam, as discussed by al-Bājūrī and his predecessors, are outlined below.

Islām: Law

Islām is the term indicating the aspect of the religion that pertains to rules and regulations governing the limbs. Al-Bājūrī says of the term *islām*, as mentioned in the Gabriel *ḥadīth*, "linguistically it means being completely tractable (*inqiyād*), and as a technical term it is being tractable and submitting (*istislām*) to that which the Prophet came with, peace and blessings of Allah be upon him."[12] One therefore submits his limbs to the message brought by the Prophet, that is, one adheres to the rules and regulations of the faith with regard to one's actions in worship or in society.

Associated with the dimension of *islām* is the science of *fiqh* (jurisprudence). Al-Bājūrī's discussion of the meaning of *fiqh* affirms that linguistically it means "understanding" and as a technical term it refers to "knowledge of the legal rulings pertaining to actions acquired from detailed proofs."[13] It is the science of determining the legal rulings for a given action, especially those that require deduction, investigation, and detailed proofs, rather than those clearly and unambiguously stated in the primary texts.

Al-Bājūrī says, regarding the legal rulings of *fiqh*:

> The legal rulings (*al-aḥkām al-sharʿiyya*) are ten. Five are based on revelation (*waḍʿiyya*), and they are [based on] the speech of Allah that is connected to making a thing a cause (*sabab*),[14] a condition (*sharṭ*),[15] a preventative (*māniʿ*),[16] valid (*ṣaḥīḥ*), or invalid (*fāsid*). [The other] five are related to imposing a duty (*taklīfiyya*), and they are obligatory, forbidden, recommended, disliked, or neutral.[17]

According to the jurists, all human actions fall under one of these five legal rulings.

When issues were not clearly stated in the primary texts, certain scholars (*mujtahids*—those who undertook *ijtihād*) developed methods for deducing the proper response to such issues and determining under which legal category they might fall. Circles of students often gathered around these scholars to study methods and rulings; these circles of students, or followers of the rulings of a given teacher, became identified as schools of thought, or *madhhabs*. According to pre-modern Muslim scholars, and a number of Western scholars of Islamic law, these schools were named after their respective founders. By al-Bājūrī's time, only four *madhhabs* were deemed properly preserved, namely those founded by Abū Ḥanīfa (d. 150/767), Mālik b. Anas (d. 179/796), Muḥammad b. Idris al-Shāfiʿī (d. 204/820), and Aḥmad b. Ḥanbal (d. 241/855).[18]

While Sunnī scholars such as al-Bājūrī have traditionally identified the beginning of the *madhhabs* with their eponymous founders, some Western Islamicists[19] have rejected this ascription to some or all of the four schools.[20] These rejections are usually based on redefining the term "founder" or "*madhhab*." Traditional Islamic scholars—as well as certain scholars in the modern Western academic tradition—assert that Islamic law began with the Prophet and was followed by his Companions, who at times reached consensus on issues and at other times differed among themselves.[21] From the regional schools that emerged around various Companions or their successors, individual schools that centered around the methodology of a key scholar then emerged. There are clear links from the founders to their immediate students and then to the later formulations of the *madhhab*s, despite changes in rulings, variable methods, or institutional support.

Numerous schools of law (*madhhab*) emerged and flourished for relatively short periods, frequently only while a scholar or his students were living. By the seventh/thirteenth century, there remained four main Sunnī schools, though small groups continued to follow the school of Dāwūd al-Ẓāhirī (d. 270/883), the Ẓāhirī school, and the school of Muḥammad b. Jarīr al-Ṭabarī (d. 310/923), the Jarīrī school. The four surviving schools are the Ḥanafī, Mālikī, Shāfiʿī, and Ḥanbalī, as noted above.

In *Tuḥfat al-murīd*, al-Bājūrī mentions several founders of the other Sunnī schools of law and offers some information on each, thus recognizing the validity of each school.[22] He does this in a conscious effort to show the significance of these schools, and confirm that validity extended beyond the four surviving schools. He also recognizes the validity of adopting the rulings of some of the defunct *madhhabs* in one's personal life, though he cites the consensus on the impermissibility of issuing rulings (*fatwā*) or deriving judicial verdicts based on them.

After naming the founders of the four schools as the guides of the community, al-Bājūrī mentions:

> There [also] includes . . . al-Imām al-Layth b. Saʿd, and Dāwūd al-Ẓāhirī, for he was a mountain of knowledge; whatever was narrated from al-Imām al-Ḥaramayn [al-Juwaynī] that he neither relied upon nor took anything from the sayings of the Ẓāhiriyya refers to a specific party [of Ẓāhirīs] such as Ibn Ḥazm. There also includes Sufyān al-Thawrī, who was given the title Commander of the Faithful (Amīr al-Muʾminīn)[23] in the science of *ḥadīth*. [There also includes] Ibn Isḥāq b. Rāhawī, Muḥammad b. Jarīr al-Ṭabarī, and Sufyān b. ʿUyayna. . . . [There also

includes] ʿAbd al-Raḥmān b. ʿAmr al-Awzāʿī . . . [There also includes] al-Imām Abū l-Ḥasan al-Ashʿarī and Abū Manṣūr al-Māturīdī.[24]

Al-Bājūrī's inclusion of the last two scholars, al-Ashʿarī and Abū Manṣūr al-Māturīdī, is not so much a recognition of their contributions to law, but rather an indication of their high rank as founders of the two main schools of Sunnī theology. Theology, discussed below, does not enter into the sphere of *islām* (which pertains to the law of the limbs in ritual and society), rather, it pertains to the second dimension of the religion of Islam as discussed in the Gabriel *ḥadīth*, namely *īmān*.

Īmān: Belief

Īmān refers to the beliefs held in the heart and mind, as found in the Qurʾān or the *ḥadīth*.[25] Al-Bājūrī defines *īmān* thus: "Linguistically it means assent (*taṣdīq*).[26] Its technical meaning is belief in[27] everything that the Prophet brought."[28] The six most crucial beliefs, according to the Gabriel *ḥadīth*, are the belief in Allah, His messengers, the revealed books, the angels, the Day of Judgment, and destiny.

The science associated with *īmān* is often called *uṣūl al-dīn* (the foundations of religion), *ʿilm al-tawḥīd* (the science of God's unity), or *ʿaqīda* (creed).[29] Within the science of *ʿaqīda*, there are two distinct methods, as mentioned earlier, one which claims to determine proper beliefs solely from primary texts such as the Qurʾān and *Ḥadīth* (a method which is in fact rare), and another which takes these primary text-based beliefs and corroborates them with the use of rational proofs (*kalām*). There are three main schools of Sunnī theology that are typically identified, namely the Ashʿarī, Māturīdī, and Atharī schools.

A school of theology, if we are to consider it analogous to a school of law (*madhhab*), must consist of constants and variables by which the contours of the school are delineated. Thus, a school of theology is a set of agreed upon beliefs and methodological bases for defending or deriving beliefs that are either not explicitly stated in primary texts or whose interpretation is not readily known because of the possibility of multiple interpretations. There must be a list of tenets and methods that one necessarily accepts in order to be considered a member of the school; rejection of these would constitute rejection of the school. At the same time, there must be other tenets or methods that can be accepted or rejected, which do not affect membership within the school. Ideally, one would also either claim to belong to a given school, or at minimum not disavow the school that the majority of his cohorts adhered to.[30]

After the Prophet Muḥammad's death, a number of theological and political issues arose in the rapidly expanding Muslim community. There was disagreement as to who was the rightful heir to political rule upon death of the Prophet. The faith of the one who committed a grave sin was debated; was he to be considered an apostate or a sinful believer? The Qur'ānic texts that ostensibly implied anthropomorphism demanded a legitimate hermeneutical approach, and several groups offered conflicting solutions. The nature of the Qur'ān and its relation to Allah's timeless and eternal speech elicited a powerful debate, while the question of whether or not the descriptions of the afterlife were literal or metaphorical also became a line of fissure. Attempts to determine the relationship between destiny and free will also resulted in sectarian divisions.[31]

There are some *ḥadīths* as well as reports from the lives of the Companions that indicate that these issues may have been discussed, in varying degrees, during the life of the Prophet and soon after his death. Over time the varying opinions on these and other issues resulted in the formation of sects such as the Mu'tazilī,[32] Khawārīj, Shī'a, and Qadariyya. The Sunnīs outlined their views on these issues, and wrote tracts against the various sects. A work of theology called *al-Fiqh al-akbar* is attributed to Abū Ḥanīfa and there are reports of Mālik b. Anas discussing matters of interpreting apparently anthropomorphic Qur'ānic verses.

These theological issues played themselves out in the political realm. In 218/833, the 'Abbāsid caliph al-Ma'mūn (r. 189–218/813–833), who had adopted the views of the Mu'tazilī regarding the createdness of the Qur'ān, instituted an oppressive inquisition (*miḥna*), threatening imprisonment and physical abuse to all who upheld the Sunnī view of the non-created eternality of the Qur'ān.

Al-Bājūrī comments on the *miḥna* thus:

> There befell a great test for many people of the Ahl al-Sunna. Al-Būkhārī fled, and said "Oh Allah, deliver me unto you unscathed by tribulation" and he died four days later. 'Īsā b. al-Dīnār was imprisoned for twenty years. . . .[33]

Al-Shāfi'ī narrowly escaped punishment, purportedly through a clever play on words that persuaded his inquisitors that he believed in the createdness of the Qur'ān, all the while allowing him to maintain his belief in the uncreatedness of the Qur'ān. Al-Bājūrī narrates:

> He [a scholar named al-Sha'bī] said [counting each of the four divinely revealed books on his fingers], "As for the Torah, the Gospel, the Psalms, and the Qur'ān, these four are created" and he intended thereby his [four] fingers. That was the reason he was saved. The same has been narrated regarding al-Shāfi'ī.[34]

Aḥmad b. Ḥanbal, on the other hand, was not so fortunate. According to al-Bājūrī:

> Imām Aḥmad was imprisoned and beaten with a whip until he fainted. It is said that the Prophet (peace and blessing of Allah be upon him) said to Imām al-Shāfi'ī in a dream "Give glad tidings of paradise to Aḥmad on account of the tribulations that afflicted him regarding the createdness of the Qur'ān." So he [al-Shāfi'ī] sent him [Aḥmad b. Ḥanbal] a letter in Baghdad. When he read it, he cried and gave to the letter-carrier his shirt which was close to his body, as he was wearing two shirts. When the shirt was given to al-Shāfi'ī, he washed it and anointed himself with its water.[35]

Aḥmad b. Ḥanbal's imprisonment and abuse, a result of his steadfast adherence to the Sunnī view, only succeeded in increasing his rank and prestige. His perseverance and survival were viewed as a victory over the Mu'tazilī inquisition, and upon their fall from power, he was viewed as the champion of Sunnī orthodoxy.

However, the Mu'tazilī continued to hold significant ideological sway, though their political influence waned. Despite their formal disappearance in the seventh/thirteenth century, many of their positions were retained by various Shi'ī sects. Al-Bājūrī and his predecessors' continued defenses against Mu'tazilī thought are often viewed as a form of scholastic preservation, and maybe an inoculation against a potential revival, but perhaps there was an awareness that some Mu'tazilī ideas were still held by the Shi'ī, thus rendering their discussions relevant to the political/theological conflicts of their day.

In the generations after Aḥmad b. Ḥanbal's victory, Sunnīs continued to debate creedal issues with the Mu'tazilī. Some scholars, such as Ibn Kullāb (d. 241/855), debated theological issues by defending the Sunnī creed with rational argumentation, while others, especially scholars from among the Ḥanbalīs, at least claimed to reject rational argumentation and relied instead on proofs from the primary texts.

In the fourth/tenth century a former Muʿtazilī, Abū l-Ḥasan al-Ashʿarī (d. 324/935) came to Baghdad, where he argued against the Muʿtazilī and others in favor of Sunnī views using rational argumentation (*kalām*). While his claim to support the views of Aḥmad b. Hanbal was not sufficient for some, who saw all rational argumentation over points of belief to be heretical, his teachings spread and eventually became associated with Sunnī orthodoxy, especially among the Shāfiʿīs and Mālikīs.

After al-Ashʿarī's death, his legacy was carried on and spread by a number of his followers. Among the most prominent early proponents of Ashʿarī thought are Abū Bakr b. Fūrak (d. 406/1015), Abū Isḥāq al-Isfarāyīnī (d. 418/1027), and Abū Bakr al-Bāqillānī (d. 403/1013), the latter two were referenced on numerous occasions in al-Bājūrī's *Tuḥfat al-murīd*. Soon thereafter, other major proponents of Ashʿarī thought appeared, such as al-Qushayrī (d. 465/1072), al-Juwaynī (d. 478/1085), al-Ghazālī, Ṣalāḥ al-Dīn al-Ayyūbī (known as Saladin, d. 589/1193), Ibn Tumart (d. ca. 524/1130), and others.[36]

Concurrent with al-Ashʿarī's efforts, Abū Manṣūr al-Māturīdī (d. 333/944) was defending the Sunnī views against the Muʿtazilī and other Muslim and non-Muslim groups of his day in Samarqand. While biographical information on al-Māturīdī is scant in comparison to al-Ashʿarī, a few of his teachers are known to have been direct disciples of the principle students of Abū Ḥanīfa. The Māturīdīs eventually became all but synonymous with the Ḥanafīs.

Regarding al-Ashʿarī and al-Māturīdī, al-Bājūrī considers them and their followers the founders of the field of *uṣūl al-dīn*, saying: "[they were the founders] in the sense that they wrote the books [on the topic] and responded to the doubts brought by the Muʿtazila, otherwise all the prophets . . . came with *tawḥīd*."[37] That is, the true founders of the discipline of theology were the prophets, however, as formalized science, al-Ashʿarī and al-Māturīdī are counted as its founders.

Those who opted out of affiliation with the Ashʿarīs and Māturīdīs are often referred to as merely a group of Ḥanbalīs—following Aḥmad b. Ḥanbal's apparent disdain for the rational sciences (*kalām*) and especially *taʾwīl*—or Atharīs, who relied on transmitted as opposed to rationally deduced sources. Their school is generally associated with an insistence on avoiding the use of rational argumentation in matters of belief, and a reliance solely on transmitted content (Qurʾān and *Ḥadīth*). While al-Bājūrī may occasionally quote an opinion from an Atharī, he does not count them among the founders of the science of *ʿaqīda*.

Thus, in the realm of theology, two main schools appeared, the Ashʿarī and Māturīdī, both associated with the use of *kalām*, and a third school, the Atharīs,[38] which remained a minority and is usually associated with an avoidance of *kalām* in favor of reliance on the Qurʾān and *Ḥadīth*.[39] However, as discussed below, this was not always the case, as a number of Atharīs delved into *kalām*, whether or not they described it as such.

Both the Ashʿarī school and the Māturīdī school took up the Sunnī creed and defended it against the Muʿtazilīs and other sects by using rational methods, or *kalām*. The Atharīs are often referred to by the other schools as a group of Ḥanbalīs who strayed too near to anthropomorphism in their literalism and hostility to rationalism; in reality their case is more complex. Furthermore, in addition to the Ḥanbalīs, the Atharīs also include a small number of followers of the other three schools of law.[40] The Shāfiʿīs and the Mālikīs in most cases adhered to the Ashʿarī school, whereas the Ḥanafīs mostly followed the Māturīdī school. As with the later followers and the founders of the legal *madhhabs*, over the years Ashʿarīs and Māturīdīs often differed with the founders of their schools.[41] A strong case can be made that later Atharīs, especially Ibn Taymiyya, also differed substantially from the early Atharīs, of whom Aḥmad b. Ḥanbal is a prime example.

Iḥsān: Spiritual Excellence

In the Gabriel *ḥadīth*, the third component of the triadic conception of the religion of Islam is called *iḥsān*. Al-Bājūrī does not discuss the linguistic or technical meanings of the word in *al-Durar al-ḥisān*, as the author of the original text, al-Zubaydī does not include *iḥsān* in his discussion. However, al-Bājūrī does narrate the entire *ḥadīth* in his commentary, without explaining its relationship to spiritual purification.

Just as *fiqh* is associated with *islām*, and *ʿaqīda* with *īmān*, the science of Sufism (*taṣawwuf*)[42] is associated with *iḥsān* and is concerned with the purification of the heart of base traits and its adornment with meritorious traits, including the realization of mystical states and realities.[43] Al-Ghazālī defines Sufism as: "The divestment of the heart for Allah, and the disdaining of all except Him," meaning, as al-Bājūrī explains, the purification of the heart for Allah, and the belief that none but He has the power to benefit or harm.[44] Al-Bājūrī defines Sufism as: "A knowledge of principles through which the rectification of the heart (*qalb*) and the rest of the senses (*ḥiwās*) are known."[45] It is the third of the three core sciences that the pre-modern super-scholar necessarily studied. *Iḥsān*, meaning perfection or beautification, complements the two other categories, namely the jurisprudential or legal aspects of *islām*, and the creedal aspects of *īmān*. The perfection or beautification that Sufism is concerned with has two faces, one turned toward *islām* and one turned toward *īmān*.[46]

Al-Bājūrī hints at these two faces when he says of Sufism ". . . for it has within it the incitement toward the purification of beliefs (*iʿtiqād*) and perfection and rightness of actions."[47] The face turned toward *islām* is the aspect of Sufism that pertains to the purification of the heart of base characteristics and the adornment of the Sufi with noble character traits. The five legal rulings of *fiqh*, mentioned above, also apply to the inward states. Thus patience is obligated of the Sufi and envy is prohibited.

In addition to these internal states of the heart, the character of the Sufi also has obligatory and prohibited aspects. Among the obligatory aspects of the Sufi's character is chivalry (*futūwwa*) and silence (*ṣamt*), except in saying what is good. Among the prohibited aspects of character, tied to the states of the heart, is the prohibition of ostentation in acts of worship.

The face of Sufism that is turned toward *īmān* pertains to the perfection of one's belief. It is to move beyond mere rational affirmation of Allah's omnipotence and existence, into a state of belief wherein one has absolute certainty (*yaqīn*) that everything perceived is the immediate creative work of Allah. A Sufi does not follow the cause-and-effect chain back to Allah, in the same way that one who is contemplating the cosmological proof for Allah's existence would; rather a Sufi's eyesight (*baṣr*) links immediately, without rationalization or contemplation, to spiritual insight (*baṣīra*), which perceives Allah as the doer, the creator of each moment and all that it contains. This is the experiential perfection of the belief that Allah is the creator of each and every contingent thing and its actions, the belief that Allah alone creates and that no existent thing has any ontological separation from Allah in the sense that nothing exists except that it was created by Allah.[48] Al-Bājūrī affirms the experience of witnessing the creation's connection to Allah's power as a high spiritual experience, though one that can often lead to controversial statements, as discussed later in this work.

Sufism, therefore, is the science of changing one's spiritual psychology. The traveler of the Sufi path transforms himself from a state of heedlessness of Allah in his inner and outer states and actions, from one who experiences the contingent things of the universe as being ontologically separate from Allah's creative power, into a person endowed with a noble character and states of the heart, who through pious devotion and love of Allah comes to know Him through the mystical experiential vision.

Not unlike the schools of jurisprudence, and the schools of theology, practitioners of Sufism eventually formed into a number schools or orders (*ṭuruq*) named after their founders.[49] However, prior to the formation of these orders, there were many foundational figures of Sufism, of whom al-Bājūrī counted al-Junayd as the most prominent.[50] The *silsila*s (chain of teachers similar to the *isnād*) of these orders usually include al-Junayd, though the Sufi orders tend to be named after later foundational figures. Some orders include the Qādirī, Shādhilī, Naqshbandī, and Rifāʿī. The biographies of many legal scholars include their Sufi affiliations, and mention that they were granted the *khirqa* (mantle) associated with a particular order, or refer to their *silsila*. Al-Bājūrī's Sufi Shaykh, Abū Ḥurayba, was trained in several orders, as discussed below, and could therefore likely produce *silsila*s to a number of different founders of the Sufi orders.

Additional sciences that are directly related to the three core sciences include those pertaining to Qurʾānic studies—the Qurʾān being the primary source for the details of *fiqh*, *ʿaqīda*, and *taṣawwūf*—as well as those pertaining to the *ḥadīth*.[51] Arabic is necessary to understand these sciences in all of their details, and thus there are a number of sciences related to the Arabic language, including, but not limited to, poetry, rhetoric, and grammar. Al-Bājūrī defines some of the linguistic sciences in his discussion of the sciences necessary for the judge to have studied, and claims that a comprehensive knowledge of their fundamentals was easy in his times, as the linguistic sciences had been compiled and written in easily accessible texts.[52] In addition to these, other ancillary sciences, such as the study of debate, syllogistic logic (*manṭiq*, on which there was a disagreement regarding its permissibility), belles-lettres, astronomy, mathematics, and others are also important.

Al-Bājūrī taught a class on Fakhr al-Dīn al-Rāzī's exegesis of the Qurʾān, and an unfinished commentary on the same work (possibly his lecture notes) is attributed to him. Furthermore, as mentioned previously, he granted *ijāza*s to others in *tafsīr* (exegesis), as well as *ḥadīth*, indicating that his expertise extended to these subjects as well. He also wrote commentaries on popular texts on logic, rhetoric, and grammar; these works illustrate his strong grounding in the foundational sciences, as well as the core sciences of the Gabrielian paradigm discussed earlier. The core, foundational, and supporting sciences that a scholar such as al-Bājūrī was required to study were, in most cases, the same sciences required of a *mujtahid*, a judge, or a *mufti*, indicating an expectation to reach for a comprehensive mastery of a broad range of knowledge.

Al-Bājūrī provides us with an example of an archetypal scholar in the late Sunnī pre-modern and early modern tradition. His advanced scholarship in law, theology, and mysticism, as well as Qur'ānic studies, *ḥadīth*, logic, grammar, and rhetoric are common indications of one's inclinations to seek authority and authenticity in the traditional sciences and their transmission, rational and revelatory harmony, and a spiritual experience that does not contradict their conceptions of orthodox theological and legal positions. While the institutionalization of this model of scholarship may have also produced great scholars who merely conformed to a socially expected convention, al-Bājūrī's life further indicates the sincerity of his pursuit and manifestation of the above mentioned qualities of the archetypal scholar of the Gabrielian paradigm (i.e., authority/authenticity, rational/revelation harmony, and *Sharīʿa* compliant spirituality).

The *Ijmāʿ–Ikhtilāf* Spectrum

An important aspect of the tradition that al-Bājūrī existed within was the recognition of a spectrum of views in matters of law, theology, and Sufism. In each of the core sciences, there are matters upon which there was consensus[53] (*ijmāʿ*), and other matters over which there were varying degrees of disagreement (*ikhtilāf*). This has been explained as stemming from the fact that primary texts are either unquestionably authentic in their transmission from the Prophet (*qaṭʿī l-wurūd*), or fall within a range of probabilistic authenticity (*ẓannī l-wurūd*). Texts in each of these categories can be of two types: those admitting only one possible interpretation, thus being texts of unquestionable proof (*qaṭʿī l-dalāla*), and those which have a range of possible interpretation, thus being texts of probabilistic proof (*ẓannī l-dalāla*).[54]

Al-Bājūrī discusses the word "*dīn*" in *Tuhfat al-murīd*, giving as one of its possible definitions "those rulings which Allah most high has legislated on the tongue of his Prophet."[55] While discussing the relationship of the rulings that stem from the derivations of the *mujtahid* scholars to the term "*dīn*," al-Bājūrī acknowledges that there are matters over which there is no disagreement, namely that which comes from texts with only one interpretation that are thereby "from the *dīn* unquestionably (*qaṭʿan*)."[56] Al-Bājūrī uses the terms *qaṭʿī* and *ẓannī* in numerous places throughout his works, indicating his recognition of the range of accepted disagreement on many topics that stem from the nature of the primary texts and their transmission.

The schools of law arose from the different approaches to, and interpretation of, the variables of certainty and probability in law, theology, and Sufism. This flowering of diverse methods and practices was seen as natural, despite the vehemence with which scholars often debated their views, and was also viewed as something sanctioned by the primary texts. The spectrum of consensus and disagreement indicates an "emphasis on correct process"[57] rather than correct answers, in keeping with the *ḥadīth* narrated by al-Bukhārī that states that a *mujtahid* receives one reward for an incorrect answer and two for a correct answer.[58]

The emphasis on correct process, and the acceptability of differing results, was generally applied to *fiqh*, whereas matters of faith were generally considered to be more fixed. Though even in such matters, it is clear that beyond certain core beliefs over which disagreement (*ikhtilāf*) was not permissible,[59] disagreement in fact existed and was permitted on a variety of secondary and interpretive issues. In the realm of Sufism, disagreement clearly existed in both explanation of spiritual states and in the means of achieving them.[60]

As various schools of law, theology, and mysticism spread throughout the Muslim populated lands, a number of permutations of the jurist–theologian–mystic emerged. By way of example, a few are mentioned here with the contexts in which they might be found:

School of Law (*fiqh*)	School of Theology (*maddhab*)	Sufi Order (*ṭarīqa*)	Region
Ḥanafī	Māturīdī	Naqshbandī	Ottoman lands (especially modern-day Turkey, Bosnia, Chechnya)
Mālikī	Ashʿarī	Shādhilī	North Africa
Ḥanbalī	Atharī	Qādirī	fifth/eleventh-century Baghdad and Damascus (also Ibn Taymiyya, Ibn Rajab al-Ḥanbalī)
Ḥanafī	Ashʿarī–Māturīdī	Chishtī	Moghul lands and Indian/Pakistani *madrasas* (for example, the Deoband)
Shāfiʿī	Ashʿarī	Naqshbandī	in Egypt, at al-Azhar (al-Bājūrī and others)

Al-Bājūrī's works often mention varying opinions in law, theology, and mysticism, as do the works of his scholarly predecessors, such as al-Suyūṭī and al-Shīrāzī.[61] It is not uncommon for al-Bājūrī to mention a Mālikī opinion as a comparison to the Shāfiʿī opinion that he espouses in a work of jurisprudence, or to list the varying opinions within the Ashʿarī school in a work of creed. In fact, a prime characteristic of Sunnī methodology (and that of other groups) involves mentioning and weighing various opinions, and offering one's own opinion, when possible, as to which is the soundest.[62]

The result of the *ijmāʿ–ikhtilāf* spectrum is the existence of inter-affiliational agreement and intra-affiliational disagreement—phenomena that problematize attempts to narrowly define a given school of law, theology, mysticism, or Sunnī thought for that matter. By way of example, it is possible to find Ḥanbalīs who agree that *kalām* is impermissible, but disagree on the permissibility of using logic (*manṭiq*) in *uṣūl al-fiqh* (i.e., Ibn Taymiyya and Ibn Qudāma). It is possible to find Shāfiʿīs who disagree on the permissibility of logic, yet agree on the centrality of the Sufism to one's religious life (i.e., al-Bājūrī and al-Suyūṭī). One can find a Shāfiʿī-Ashʿarī and a Ḥanbalī who agree on the permissibility of *taʾwīl*, but disagree on the validity of the Sufi concept of *fanāʾ* (i.e., al-Bājūrī and Ibn al-Jawzī). One can find Sufis who disagree on the use of *kalām* but agree on the heresy of al-Ḥallāj (i.e., al-Bājūrī and Ibn Taymiyya).

I believe that with the passage of time, the breadth of diversity of opinion may have narrowed within a *madhhab* or across *madhhab*s on some issues; however, one can argue that in some matters the pool of topics that required an opinion, and the diversity of opinions on a given topic, increased, thus broadening the scope of diverse perspectives. This is, perhaps, partially due to differing intellectual trends in various regions of the Muslim world; intellectual trends that converged over time, perhaps in Mecca, perhaps at centers of learning like al-Azhar, and then required discussion, refutation, synthesis, or change.

The legacy al-Bājūrī inherited was characterized by a cycle of cross-fertilization and development that is still little understood or studied today. Centuries of reflection and discussion across the *ijmāʿ–ikhtilāf* spectrum had produced volumes of texts, commentaries, and super-commentaries, many of which needed to be referenced and processed before a scholar could adequately treat a subject in his own classes or books. These books, passed on from earlier scholars, represented not just explanation and preservation of past teachings, but also included developments in technical terminology, method, and thought.

Al-Bājūrī's scholarly mission was one of clarification and verification of a number of core texts that contain essential details of a variety of sciences, and areas of scholarly contention, with an aim to educate the students of his time with a broad-based knowledge of the necessary Islamic sciences. His work evidences a familiarity not just with the preeminent scholars of each field, but also with diverse post-ninth/fifteenth-century[63] scholars of law, theology, mysticism, and especially the rational sciences as they related to *manṭiq*, *kalām*, and *uṣūl al-fiqh*.

Al-Bājūrī was a Shāfiʿī *faqīh*, an Ashʿarī *mutakallim*, and a Naqshbandī Sufi. His *fiqh* was firmly rooted in a tradition of authentication and authorization that stretched back through the *isnād*/*ijāza* system to the forebearers of the schools of law. Likewise, his *kalām*, also authenticated and authorized through the chains of transmission via the scholars of Ashʿarī thought, was, in his view, in full agreement with the dictates of both the intellect and revelation. His Sufism was equally authentic and also based on authorization, but best transmitted through observation of the spiritual state (*ḥāl*) of the fully realized gnostic (*ʿārif*, or knower of God). For centuries, this particular manifestation of the Gabrielian paradigm was a normative model of Islamic scholarship in the Islamic world, and especially in al-Bājūrī's Egypt.

The Egyptian Milieu

Al-Bājūrī fit into a tradition of Shāfiʿī–Ashʿarī–Sufi scholarship that had been prominent in Egypt for many generations. Al-Shāfiʿī and his immediate followers and transmitters, such as al-Muzanī and al-Buwayṭī (d. 231/846), continued to teach in Egypt after their teacher's demise.[64] While the exact nature of the Shāfiʿī school during the third/ninth century is still in question,[65] it was prominent in Egypt, though in a form that may not have resembled the later commentary-based definitions of *madhhab*s defined by Melchert and others.

The Shāfiʿī School in Egypt

Al-Shāfiʿī moved to Egypt five or six years before he died. During that time he founded a new school of jurisprudence, wherein he changed much of his earlier legal rulings and methods. He challenged the old guard in Egypt, primarily the Mālikīs. His new ideas, especially the grounding of legal normativity in primary texts, rather than the living transmission (*ʿamal*) of an area, met with much resistance, though he did receive some patronage. He was granted a primary place of teaching in the central mosque of Fustat, and he developed a significant group of students who transmitted his works, wrote abridgments, and critically engaged with his teachings, even offering alternate opinions in some cases.

Though still a minority among the state-sponsored Ḥanafīs and the Mālikī scholars, certain students of al-Shāfiʿī held positions of scholarly influence, such as al-Buwayṭī, who was consulted by the governor and others on legal matters.[66]

Under the rule of the governor Ibn Ṭūlūn (d. 270/884), the Shāfiʿī *madhhab* rose in prominence, largely a result of its promotion by the Shāfiʿī judge Muḥammad b. ʿUthmān Abū Zurʿa (d. 302/914 or 915).[67] Ibn Ṭūlūn sent his own family members to study Shāfiʿism and some even went on to teach Shāfiʿī doctrine as far afield as Baghdad.[68] Though state-sponsorship under the Ṭūlūnids was short-lived, Shāfiʿism gained momentum and spread to the far reaches of the Muslim world.[69]

Under the Shīʿī Fāṭimid dynasty in the fourth/tenth cenury, the Shāfiʿīs continued to teach, though under somewhat strained circumstances. After confirming a Mālikī chief justice for a few years, the Fāṭimids eventually appointed their own judges, although Shāfiʿīs and Mālikīs were at times appointed to the chief judgeship alongside Shīʿī judges.[70]

With Ṣalāḥ al-Dīn al-Ayyūbī's Sunnī revival, the Shāfiʿī school was made paramount. The Ḥanafīs and Mālikīs were supported, but not to the same degree as the adherents to Ṣalāḥ al-Dīn's own *madhhab*, that of al-Shāfiʿī. *Madrasa*s were built for the promotion of Sunnī law and theology and the Ḥanafīs, Mālikīs, and Shāfiʿīs each had their own colleges established for their adherents. After Ṣalāḥ al-Dīn's time, the Shāfiʿīs tended to dominate the *madrasa*s.[71] In 566/1170 Ṣalaḥ al-Dīn designated that the office of chief judge be occupied by a Shāfiʿī, and this remained the case until 660/1262 when the Mamlūk governor, Baybars, began a series of reforms that included the appointment of four chief judges, one for each Sunnī *madhhab*.[72] The Mamlūk tradition of appointing four chief judges was still in effect in al-Suyūṭī's time (ninth/fifteenth century), though, as discussed below, he took issue with this.

With the rise of the Ottomans in Egypt in the tenth/sixteenth century, the tradition of appointing four chief judges (*qāḍī*) faded from Egypt, as did the Ḥanbalī presence, although each of the three remaining *madhhab*s had a chief *muftī*.[73] Throughout the tenth/sixteenth through thirteenth/nineteenth centuries, the Shāfiʿīs remained dominant, although the official *madhhab* of the Ottomans was that of the Ḥanafīs. The Mālikīs never regained the level of dominance they had in al-Shāfiʿīs time, although there were consistently important scholars, *muftīs*, and rectors of al-Azhar who adhered to the Mālikī school, including some of al-Bājūrī's contemporaries.

Al-Bājūrī's Egypt, therefore, was still one of Shāfiʿī dominance, with significant representation from the Mālikīs and the state-sponsored Ḥanafīs, some of whom were students of al-Bājūrī. Although, after his death, Mālikīs and Ḥanafīs began to play a more dominant role,[74] al-Bājūrī's recension of the Shāfiʿī school (including texts, rulings, and so forth) remains influential and well-represented to this day. The Shāfiʿī school of his time was not, however, one that developed solely within Egypt. Rather, it had been exported and developed in many parts of the Muslim world: in Baghdad, Nishapur, Khurasan, Persia, the Levant, Mecca, and Medina, and then returned, so to speak, to its origins in Egypt. Thus, al-Bājūrī inherited a Shāfiʿī school that had been affected by al-Ashʿarī, al-Juwaynī, al-Shīrāzī, al-Ghazālī, al-Taftazānī, Ibn Ḥajar, al-Ramlī, al-Nawawī, al-Rāfiʿī, al-Āmidī, al-Suyūṭī, and others, each hailing from and imbued with the wisdom of a variety of lands and intellectual environments.

In addition to the prominent personalities of the Shāfiʿī school, al-Bājūrī's thought was also affected by lesser-known Shāfiʿī scholars, such as al-Shabrāmallisī (d. 1086/1676–7), as well as his teachers who passed down additional teachings, not found in earlier works. One example is al-Bājūrī's reference to al-Dayrabī's[75] (d. 1151/1738) opinion that in addition to the well-known Prophetic practice of reciting the call to prayer in a newborn's right ear, and the call to commence the prayer in the left, one should also recite Sūrat al-Qadr from the Qurʾān in order to protect the child from ever committing adultery.[76] This appears to have been an oral transmission of al-Dayrabī's opinion, as al-Bājūrī says "he [al-Dayrabī] said it thus, and we took it [this narration] from our shaykhs."[77]

Al-Bājūrī mentions the teachings of each of these past and contemporary scholars in various contexts, in the process of incorporating their thought into his own. This infused al-Bājūrī's Shāfiʿism with a diverse blend of the intellectual developments in the Shāfiʿī school that spanned the vast stretches of Muslim lands and history, while remaining deeply rooted in the traditions of his native soil.

Ashʿarī Thought and the Egyptian Madrasas

Al-Bājūrī was Shaykh al-Azhar from 1847 to 1861, and one of many Ashʿarīs (and Māturīdīs)[78] who held this title. Al-Azhar has long been considered one of the leading Sunnī institutions of learning and an authoritative source of teachers and rulings. George Makdisi suggests that Ashʿarī thought was excluded from the major institutions of learning as early as the fifth/eleventh century, indicating that it was viewed as heterodox.[79] Why then would al-Bājūrī, his teachers, and his heirs down to the present day proclaim Ashʿarī thought as their creed? Was al-Azhar an Ashʿarī institution from the time it became Sunnī, or did it become so at a later date? And is the Ashʿarī thought of al-Azhar representative of other institutions of learning, or were others staunchly "traditionalist," abhorring Ashʿarī thought and all things rational? As many scholars have been influenced by Makdisi's thesis, in order to answer these questions, and to understand whether or not al-Bājūrī's Shāfiʿī-Ashʿarī-Sufi paradigm was normative, rather than a later anomaly or the result of a coup against the bulwark of anti-rationalist traditionalism that Makdisi argues had become the representative of orthodox Sunnī institutions, an overview of the historical relationship between Muslim institutions of learning and Ashʿarī thought must be presented.

Egypt was, from al-Shāfiʿī's time, throughout Fāṭimid rule, and through the sixth/twelfth century, dominated by Shāfiʿīs, Mālikīs, and Ḥanafīs; Ḥanbalīs had a very limited presence until the sixth/twelfth century,[80] and even this waned under Ottoman rule. While there were Shāfiʿīs who did not follow al-Ashʿarī, such as Ibn al-Kīzānī (d. c. 562/1166–67), there were a number of others who did. In fact, the presence of Ashʿarī thought was sufficiently great during the late Fāṭimid rule to have caused some protest from the rising Ḥanbalīs and their non-Ashʿarī Shāfiʿī allies. However, even the non-Ashʿarī Shāfiʿīs and the Ḥanbalīs at times clashed in riots over theological issues; there was not a unified block of Atharī "traditionalists" against the Ashʿarīs.[81]

Al-Azhar was founded by the Fāṭimids in 359/970 and prospered as a Shīʿī institution for some two hundred years. It was, however, converted to a Sunnī institution with the founding of the Ayyubid dynasty by Ṣalāḥ al-Dīn.[82] Ṣalāḥ al-Dīn was an Ashʿarī; he memorized a treatise on Ashʿarī thought as a child, was reportedly a student of the great Ashʿarī apologist Ibn ʿAsākir,[83] and established several Ashʿarī institutions. Among the largest of these institutions was the Ṣalāḥiyya, whose "surviving inscription states that it had been constructed for Ashʿarī jurists."[84] In fact, he ordered that Ashʿarī thought be the official creed of all of the institutions, including those that taught Mālikī and Ḥanafī law[85] (there being no established Ḥanbalī *madrasa* in Egypt until 641/1243–44).[86]

The Ashʿarī presence in al-Azhar and other Egyptian institutions was, apparently, substantial from the sixth/twelfth century, throughout al-Bājūrī's time, and to the present day. To the west of Egypt, we also find a strong Ashʿarī presence as early as al-Qayrawānī (d. 386/996); this was boosted by Ibn Tumart's Muwaḥḥidūn dynasty.[87] Al-Qayrawānī was the leader of the Mālikī school in Qayrawān (present-day Tunisia), and was also an active proponent of Ashʿarī thought.[88] Ibn Tumart, a contemporary of al-Ghazālī, founded the Muwaḥḥidūn dynasty and required all of his followers to memorize, reportedly under threat of death, Ashʿarī texts he had composed.[89] By the time of al-Sanūsī (d. 895/1490), Ashʿarī thought was still dominant in North Africa, and his own writings continued to be used in educational institutions, from Qayrawān to Cairo, until the twentieth century. Al-Sanūsī represents a significant change in the Ashʿarī tradition, one in which the use of the syllogistic logic of the later logicians[90] became more firmly established across the Ashʿarī world, despite al-Ghazālī having already composed books of creed drawing from the principles of syllogistic logic of the early logicians. The effect of al-Sanūsī's works on al-Bājūrī and later Ashʿarī thought cannot be overstated.

In Baghdad and Khurasan during the fifth/eleventh century, though Ashʿarīs had disagreements with the Muʿtazilīs and Ḥanbalīs, they were also a strong presence in the educational institutions, especially the Niẓāmiyyas. Among the prominent teachers of the Niẓāmiyyas, we find al-Shīrāzī, who by most accounts was an Ashʿarī, and certainly not anti-rationalist, as his text *al-Lumaʿ* clearly indicates. Al-Juwaynī, al-Ghazālī, and al-Qushayrī—Ashʿarī luminaries of *fiqh*, *uṣūl-al fiqh*, and Sufism—all had important teaching appointments. Considering the fundamental role of *kalām* in their *uṣūl al-fiqh*, as well as the interrelatedness of the subjects taught, it is quite probable that their Ashʿarī perspective influenced their teaching of *fiqh*.[91] Later teachers at the Niẓāmiyyas were also Ashʿarīs, including scholars such as al-Zanjānī (d. 656/1258), whose writings on *uṣūl al-fiqh* are clearly Ashʿarī.

In addition, some of the original teachers at the Dār al-Ḥadīth colleges in Syria and elsewhere were Ashʿarīs; at Dār al-Ḥadīth al-Nūriyya the first professor of *ḥadīth* was Ibn ʿAsākir (followed by his son).[92] Despite the fact that these colleges were later taken over for a time by those hostile to the Ashʿarīs, the tradition of Ashʿarī thought in the *madrasa*s continued with Ibn ʿAsākir's student, Ṣalāḥ al-Dīn, in Egypt and elsewhere.[93]

Even this cursory glance at Ashʿarī institutional history sufficiently indicates that Ashʿarī thought played a prominent role in the *madrasas* from pre-sixth/twelfth-century institutions in Qayrawān, Cairo, Baghdad, and Nishapur to the present day. While the influence of the Ashʿarīs may have waned for a time in Baghdad, and perhaps in Damascus after the Ḥanbalīs rose to prominence, it certainly was not excluded from the *madrasas* in many of the above-mentioned lands during that time or afterward.

Thus, the notion that the colleges of law or the *ḥadīth* schools were formed to exclude Ashʿarī views is only true in a limited geographical and chronological scope, specifically during a few centuries of pre-Mongol Baghdadī history, and in only a handful of Ḥanbalī-dominated institutions. The purported two-hundred-year silence between the two great Ashʿarī apologists, Ibn ʿAsākir (d. 571/1176) and al-Subkī (d. 771/1370), was hardly due to a lack of proponents of Ashʿarī thought, but is most likely the result of a lack of sufficient challenges to it, pace Makdisi. In fact, it was during this time that Ṣalāḥ al-Dīn and his successors instituted Ashʿarī thought as the sole representative of orthodoxy.

Thus, al-Bājūrī's Ashʿarī thought was characteristic of Shāfiʿī and Mālikī institutions across the Muslim world, both in his day and for centuries prior. Like the Shāfiʿī school as taught in Egypt, the Ashʿarī school of al-Bājūrī's time was a diverse blend of intellectual developments that originated in varying times and lands, coming to and spreading from Egypt with the movement of scholars and their books. The Ḥanafī school also underwent significant development, and was often associated with the Māturīdī school, a combination of the Ashʿarī and Māturīdī schools (as in the former Moghul lands), or even the Ashʿarī school—as they were required to be in Egypt during Ṣalāḥ al-Dīn's time. The Atharī Ḥanbalīs and those non-Ashʿarīs of the other *madhhabs* only represented themselves and a limited number of institutions, certainly not the entirety of Sunnī thought. Indeed, a study of Atharī intellectual history indicates significant development, change, and internal disagreement.

The history of the theological schools and their relationships to the major educational institutions indicates that all three perspectives—Ashʿarī, Māturīdī, and Atharī—vied for influence, often through political allegiances, and all three were generally tolerated, despite the harshness and intolerance of certain individual thinkers and rulers. In Egypt and elsewhere throughout the Muslim lands, Ashʿarī and Māturīdī thought dominated for much of Islamic history. Al-Bājūrī himself pays little attention to the Atharīs, with only occasional reference to their views, perhaps reflecting the Egyptian Shāfiʿī scholar Ibn Ḥajar al-Haytamī's *fatwā* that the Ahl al-Sunna are the followers of the Ashʿarī and Māturīdī schools.[94] In any case, he had students who were descendants of Muḥammad b. ʿAbd al-Wahhāb, who must have seen al-Azhar as an important center of learning despite its Ashʿarī affiliations; though some may have gone to proselytize the teachings of ʿAbd al-Wahhāb.[95] Additionally, al-Bājūrī gave an *ijāza* to the Damascene Ḥanbalī scholar ʿAbd al-Salām b. ʿAbd al-Raḥman al-Shaṭī.[96] While family descent and place of origin did not determine one's beliefs and affiliations, it is unlikely that Ḥanbalīs would lack some sympathies for the many Atharīs that populated their *madhhab*.

The Ashʿarī and Māturīdī dominance in many of the institutions of learning throughout Egypt, North Africa, and much the Islamic world from the sixth/twelfth century onward indicates that al-Bājūrī's Ashʿarī thought in particular, though representative of generations of development, and *kalām*-based theology in general, was normative not just in his time, but for centuries prior.

Sufism in Egypt

Al-Bājūrī's appointment as Shaykh al-Azhar appears to have been conditioned on his agreement to leave the supervision of the officially recognized *ṭarīqas* to someone else. These *ṭarīqas* had been under the sphere of control of previous holders of the position of Shaykh al-Azhar, indicating that the role of these orders had become significant enough to require government recognition and supervision. In addition, al-Bājūrī was required to consult other scholars before making major institutional decisions within al-Azhar.[97]

Al-Bājūrī was a disciple of Abū Ḥurayba Aḥmad al-Shintināwī (d. 1852), from the village of Shintinā in the Mānufiyya discrict, as was his teacher al-Quwaysnī. Abū Ḥurayba is described by al-Bājūrī, as narrated in ʿAlī Mubārak's *Khiṭaṭ*, as a pious *fallaḥ*[98] from Upper Egypt, who, despite having memorized the Qurʾān in his youth, never attended institutions of formal education. Nonetheless, he was known to respond to religious questions with the proper answers and cite the texts in which these sources could be found. He was affiliated with multiple orders, including the Naqshbandī, Shādhilī, Khalwatī, Khātimī, and Qādirī orders.[99]

Although various orders reached Egypt at different times after the seventh/thirteenth century, Sufism in general had an early presence in Egypt, with mystics such as Dhūl Nūn al-Miṣrī (d. 245/859). Although the people of Egypt initially resisted his teachings, al-Suyūṭī reports that Dhūl Nūn was later revered among them.[100] Sufism was fully institutionalized, accepted, and included in Ṣalāḥ al-Dīn's reforms in the post-Fāṭimid era. Al-Shādhilī (652/1258) and his prominent students lived and taught in seventh/thirteenth-century Egypt, and it was the norm in al-Suyūṭī's time (ninth-tenth/fifteenth-sixteenth centuries) for a scholar to have Sufi affiliations, there being numerous institutions for the study and practice of Sufism in Mamlūk Egypt. Egypt under Ottoman rule saw the growth of various non-Arabic orders (that is, those orders whose primary works were not originally written in Arabic) including the order to which al-Bājūrī belonged, the Naqshbandiyya.

We can argue that the archetypal scholar of the Gabrielian paradigm, in its most general sense, existed in Egypt from the earliest days of Islam's arrival, though the more specific jurist–theologian–mystic who adhered to systematized schools did not appear until the formation of the *madhhab*s and theological schools. As for the presence of the Shāfiʿī–Ashʿarī–Sufi paradigm, we expect to find it from the earliest time in which each tradition was simultaneously present in Egypt. That is to say, from the moment there existed the simultaneous presence of the Shāfiʿī school, the Ashʿarī school, and some form of Sufism, it is likely, or at least possible, that there existed scholars who ascribed to all three. Al-Ashʿarī died in the fourth/tenth century, over a century after al-Shāfiʿī, yet Sufism existed in al-Shāfiʿī's time. Therefore, we can tentatively place the beginning of this specific paradigm (Shāfiʿī–Ashʿarī–Sufi) around the mid-fourth/tenth or early fifth/eleventh centuries,[101] with al-Bājūrī's more specific Shāfiʿī–Ashʿarī–Naqshbandī paradigm taking root upon the arrival of the Naqshbandī order, possibly as late as the eleventh/seventeenth century.[102]

By al-Bājūrī's time, the Shāfiʿīs (along with the Mālikīs, and the Ottoman-sponsored Ḥanafīs),[103] Ashʿarīs, and a multitude of Sufi orders, were firmly entrenched in Egypt and its institutions. Given the strong presence of all three as early as the mid-fourth/tenth century, and their clear interconnection before and after Ṣalāḥ al-Dīn's time in the sixth/twelfth century, al-Bājūrī's adherence to Shāfiʿī *fiqh*, Ashʿarī thought, and Sufism had a thousand years of precedent. He wrote at a time when these schools of law, theology, and mysticism were still taken as the norm, before major reformist tendencies had spread to the degree that they did shortly thereafter. He lived and wrote on the cusp of the modern era, representing a long entrenched tradition that would soon be challenged at its core, by reformers such as Muḥammad ʿAbduh (d. 1905) and Jamāl al-Dīn al-Afghānī (d. 1897).

As el-Rouayheb indicates, the interpretation of al-Bājūrī's predecessors in the *taḥqīqī* (scholarly verification) tradition is often skewed in Western treatments that seem to have accepted the generalizations and descriptions of them offered by their reformist challengers, such as ʿAbduh or al-Afghānī, among the late nineteenth- and early twentieth-century reformers.[104] Al-Bājūrī, however, saw his tradition to be the truth, superior to any proto-reform efforts. It was a vibrant tradition, a continuing discussion, certainly not a mere repetition of all that had been said between the ninth and twelfth centuries.[105] As discussed in the next chapter, al-Bājūrī's Egyptian Islam was the result of cross-fertilization, a diverse blend of Nishapuri, Baghdadī, Egyptian, and Yemeni Shāfiʿī *fiqh*, Baghdadī, Nishapuri, and North African Ashʿarī thought, and Baghdadī, North African, Central Asian, and Egyptian Sufism. Both the vibrancy, diversity, and three dimensionality of the Gabrielian paradigm was normative and dominant in the culture of al-Azhar, certainly at the level of its top teachers and administrators.

3

Al-Bājūrī in Dialogue with His Archetypal Predecessors

As Islam spread and regional centers of learning gave way to a variety of schools centered around the methods and rulings of various individual scholars, a flowering of diverse ideas and practices emerged across the Muslim world. After the foundational period of the institutionalized sciences of Islam, the various schools of thought spread from their original homelands, often to distant regions of the Muslim world. The Mālikī school moved beyond its roots in Medina and became firmly grounded in North and West Africa, as well as Spain. The Ashʿarī school spread beyond Baghdad and Nishapur, from Fez to Timbuktu to Java. The Ḥanafī school, though also established in the Muslim heartlands, spread as far as China and India, and was usually accompanied by the Māturīdī school of theology. The Ḥanbalī school, often including prominent Atharīs, established itself at various times in Baghdad and Damascus, and eventually made headway into Egypt. The Shāfiʿī school spread from Egypt, and eventually reached southeast Asia and elsewhere. Baghdadī Sufism, and its related ascetic and spiritual movements spread to Egypt, North and West Africa, the Balkans, India, southeast Asia, and elsewhere. Indeed, regardless of the legal or theological schools that held sway in a given area, Sufism was often firmly rooted across the Muslim world.

The spread of these schools resulted in a cycle of cross-fertilization, and thus the Sufism that spread to North Africa and reached the likes of al-Shādhilī eventually returned to Baghdad in its new form. The developments that occurred in Ashʿarī thought in northwest Africa, after being touched by Persian influences, returned to Egypt, Mecca, Baghdad, and Damascus, in an altered and advanced form. The Shāfiʿī school, firmly grounded in Egypt in al-Shāfiʿī's time, was influenced by the ideas of later Shāfiʿī scholars of Baghdad and Khurasan.

Al-Bājūrī inherited this rich legacy that had spread to diverse geographic regions, developed, and returned to Egypt, only to be exported again and further interpreted with each generation of Azharī graduates returning to their homelands. With so many generations of cross-fertilization, consensus and disagreement, writing and commentating, an original work was often laden with references to previous scholars and their opinions. Indeed, familiarity with the *ijmāʿ–ikhtilāf* spectrum was a necessary component of qualified scholarship in many fields.

Al-Bājūrī's commentaries show a broad exposure to the thought, if not always the original works, of generations of previous scholars. The scholars that he mentions in his commentaries include the founders of the *madhhab*s, schools of theology, and Sufi orders, and their later inheritors throughout the generations, as well as scholars of Qurʾānic exegesis, logic, and grammar.

A number of scholars are cited in al-Bājūrī's works, either as the author of the text he comments upon, or by reference in the commentaries themselves. When he refers to a scholar in his commentaries, there is often a sense of familiarity between him and the given scholar; al-Bājūrī often mentions them, as is customary in commentary literature, on a first name basis or by their *kunya* (a type of honorific epithet). For example, in his discussion of Allah's attribute of *qidam* (beginningless eternality) al-Bājūrī writes: "And that is what is understood from the words of Saʿd," whom the reader presumably already knows is the scholar Saʿd al-Taftazānī (d. 792/1390).[1] Other scholars may not be mentioned individually by name, such as when al-Bājūrī refers to "a group of Ḥanbalīs" whose general legacy, if not individual opinions, is important enough to warrant mention.

As Sachau wisely cautions, "If one wanted to just briefly examine the authorities cited by al-Bājūrī, such a study would rapidly grow into an exposition of the major part of the Shāfiʿī legal literature."[2] Indeed the same could be said, though perhaps to a lesser extent, regarding the Ashʿarī theological literature. Among the scholars whose views al-Bājūrī cites, at times through direct quotation and at others through references to an opinion or ruling, are al-Sanūsī, al-Laqānī, al-Akhḍarī, al-Haytamī, al-Ramlī, al-Nawawī, Fakhr al-Dīn l-Rāzī, al-Shaʿrānī, al-Suyūṭī, al-Taftazānī, Ibn Qayyim al-Jawziyya, al-Muzanī, and many others.

Although he refers to scholars from the vast continuum of previous archetypal scholars of the Gabrielian paradigm, as well as others from outside this paradigm, al-Bājūrī was probably most influenced by those whose works represent the later recensions of the Ashʿarī school of theology, those whose thought was tied to the logic of the later logicians (*muta'akhkhirūn*), the refining and weighing (*tarjīḥ*) of later jurists of the Shāfiʿī *madhhab*, and the later scholars of the Naqshbandī order whose thought and methods may have been cross-fertilized by other orders. However, al-Bājūrī does not merely narrate the opinions of these masters of the later legal, theological, and Sufi traditions; he often disagrees with them or offers others' opinions which contradict al-Sanūsī, Ibn Ḥajar, or others. Nor does he dismiss all pre-Mamlūk scholarship, rather he sometimes engages the past masters from the founders of the *madhhabs*, the Saljūq-era scholars of law, theology, and Sufism, those of the Ayyubid, Mamlūk, and Ottoman eras, including Azharīs of recent centuries, down to his own teachers and colleagues. Whether or not he is merely citing from more recent commentaries, or reading directly from these texts is at times easy to determine by comparing commentaries, while at other times it is not possible to determine with certainty. Nonetheless, I believe it is a combination of the two possibilities, since we will see that he had access to several pre-Mamlūk texts which he taught from directly or cites in commentaries, though quoting from previous commentaries' citations of earlier texts was his more common tendency.[3]

In the current chapter, I address several scholars of the later recensions of al-Bājūrī's legal, theological, philosophical, and mystical affiliations, as well as a sample of earlier scholars who nonetheless influenced (directly or indirectly) al-Bājūrī's thought. The scholars I have chosen to discuss in this chapter are either authors of a text upon which al-Bājūrī has commented, scholars referenced in his commentaries, or those who may or may not be mentioned by name, but whose intellectual legacy affects a given topic treated by al-Bājūrī. In all cases, these contribute to our understanding of the archetype of the premodern Muslim scholar and his[4] place in the continuum.

First, I discuss those theologians who influenced al-Bājūrī, or whose contrasting views help to better understand al-Bājūrī's. This gives us a deeper understanding of al-Bājūrī's logic-based Ashʿarī theology (*kalām*) that allows for metaphysical interpretation (*ta'wīl*) and consignment of meanings (*tafwīḍ*), and its relation to the earlier *kalām* of Ashʿarīs and Atharīs who wrote before the important developments in logic that al-Bājūrī considers to have occurred. Some of the scholars discussed in relation to their theological work overlap with the discussion of al-Bājūrī's predecessors in law, while additional scholars of great importance and potentially less fame are also mentioned. I follow this with a brief exploration of some of the lesser-known Sufis who influenced al-Bājūrī, as well as those scholars whose thought is largely in agreement with that of al-Bājūrī, despite being considered by many to be opponents of Sufism.

Al-Bājūrī's Theological Predecessors

Al-Bājūrī's theology was deeply impacted by the developments ushered in by the likes of Fakhr al-Dīn al-Rāzī, and firmly established by the likes of Ibrāhīm al-Laqānī, ʿAbd al-Raḥmān al-Akhḍarī, Saʿd al-Dīn al-Taftazānī, and, perhaps most importantly, Muḥammad b. Yūsuf al-Sanūsī. The following biographies address a few of these important post sixth/twelfth-century theologians who had a major impact on al-Bājūrī's thought, and the discipline of theology and logic in general.

Fakhr al-Dīn al-Rāzī

Abū l-Faḍl Muḥammad b. ʿUmar, popularly known as Fakhr al-Dīn al-Rāzī (d. 606/1210), was born in Rayy (in modern-day Iran). He is credited with founding a new school of *kalām* and its supporting science of logic (*manṭiq*), as well as being an important jurist of the Shāfiʿī school, and, especially later in his life, a Sufi.[5] His influence on al-Bājūrī cannot be understated, yet it may not seem as obvious as that of al-Sanūsī, al-Laqānī, Ibn Ḥajar, or al-Shaʿrānī. Al-Bājūrī taught al-Rāzī's tafsīr (entitled Mafātiḥ al-ghayb) for a time, until he was no longer able due to health problems. Al-Rāzī's exegetical effort was not limited to grammar, ḥadīth, or the works of previous exegetes, but is rather viewed primarily as a theological and philosophical commentary. Al-Bājūrī had firsthand exposure to al-Rāzī's legal, theological, and philosophical thought, along with his exegetical ideas via his commentary on the Qurʾān, yet al-Rāzī's influence was also present in the rational sciences, specifically *manṭiq* and *kalām*, as they effected theology and legal methodology (*uṣūl al-fiqh*). Indeed, al-Rāzī is known and referred to in *manṭiq* texts as al-Imām (the leader).

It is reported that only the Baghdadī scholar Ibn Yūnus (d. 639/1242) was able to interpret the technical terminology of al-Rāzī's theological and philosophical writings in that day, when al-Rāzī's writings were first dispersed in Baghdad.[6] Al-Rāzī probably sparked the beginning of a new era in *manṭiq* and therefore *kalām* and *uṣūl al-fiqh*, or at minimum gave the developing school of later logicians a significant boost. Indeed, he is credited with starting a new school of *kalām* and is considered to be "the third teacher after Aristotle and al-Farābī."[7]

Among al-Rāzī's influential ideas was his theory of interpreting problematic primary texts, which held that there were four possible responses to an apparent conflict between reason and revelation: acceptance of both, rejection of both, preferring revelation to reason, or reason to revelation. The first is rejected as it confirms two contradictory opinions. The second too is rejected, for, in the absence of a third option, one claim must be preferred. The third, which seems like the right choice to many, is rejected, as revelation is grounded in reason, for without reason, revelation cannot be understood. This leaves only the fourth possibility, that reason is preferred, and a problematic text is either metaphorically interpreted (*ta'wīl*) or its problematic implication is rejected while its actual meaning is confined to its speaker (*tafwīḍ*).[8]

This approach to those Qur'ānic verses whose apparent meaning implies anthropomorphism or some other rational absurdity entails that one hold the revealed text (*naql*) to the light of the intellect (*ʿaql*) in order to deduce its meaning. In short, it burdens the intellect with the task of interpreting such verses, since the Qur'ān was revealed to those who can have the capacity of rational reflection (*al-ʿāqilūn*).

This approach to *ta'wīl*, as well as the post-Rāzī developments in *manṭiq* which al-Bājūrī considered substantial, colored al-Bājūrī's approach to the rational sciences and their relationship to the revealed sciences. Although he does not agree with al-Rāzī in every issue, he nonetheless is indebted to him, as al-Suyūṭī declared himself to be as well, due to al-Rāzī's profound impact on most of the core and supportive sciences (i.e., *tafsīr*, *fiqh*, *uṣūl al-fiqh*, *kalām*, and *manṭiq*).

Al-Suyūṭī considered al-Rāzī to have been the centennial renewer (*mujaddid*) of his age, despite the former's rejection of *kalām* and *manṭiq* and the latter's instrumental role in ushering in a new age of scholarship and sustained interest in these sciences.[9] His influence can be found not only in Qur'ānic studies, but also in the *kalām* and *manṭiq* works of later scholars, such as al-Taftazānī and al-Jurjānī, on down to al-Bājūrī's time, as well as in Shāfiʿī legal works.

Al-Bājūrī, having written on or taught each of the aforementioned sciences in which al-Rāzī's influence is weighty, did not escape his influence, though at times they differed. As fellow Shāfiʿī-Ashʿarīs, their paths were destined to cross. It is difficult to imagine al-Bājūrī being who he was, had al-Rāzī never lived.

Al-Taftazānī

Sa'd al-Dīn Mas'ūd b. 'Umar al-Taftazānī (d. 792/1390), was a Shāfi'ī (or Ḥanafī)[10] in law, an Ash'arī in theology,[11] and expressed clear sympathies with Sufism. He was a student of the Shāfi'ī jurist, exegete, and logician Quṭb al-Dīn al-Rāzī (d. 776/1364), and was affiliated with the court of Timur.[12] Two important works, among his many books, are his commentary on the creed of al-Nasafī (d. 537/1142), and his commentary on al-Kātibī's (d. 675/1277) logic primer entitled *al-Shamsiyya* (for which his teacher Quṭb al-Dīn also provided a commentary).

Al-Bājūrī cites al-Taftazānī in a number of places throughout his works, including *Tuḥfat al-murīd,* referring to him, as noted, as Sa'd. He also wrote a lengthy *Ḥāshiya* on al-Taftazānī's commentary on al-Nasafī's creed (*Sharḥ al-Taftazānī 'alā 'aqīdat al-Nasafī*), which, despite being unfinished, amounts to over two hundred pages.

Al-Taftazānī's commentary on al-Nasafī has been studied in *madrasas* across the Muslim world—in traditionally Ash'arī and Māturīdī lands—until the present day. His impact on theology was immediate and long-lasting; Ibn Khaldūn, al-Taftazānī's contemporary, reports:

> I found in Egypt numerous works on the intellectual sciences composed by the well-known person Sa'd al-Dīn al-Taftazānī, a native of Harat, one of the villages of Khurasan. Some of them are on *kalām* and the foundations of *fiqh* and rhetoric, which show that he had a profound knowledge of these sciences. Their contents demonstrate that he was well versed in the philosophical sciences and far advanced in the rest of the sciences which deal with Reason.[13]

Al-Taftazānī's willingness to adopt and familiarity with Ash'arī or Māturīdī opinions, or Shāfi'ī or Ḥanafī opinions, almost five hundred years before al-Bājūrī, reflect a long-established view that the *ijmā'–ikhtilāf* spectrum did not necessitate absolute conformity to one set of beliefs or legal rulings; this is a view that al-Bājūrī maintained in his own works.

Regarding Sufism, al-Taftazānī recognized that there were legitimate Sufis who sought to purify themselves of base and immoral traits and adorn themselves with the meritorious traits of which the Prophet spoke.[14] Al-Taftazānī supported the unitive experience of Sufism, the annihilation in the Oneness of Allah, and the resultant spiritual intoxication that this witnessing of Allah's "unfathomable Oneness" produced.[15] However, he rejected any notion that this experience of Oneness should imply that the universe and its creator are one and the same, that is to say, he rejected those who interpreted *waḥdat al-wujūd* as the monistic belief that everything in the universe shared in its existence with Allah. This view of monism was what al-Taftazānī considered Ibn al-ʿArabī's (d. 638/1240) teachings to imply, and he, like his teacher Aḍūḍ al-Dīn al-Ījī (d. 756/1355) and Ibn Taymiyya before him, declared Ibn al-ʿArabī a heretical disbeliever.

Al-Taftazānī, unlike al-Suyūṭī, was a proponent of *manṭiq* but an opponent of Ibn al-ʿArabī. Al-Suyūṭī was against *manṭiq* yet emphatically defended Ibn al-ʿArabī's orthodoxy. In this sense, al-Taftazānī was in agreement with Ibn Taymiyya on Ibn al-ʿArabī's thought, but entirely opposed to Ibn Taymiyya's and al-Suyūṭī's views on *manṭiq* and *kalām*. This is yet another example of inter-affiliational agreement and intra-affiliational disagreement, further complicating any effort to declare a single official Sunnī stance on any of these issues, as such diversity of views could be found in each individual. Al-Suyūṭī, who deeply impacted al-Bājūrī, is a prime example of such diversity of thought and influences, and will be discussed in greater detail below. A scholar of less fame than al-Suyūṭī or Ibn Taymiyya, but of significant scholarly impact is Ibrāhīm al-Laqānī, an Egyptian Mālikī Ashʿarī Sufi who had a direct and profound impact on al-Bājūrī's theological thought and whose works are still read today from Morocco to Indonesia.

Al-Laqānī

Ibrāhīm al-Laqānī (d. 1041/1631) was a *muftī* of Mālikī law, a scholar of *ḥadīth*, a *mutakallim*, and author of one of the most popular didactic poems on Ashʿarī theology (*Jawharat al-tawḥīd*), and a Sufi who "joined between the sacred law (*sharīʿa*) and the ultimate spiritual reality (*ḥaqīqa*)."[16] He studied under notable Ḥanafīs, Mālikīs, and Shāfiʿīs, but issued *fatwā*s in the Mālikī school. He also took knowledge of Sufism from a number of scholars including Shaykh Aḥmad al-Bulqīnī l-Wazīrī, Shaykh Muḥammad b. al-Tarjamān, and others.

Al-Laqānī wrote many works, including the *Jawḥarat al-tawḥīd* as well as some commentaries on it. He also wrote on *ḥadīth*, issued *fatwā*s, and delved into Arabic grammar. He was an archetypal scholar of law, theology, and Sufism who embraced the rational sciences as well as *ḥadīth* and despite following one *madhhab*, did not hesitate to study under those of other *madhhab*s. He saw Sufism as a necessary dimension of one's faith, mentioning in his didactic poem on Ashʿarī *aqīda* some of ruinous traits one must eliminate in oneself, and some of the meritorious traits with which one must adorn oneself.

In addition to his popular commentary on al-Laqānī's *Jawharat al-tawḥīd*, al-Bājūrī also narrates in his *al-Musalsalāt* a *ḥadīth* whose chains of narration (*isnād*) go through al-Laqānī via his son.[17] Although he disagreed with al-Laqānī on some issues, their views of the Islamic sciences are quite similar. Both affirm the necessity to follow a *mujtahid*, the Ashʿarī or Māturīdī schools of theology, and one of the recognized Sufi orders (*ṭarīqa*s).

While al-Laqānī's *Jawharat al-tawḥīd* is a popular, oft-memorized, and frequently commented-upon *arjūza* poem, perhaps the most influential theologian from the ninth/fifteenth century onward was Muḥammad b. Yūsuf al-Sanūsī, whose life and works will now be discussed.

Muḥammad b. Yūsuf al-Sanūsī

Muḥammad b. Yūsuf al-Sanūsī (d. 895/1490) was a Mālikī–Ashʿarī–Junaydī[18] of Tlemcen whose greatest influence on the Muslim world was, perhaps, his theological works, especially the widely studied *Umm al-barāhīn*—a short summary of Ashʿarī theology, specifically addressing the subject of *tawḥīd* and the attributes of the prophets of Islam. An archetypal scholar in the sense that he had a mastery of the legal, theological, and mystical sciences, his legacy touched later scholars of various sciences and he was also remembered locally (in Tlemcen) as a great saint (*walī*) whose tomb became a place of visitation and supplication associated with miraculous wonders (*karāmāt*).

Al-Bājūrī wrote commentaries on al-Sanūsī's *Umm al-barāhīn* and on his *manṭiq* text known as *al-Mukhtaṣar* or *Mukhtaṣar al-Sanūsī fī ʿilm al-manṭiq*. In addition to this, al-Bājūrī refers to al-Sanūsī on over twenty occasions in his commentary on the *Jawharat al-tawḥīd*. At times these are references to his opinions on a matter and mention in which book they can be found; at other times, he uses al-Sanūsī's elucidations of certain topics, as in al-Sanūsī's differentiation between students and followers (*muqallidīn*), where the former are shown through signs and indications from their teachers, and the latter blindly follow reports without knowing the evidence.[19]

Al-Sanūsī's works were among the influential texts that helped further spread or fortify Ashʿarī thought from the ninth/fifteenth century onward, especially in West Africa. His text, *al-Mukhtaṣar*, was used to teach logic in Fez[20] and elsewhere up until the twentieth century,[21] when colonial and Salafi influences began to alter the curriculums of traditional learning institutions. His five texts on creed, namely, the Introductions (*al-Mutaqaddimāt*), the Smallest, (*Ṣughrā al-ṣughra*), the Mother of Proofs, or the Lesser (*Umm al-barāhīn* or *al-Ṣughrā*), Middle (*al-Wuṣṭā*), and Advanced (*al-Kubrā*), along with their commentaries, were taught at learning institutions all across North Africa. Notably, at al-Azhar, *Umm al-barāhīn* came to be taught with the commentary of al-Faḍālī (d. 1236/1821)—the teacher of al-Bājūrī—and that of al-Bājūrī himself.[22] Al-Sanūsī's texts continued to influence post-Napoleonic Egyptian scholars, including Muḥammad ʿAbduh, and have received some attention from Western scholars, among them Montgomery Watt,[23] Joseph P. Kenny,[24] J. D. Luciani, and others.[25]

His lesser work on *ʿaqīda* (*ʿAqīdat al-ṣughrā*), which is based largely on al-Juwaynī and al-Ghazālī's works, "spread through West Africa to the Niger under the Fulani name *kabbe*."[26] His teachings spread to Timbuktu through the renowned Mālikī scholar Aḥmad Baba in the tenth/sixteenth century,[27] and in northern Nigeria by way of Uthman Dan Fodio in the eighteenth century, though it is possible though that the latter was based on Ibn ʿĀshir's *Murshid al-muʿin*, the *ʿaqīda* portion of which is a didactic poem summarizing al-Sanūsī's text. Additionally, al-Sanūsī's *ʿaqīda* texts made their way to Malaysia and Indonesia and often include "interlinear Malay and Javanese translations."[28] They continue to be taught in the *madrasas* on "old, original texts (*matn*)."[29]

A contemporary of al-Suyūṭī, whose works also spread far and wide, al-Sanūsī's views on *manṭiq* and *kalām* seem to have eclipsed those of al-Suyūṭī.[30] Indeed, al-Sanūsī's texts became standard in the curriculum in Islamic institutions across West, sub-Saharan, and North Africa, and stretching as far as Malaysia and Indonesia. Many of the major centers of Mālikī and Shāfiʿī learning were thus committed to teaching both *manṭiq* and Ashʿarī *kalām* during and after al-Sanūsī's time.

Although his theological and mystical legacy is more pronounced, it cannot be forgotten that al-Sanūsī was well trained in other sciences, including *fiqh*, *ḥadīth*, Qurʾānic recitation, and ancillary sciences such as mathematics. In fact, al-Sanūsī produced books and commentaries on a variety of subjects, including one on the *Ṣaḥīḥ* collection of Muslim b. Ḥajjāj, thus continuing a long tradition of *ḥadīth* studies by Ashʿarī scholars.[31]

Al-Sanūsī was an important intellectual forefather of al-Bājūrī, who relied heavily upon his works. Al-Bājūrī's theological thought is deeply indebted to al-Sanūsī, at least in the sense that al-Sanūsī distilled the teachings of earlier Ashʿarīs into a form that al-Bājūrī readily adopted. Despite this debt, al-Bājūrī did not hesitate to disagree with al-Sanūsī on the issue of the legal necessity of learning *kalām* proofs for the obligatory points of creed.[32]

Al-Sanūsī, like al-Bāqillānī before him, believed that the *kalām* proofs and what they proved were reversible, in that it was equally necessary to know what was used to prove something as that which was proven.[33] That is to say, to know the proof for the correctness of an obligatory belief X is as much an obligation as knowing belief X itself.[34] Since the core creedal points were among those aspects that were incumbent for all Muslims to know (*farḍ ʿayn*), al-Sanūsī and al-Bāqillānī opined that one who does not know the proof for the necessary beliefs was like one who did not know the necessary beliefs, that is to say a disbeliever.[35] Al-Bājūrī, however, disregarded al-Sanūsī and al-Bāqillānī, opting instead for the opinion that one who is capable of reflecting on and comprehending the general (rather than specific) *kalām* proofs is obligated to know them, and his failure to do so is a potentially forgivable sin, but not disbelief.[36]

Al-Bājūrī reports al-Sanūsī's opinion in his commentary on *Jawharat al-tawḥīd* by first mentioning *qīla* ("it was said"), the past tense passive verb indicating, in the parlance of jurists, that the opinion following the word *qīla* is considered a weaker opinion, not the relied upon opinion.[37] While al-Bājūrī cites al-Sanūsī's *Sharḥ al-kubrā* as the source for this opinion, he also mentions that it is reported that al-Sanūsī returned to the stronger opinion of *kifāyat al-taqlīd* (the sufficiency of following the proofs of another).[38]

As el-Rouayheb notes, al-Sanūsī was a scholar of the *taḥqīqī* tradition,[39] which places a special emphasis on independent reasoning (*ijtihād*, in its broadest sense).[40] His thinking on theology and the rational sciences had a profound effect on scholars and learning institutions across the Muslim world. Al-Bājūrī grew out of this same tradition, and in the same spirit of independent reasoning, he comfortably disagreed with al-Sanūsī on certain matters. Al-Bājūrī, continuing in the long tradition of which al-Sanūsī was also a part, commented on earlier works of theology, using the terminology commonly used by the *fuqahāʾ* and scholars of other Islamic sciences (*qīla, ʿalā al-aṣaḥ*), measuring and weighing various opinions and choosing the one he believed was strongest.

The legacy of al-Sanūsī is an important facet of the current study of al-Bājūrī and his role in the continuum of archetypal scholars of Sunnī Islam because al-Sanūsī represents an important link in the chain (*sanad*) to earlier Ashʿarī learning in North Africa (i.e., al-Qayrawāni and Ibn Tumart).

Like many of his contemporaries and predecessors, al-Sanūsī was a scholar of many different sciences, but especially the three core sciences of law, theology, and mysticism. The fact that he was a proponent of the *ʿaqlī* sciences, including *manṭiq*, did not negate his being a scholar of *ḥadīth* and the other *naqlī* sciences. Like al-Qayrawānī (d. 386/996) and many other North African Mālikīs before al-Sanūsī's time, the scholars and the *madrasas* in which they studied were proponents of Ashʿarī thought. There was, however, an apparent split between some of the Persian-influenced *taḥqīqī* Ashʿarī scholars, among whom al-Sanūsī was counted, and those Ashʿarīs, such as al-Suyūṭī, who followed the "method of the Arabs" rather than the Persians, and rejected some of the *ʿaqlī* sciences promoted by the *taḥqīqī*s.[41]

Al-Sanūsī, in the context of his contemporaries, such as al-Suyūṭī, indicates that the Ashʿarīs themselves disagreed over some issues, and thus were not a monolithic entity. Furthermore, al-Bājūrī's frequent reliance on al-Sanūsī in his commentary on *Jawharat al-tawḥīd*, and his written commentaries on al-Sanūsī's works further indicate that Ashʿarī thought, like any *madhhab* of law, admitted and accepted a wide scope of *ikhtilāf*.

The aforementioned scholars are Ashʿarīs who wrote in a post-Ghazālīan world, in which some of Ibn Sīnā's thought was channeled into the *kalām* discourse, and in which the developments in the science of *manṭiq* had occurred, such that one could speak of a logic of the earlier logicians (in my opinion, pre-Rāzī) and a logic of later logicians (beginning with al-Rāzī, and culminating in al-Akhḍarī, al-Sanūsī, al-Khūnājī, and others). These two factors, the tendency toward Ibn Sīnā and the development of "the logic of the later logicians," marry Ashʿarī theology to a set of methods and topics, which make it subtly different from the Ashʿarī thought of al-Ashʿarī, al-Bāqillānī, al-Juwaynī, and even al-Ghazālī. However, this does not mean that al-Bājūrī or other Ashʿarīs were unable to express their own opinions and disagree with any of these previously mentioned founders of post sixth/twelfth-century Ashʿarī theology. He can be found differing from al-Laqānī, al-Rāzī, or al-Sanūsī, as discussed previously, without any sense that doing so was problematic for his Ashʿarī affiliations.

Al-Bājūrī's Predecessors in Law

Al-Bājūrī's predecessors in *fiqh* and *uṣūl al-fiqh* represent a broad pool of perspectives and opinions. His theology was deeply influenced by post seventh/thirteenth-century Persian Shāfiʿī and North African

Mālikī theologians and logicians. Some of these scholars, if not all, also impacted his legal thought, along with the major scholars of the Shāfiʿī school. He inherited, and quotes from, the teachings of al-Shāfiʿī's early followers, such as al-Muzanī and al-Buwayṭī, as well as others from the historical continuum of Shāfiʿī scholars. Sachau's comment, noted earlier, that an examination of just the Shāfiʿī scholars cited by al-Bājūrī would be a major exposition of Shāfiʿī intellectual history is accurate, and therefore any discussion of al-Bājūrī's Shāfiʿī predecessors is necessarily incomplete. Sachau's very useful classification of the popular works of Shāfiʿī *fiqh* divides the popular Shāfiʿī works into five categories, with each category (except one), consisting of works with which al-Bājūrī is familiar, or consisting of texts on which al-Bājūrī has written commentaries. The five categories of Shāfiʿī works as noted by Sachau are:

1. The *Taḥrīr* group, consisting of *al-Lubāb fī fiqh al-Shāfiʿī* by al-Maḥāmilī (d. 415/1034), and its various commentaries and super-commentaries, including that of Zakariyya al-Anṣārī, whom al-Bājūrī often cites.
2. The *Tanbīh* group, consisting of al-Shīrāzī's *Tanbīh* which received commentaries by al-Zarkashī (d. 794/1392) and al-Nawawī, from whose commentary al-Bājūrī often cites.
3. The Abū Shujāʿ group, consisting of *Matn Abī Shujāʿ* and its various commentaries, as well as super-commentaries, including al-Bājūrī's gloss on the commentary of al-Ghazzī, which was inspired by an earlier commentary of al-Barmāwī. Another popular commentary is that of al-Shirbīnī (977/1570), often referenced by al-Bājūrī.
4. The *Minhāj* group, based on al-Nawawī's abridgment of al-Rāfiʿī's *al-Muḥarrar*. Al-Bājūrī often cites this work, as well as those scholars who have written commentaries on it, such as al-Shabrāmallisī (d. 1087/1676).
5. The *Fatḥ al-Muʿīn* group based on the text by Zayn al-Dīn al-Malibārī (d. 928/1522), was apparently unknown to Sachau; neither it nor its commentaries figure prominently in al-Bājūrī's works, though a popular commentary by the Egyptian scholar al-Dimyāṭī (d. 1893) often cites al-Bājūrī.[42] Al-Malibārī's text was more popular outside Egypt, in East Africa and, perhaps, in al-Malibārī's native India (although he was of Yemeni descent).[43]

I discuss below those scholars whose thought influenced al-Bājūrī's and who wrote in four of the five categories of Shāf ʿī texts listed above; I also note additional references to later scholars who parsed the works in these categories, and others who offered their own important contributions to the discussion. Through an examination of these scholars, whose thought so influenced that of al-Bājūrī, we find further evidence of the normativity of the Gabrielian paradigm, the acceptance of the *ijmāʿ–ikhtilāf* spectrum, and the myriad of diverse derivations produced from the individual investigations of each scholar, producing inter-affiliational agreement and intra-affiliational disagreement.

The *Minhāj* Group: Al-Nawawī and al-Rāfiʿī

The *Minhāj* group consists of commentaries, abridgments, and glosses on al-Nawawī's *Minhāj al-ṭālibīn wa ʿumdat al-muftīyīn* (The method of the seekers and reliance of the muftīs). Abū Zakariyya Yaḥyā b. Sharaf al-Nawawī (d. 676/ 1277), author of the *Minhāj*, studied, lived, taught, and wrote in Damascus. He was one of the foremost scholars of the Shāfiʿī school in his time, and his opinions, along with those of his contemporary al-Rāfiʿī, are often considered authoritative in the Shāfiʿī school. In addition to his legal works, al-Nawawī also wrote commentaries on several canonical collections of *ḥadīth*, including that of Muslim b. Ḥajjāj (i.e., *Ṣaḥīḥ Muslim*), as well as works on Sufism, including his *Bustān al-ʿārifīn*, wherein he relates with an *isnād* (chain of narration) from the work of al-Qushayrī (a Shāfiʿī-Ashʿarī-Sufi), *Risālat al-Qushayrī*. Al-Nawawī was an archetypal scholar, a Shāfiʿī-Ashʿarī-Sufi himself, whose scholarship has affected countless jurists, *ḥadīth* specialists, theologians (especially given his conditioned support for *kalām* and *taʾwīl*, and his condemnation of *manṭiq*), Sufis, and laymen alike. For the latter, his work *Riyāḍ al-ṣāliḥīn* (Gardens of the righteous) remains extremely popular.

ʿAbd al-Karīm b. Muḥammad b. ʿAbd al-Karīm b. al-Faḍl b. al-Ḥasan, Abū l-Qasim al-Rāfiʿī (d. 623/1226) was born in Qazvīn in modern day Iran.[44] He and al-Nawawi were the two principle scholars of the Shāfiʿī school in their time, having researched and established the main opinions of the school. He was a great scholar of Islamic law as well as Qurʾānic exegesis. Tāj al-Dīn al-Subkī praised him for his profound knowledge of the sciences of law, Qurʾānic exegesis, and *ḥadīth*. He was also known as a pure-hearted ascetic and mystic. Al-Nawawī said of him: "[he] had a firm standing in righteousness, and many miracles were vouchsafed to him."[45] Al-Rāfiʿī taught

Qur'ānic exegesis and *ḥadīth* in Qazvīn, and wrote books on law and history, his main work being a commentary of al-Ghazālī's *al-Wajīz*, is entitled *Fatḥ al-ʿAzīz fī sharḥ al-Wajīz* [The victory of the invincible: An exegesis of "The synopsis"]. Al-Nawawī used this book, as discussed below, as a source for his *Minhāj*.

The *Minhāj* itself is an abridgment of al-Rāfiʿī's *al-Muḥarrar*, which is considered an abridgment of al-Ghazālī's *al-Wajīz*. Al-Ghazālī's *al-Wajīz*, via a series of his own abridgments, eventually reaches its core text, the *Nihāyat al-maṭlab fī darāya al-madhhab* of al-Juwaynī, which is a commentary on al-Muzanī's abridgment of al-Shāfiʿī's *al-Umm*. In addition to the *Minhāj*, al-Nawawī also penned *Rawḍa al-ṭālibīn wa ʿumdat al-muftīyīn* (The garden of the seekers and reliance of the *muftīs*), which was an abridgment (*mukhtaṣar*) of al-Rāfiʿī's commentary on al-Ghazālī's *al-Wajīz*. Due to its relation to the *Minhāj*, in that both return to al-Rāfiʿī's recension and reflection on al-Ghazāli's *al-Wajīz*, it is therefore fitting to include the many commentaries of *al-Rawḍa* under the *Minhāj* group, though with the disclaimer that at times al-Nawawī's views in one might not agree with his views in the other.

According to ʿAlī Jumʿa and others, the era and efforts of al-Nawawī (and al-Rāfiʿī) represent an important stage in the recension, processing, judging, and weighing of the plethora of Shāfiʿī writings and teachings, especially the Khurasanī tradition of al-Ghazālī and al-Juwaynī, and the Baghdadī tradition of al-Shīrāzī. Through the chain of abridgments and commentaries of the *Minhāj* group, one can trace the development of the Shāfiʿī school through the Khurasanī scholars, as received, processed, judged and weighed by al-Nawawī and al-Rāfiʿī. Their works were then discussed for generations, until Ibn Ḥajar al-Haytamī and al-Ramlī took up the task of discussing various texts from the *Minhāj* group, including those based on *al-Rawḍa*.

The *Minhāj* (and *Rawḍa*), by way of its predecessors (i.e., the books it is based on), reflects the following lineage: al-Shāfiʿī's *al-Umm*, al-Muzanī's *Mukhtaṣar* of *al-Umm*, al-Juwaynī's *Nihāya* (based on al-Muzanī), al-Ghazālī's *al-Wajīz* (based on al-Juwaynī), al-Rāfiʿī's *al-Muḥarrar* (being an abridgment of *al-Wajīz*) and *Sharḥ al-kabīr* (being a commentary on *al-Wajīz*), and finally al-Nawawī's *al-Minhāj*, based on *al-Muḥarrar*, and his *Rawḍa*, based on *Sharḥ al-kabīr*. With al-Juwaynī and al-Ghazālī in the lineage, we see a Khurasanī chain, though according to al-Nawawī, he and his colleagues busied themselves with both Ghazālī's *al-Waṣīṭ* (of which is *al-Wajīz* is an abridgment) and al-Shīrāzī's *al-Muhadhdhab*, the latter having been one of the main sources of *fatwās* in the Shāfiʿī school until the era of al-Rāfiʿī and al-Nawawī.[46]

Al-Nawawī addressed the teachings of the Baghdadī school represented by al-Shīrāzī in his commentary on *al-Muhadhdhab*, called *al-Majmū*ʿ, which al-Bājūrī often cites. If al-Bājūrī was citing from *al-Majmū*ʿ, rather than from previous commentaries that cited *Majmū*ʿ, he was clearly reading from al-Shīrāzī directly, even if via the interlinear commentary of al-Nawawī, further challenging Delanoue's claim that al-Bājūrī did not consult pre-Mamlūk era texts.[47] In addition to his commentary on *al-Muhadhdhab*, al-Nawawī also commented on al-Shīrāzī's *al-Tanbīh*, which Sachau mentions as a separate category of Shāfiʿī texts, discussed below.

Al-Nawawī and his colleagues were involved in a process of sorting through and interpreting the Baghdadī and Khurasanī Shāfiʿī heritage. The *Wajīz* itself offers views from al-Shāfiʿī, his student al-Muzanī, and Abū Ḥanīfa, thus the pool of disagreed upon opinions is vast. None of these texts, however, offer the final word on all matters. By way of example, al-Ghazzī discusses, in his commentary on *Matn Abī Shujā*ʿ, what one should do with the meat of a sacrificed animal (*uḍḥiyya*), when the sacrifice is voluntary, rather than the result of a binding vow. Al-Shāfiʿī's opinion, according to his "new school," is that one keeps a third of it for oneself. As for the remaining two-thirds, there is a debate. Some say that one should give it away in charity, an opinion for which al-Nawawī gives preference (*rajaḥḥahu al-Nawawī*) in his commentary on al-Shīrāzī's *al-Tanbīh*. Others have said that one-third should be given to wealthy Muslims, and one-third should be given in charity to poor Muslims. Al-Ghazzī tells us that al-Nawawī does not give preference to either opinion in his *al-Rawḍa*, nor does its *aṣl* (the original text on which it is based), meaning al-Rāfiʿī's *Sharḥ al-kabīr*.

Al-Bājūrī comments on al-Nawawī's preference for giving the remaining two-thirds away, as mentioned in al-Nawawī's commentary on al-Shīrāzī's *Tanbīh*, declaring this opinion weak (*ḍaʿīf*). As for the opinion that one-third is given to rich Muslims and one-third to the poor, al-Bājūrī declares this the relied upon position (*muʿtammad*), apparently relying on al-Barmāwī.[48] It is possible that al-Nawawī's conflicting positions on this issue may come from the fact he was in the process of integrating the Baghdadī position when commenting on the *Tanbīh*, and the Khurasanī position when discussing it in *al-Rawḍa*. The fact that al-Ghazzī, al-Barmāwī, and al-Bājūrī continued to discuss it, indicates that the issue may not have been fully decided, despite eventually having been declared the relied upon position. In any case, the issue indicates al-Bājūrī's continued interaction with the *Tanbīh* and *Minhāj* traditions, as well as earlier expressions of Shāfiʿī doctrine, as he mentions a few sentences later al-Buwayṭī's position on restricting the recipients of the sacrificial meat to Muslims, in contrast to al-Nawawī's position in *al-Rawḍa* that poor non-Muslims may eat from the donated third. In this case, al-Bājūrī adopts al-Buwayṭī's opinion, not al-Nawawī's.

A Shāfiʿī-Ashʿarī-Sufi like al-Nawawī, al-Bājūrī is in frequent discourse with his fellow archetypal scholars. However, he does not hesitate to oppose al-Nawawī in one case, as mentioned above, or to cite al-Nawawī to buttress his opinion against a conflicting position in another. Both Ashʿarīs accept the utility of *kalām*, but al-Nawawī appears to consider it bitter medicine, only to be used in an emergency, whereas al-Bājūrī considers it a *farḍ kifāya* (communally obligatory) in terms of its detailed proofs, and *farḍ ʿayn* (personally obligatory) in terms of its general proofs. Both considered *ta'wīl* to be valid, but, as discussed later, al-Bājūrī considers it the stronger approach, compared to *tafwīḍ*. Despite being Ashʿarīs who supported *kalām*, al-Nawawī considered *manṭiq* to be forbidden (*ḥarām*), while al-Bājūrī understood al-Nawawī's condemnation to be restricted to the earlier logicians' systems, which were not devoid of heretical philosophical beliefs, rather than the methods of the later logicians who were engaged in a communally obligatory science.

Both traveled the Sufi path, and while al-Nawawī may not have been as devoted to an individual shaykh as al-Bājūrī had been with Ibn Ḥurayba, they were both deeply imbued with Sufi teachings and wrote on its benefits and teachings.

In al-Nawawī and al-Rāfiʿī's time, the Shāfiʿī-Ashʿarī-Sufi tradition was strong and influential; al-Nawawī in particular was little concerned with Atharī critiques of *kalām* in general or *ta'wīl* in particular. They did not live in a post-rationalist age, after its supposed defeat at the hands of "traditionalists." Indeed, their Shāfiʿism, as discussed above, is rooted in al-Ghazālī and al-Juwaynī's tradition of Khurasan and al-Shīrāzī's tradition of Baghdad, both centers claiming many Ashʿarīs in their ranks, including these three scholars. Al-Nawawī and al-Rāfiʿī mine the *ijmāʿ–ikhtilāf* spectrum and parse its various derivations; no one individual is found to agree in totality with another in all matters, nor would one expect it.

Ibn Ḥajar al-Haytamī and Shams al-Dīn al-Ramlī

A number of important scholars contributed to the *Minhāj* group of Shāfiʿī texts, as well as other categories. Two in particular were Ibn Ḥajar al-Haytamī and Shams al-Dīn al-Ramlī, who represent a later stage of Shāfiʿī recension. Like al-Nawawī and al-Rāfiʿī before them, their agreement on an issue often became a relied-upon position, and their disagreement indicated greater choice for the *muftī* or layman. A useful tabulation of their disagreements on matters of worship has been produced by ʿAlī b. Aḥmad Bāṣabrayn, called *Ithmid al-ʿaynayn fī baʿaḍ ikhtilāf al-shaykhayn,* although their disagreements extended well beyond such matters.[49]

Shihāb al-Dīn Abū l-ʿAbbās Aḥmad b. Muḥammad, known as Ibn Ḥajar al-Haytamī (d. 974/1566–67), was born in Mahallat Abī l-Haytam in Western Egypt. He began his studies with the memorization of the Qurʾān and al-Nawawī's *Minhāj,* later continuing in the revered Sufi shrine of Sayyid Aḥmad al-Badawī in Tanta, and eventually at al-Azhar. Among his important teachers were Shaykh al-Islām Zākariyya al-Anṣārī, who also contributed to the *Minhāj* group via an abridgment and its accompanying commentary, as well as a commentary on Ibn al-Muqrī's (d. 837/1444) abridgment of *al-Rawḍa.* Al-Anṣārī, as discussed below, also contributed to the *Taḥrīr* group. Ibn Ḥajar also studied with Shihāb al-Dīn al-Ramlī, the father of Shams al-Dīn al-Ramlī. He later left Egypt to settle in Mecca, which may partially explain the popularity of his rulings outside Egypt, such as among some of the Shāfiʿīs in Yemen, who prefer his rulings in many cases to those of al-Ramlī.

An avid proponent of Sufism, he, like his counterpart al-Ramlī, considered singing and dancing in *dhikr* ceremonies to be permissible.[50] Ibn Ḥajar was also a supporter and defender of Ibn al-ʿArabī; he discussed his case at length in his collection of *fatwā*s entitled *Fatāwā al-ḥadīthiyya.* He was an avid supporter of the *mawlid,* or celebration of the birth of the Prophet Muḥammad, and penned a work in support of this practice. Al-Bājūrī provided a commentary on this, entitled *Ḥāshiya ʿalā mawlid al-Muṣṭafā li Ibn Ḥajar al-Haytamī* [A gloss on Ibn Ḥajar al-Haytamī's "The birthday of the chosen one (the Prophet Muḥammad)"].[51]

On matters of theology, he was an Ashʿarī *mutakallim* who considered the study of logic to be a communal obligation, as it served *kalām* as well as *uṣūl al-fiqh.*[52] His definition of the Ahl al-Sunna was more restricted than that of others, at least at first glance, as he declared the followers of al-Ashʿarī and al-Māturīdī to be the sole representatives of the Ahl al-Sunna, although he declares Aḥmad b. Ḥanbal free of anthropomorphism, citing Ibn al-Jawzī's defense of Ibn Ḥanbal.[53] In doing so, he also declares Ibn Taymiyya and his student Ibn Qayyim al-Jawziyya to be heretics.[54] Although al-Bājūrī does not explicitly mention Ibn Taymiyya, it is likely that Ibn Taymiyya's influence had waned in Egypt (and had not yet been revived in the Egypt of al-Bājūrī's time) and that al-Bājūrī inherited his stance on Ibn Taymiyya from Ibn Ḥajar, despite citing Ibn Qayyim al-Jawziyya as a source in his *Mawāhib al-laduniyya sharḥ al-shamā'il al-Muḥammadiyya*, as mentioned below.

Shams al-Dīn Muḥammad b. Aḥmad al-Ramlī (d. 1004/1596) was born in Ramla, not far from al-Bājūrī's hometown of Bājūr. His father, a notable *faqīh* and *muftī* taught him, as did Ibn Ḥajar's teacher Zakariyya al-Anṣārī. Additionally, he studied with al-Khaṭīb al-Shirbīnī, who contributed to the *Minhāj* group with *Mughnī l-muḥtāj ila maʿrifat al-maʿāni alfaẓa Sharḥ al Minhāj*, being a commentary on al-Nawawī's *Minhāj*, in which al-Shīrbīnī often differs with al-Nawawī's text. Al-Shīrbīnī also contributed to the Abī Shujāʿ group with his commentary entitled *al-Iqnāʿ fī ḥāl alfāẓ Abī Shujāʿ*, which al-Bājūrī frequently references.

Al-Ramlī became the *muftī* of the Shāfiʿīs in Egypt, a position his father had held before him. He also penned a commentary, like his teachers before him, on al-Nawawī's *Minhāj*, entitled *Nihāyat al-Muḥtāj Sharḥ al-Minhāj*. His commentary became popular with Shāfiʿīs at al-Azhar after him, and a number of super-commentaries were written on it, including that of al-Shabrāmallisī, whom al-Bājūrī often cites.

Shihāb al-Dīn al-Ramlī, Zakariyya al-Anṣārī, al-Khaṭīb al-Shirbīnī, Shams al-Dīn al-Ramlī, and Ibn Ḥajar al-Haytamī busied themselves with al-Nawawī's *Minhāj* and the works it inspired (i.e., previous commentaries and abridgments). In the works of Shams al-Dīn al-Ramlī and Ibn Ḥajar, we find the next stage in determining the relied upon position (*muʿtammad*) on many issues, the previous stage having been the works of al-Nawawī and al-Rāfiʿī. In some cases al-Ramlī and Ibn Ḥajar contradict al-Nawawī's preferred positions. It is important to note that these scholars, writing centuries after al-Nawawī and al-Rāfiʿī, were engaged in the critical assessment of the Shāfiʿī legacy as it had been passed down via al-Juwaynī and al-Ghazālī through al-Nawawī and al-Rāfiʿī, and via al-Ghazzī (who also cites al-Nawawī's *al-Minhāj* and *al-Rawḍa*), and al-Shīrāzī. They continued the process of assessing the Baghdadī and Khurasanī schools, and incorporated and critiqued developments between the time of al-Ghazālī and al-Shīrāzī and that of al-Nawawī and al-Rāfiʿī, such as those found in the *Taḥrīr* group.

For example, regarding one point of disagreement between the scholars of the Shāfiʿī school, al-Bājūrī appears to disagree with al-Ramlī, and tells the reader to review al-Ramlī's discussion of the matter at hand. The issue regards whether a ritual sacrifice offered by one member of a household suffices for the entire family under his wing (i.e., the request to sacrifice is satisfied for the remainder of the family), thus meaning that the reward is given to all family members on account of the actions of one member.[55]

Al-Bājūrī appears to give preference to the opinion that the requirement is fulfilled for the rest, but the reward is only for the one who sacrifices, whereas al-Ramlī gives preference to the opinion that the reward is for all members. Again, al-Bājūrī's confidence in differing with one of the past masters of the Shāfiʿī school indicates a continued dynamism in the legal discourse, even if recourse to precedent is more prevalent than in the foundational times of *madhhab*-development. Regardless of the disagreement, the fact that al-Bājūrī orders his reader to review al-Ramlī and the issue in general, alongside his many quotes from a number of previous commentaries on the *Minhāj* and earlier works, indicates that the reader's job is not merely to quote al-Bājūrī's commentary, but to follow up on its sources, so that one reads and understands for oneself. It is important to note that al-Bājūrī does not appear to believe that a commentary is in and of itself sufficient, but rather, the scholar should delve into the original sources.

Ibn Ḥajar, al-Ramlī, and other contemporaneous scholars who produced abridgments and commentaries on al-Nawawī's *al-Minhāj*, and the works related to it (such as *al-Rawḍa*), mark a very important stage in the development of the Shāfiʿī school, in terms of its legal thought, but also its affiliations with Ashʿarī thought and Sufism. Listed among al-Anṣārī's students is Ibn Ḥajar, as well as al-Shaʿrānī, a great legal scholar but primarily known for his Sufi thought and often cited by al-Bājūrī in his discussions of Sufism. Among al-Ramlī's students was Ibrāhīm al-Laqānī, a Mālikī-Ashʿarī-Sufi (discussed above) who was the author of the Ashʿarī manifesto *Jawhարat al-tawḥīd* upon which al-Bājūrī's *Tuḥfat al-murīd* is a commentary. While al-Bājūrī and his colleagues did not universally agree with every statement made by these scholars, this clustering of highly influential scholars around the ninth–eleventh/fifteenth–seventeenth centuries indicates that it was a vibrant time of individual investigation and thought. Al-Bājūrī was deeply affected by these scholars, and their investigation of *al-Minhāj*, as well as those in the *Taḥrīr* and Abī Shujāʿ group, to which we now turn our attention.

The *Taḥrīr* Group

The *Lubbāb fī Fiqh al-Shāfiʿī* serves as the base text of the *Taḥrīr* group, and was written by Abū l-Ḥasan Aḥmad b. Muḥammad al-Maḥāmilī (d. 415/1034). Al-Maḥāmilī was a *qāḍī* in the Shāfiʿī school, a well-regarded scholar and the author of multiple works on Shāfiʿī *fiqh*, and the student of Abū Ḥāmid al-Isfaraʿīnī (d. 406/1016), a famous Shāfiʿī *faqīh* and Sufi shaykh. This book enjoyed great popularity as an introductory text, and has received many abridgments and commentaries. Abū Zurʿa b. al-Ḥāfiẓ al-ʿIrāqī wrote an abridgment (*mukhtaṣar*) of it called *Tanqīḥ al-lubāb*, which was in turn abridged by Zakariyya al-Anṣārī in a work entitled *Taḥrīr Tanqīḥ al-lubāb*. Al-Anṣārī then wrote a commentary on his abridgment called *Tuḥfat al-Ṭulāb bi sharḥ taḥrīr tanqīḥ al-lubāb*.[56] It is from al-Anṣārī's abridgment that we take the name of this group of texts (i.e., the *Taḥrīr* group). His thought is a fitting study within the *Taḥrīr* group because he, along with his contemporaries al-Shīrbīnī, Ibn Ḥajar, and al-Ramlī, played an important role in the later recensions of the Shāfiʿī school, and was deeply tied to the Ashʿarī school and Sufism.

Zakariyya al-Anṣārī

Zakariyya al-Anṣārī was a Shāfiʿī-Ashʿārī-Sufi who studied at al-Azhar University, and eventually became the *qāḍī* of the Shāfiʿīs, a position he held for twenty years. He wrote a number of works on Shāfiʿī *fiqh* and *uṣūl al-fiqh*, substantially contributing to the *Minhāj* group and the *Taḥrīr* group.

Al-Anṣārī abridged Tāj al-Dīn al-Subkī's *Jamʿ al-jawāmiʿ*—a work on which al-Bājūrī began, though did not complete, a commentary—and then commented on his abridgment in a book called *Ghāyat al-wuṣūl fī sharḥ lubb al-uṣūl*. In his commentary, he lays out his view of Sunnī Islam, basing himself on al-Subkī, wherein he declares the founders of the *madhhab*s to be rightly guided, along with al-Ashʿarī in matters theological, and al-Junayd as the master of Sufis (*sayyid al-ṣufiyya*).[57] A very similar, though slightly more involved and expansive declaration is made by al-Bājūrī in his *Tuḥfat al-murīd*, as discussed earlier.[58]

Al-Bājūrī began a gloss on al-Anṣārī's *Manhaj fī fiqh al-Shāfiʿiyya*, itself an abridgment of al-Nawawī's *Minhāj*, both texts figuring prominently in al-Bājūrī's writings. Although he did not complete the work, entitled *Ḥāshiya ʿalā matn al-manhaj fī fiqh al-Shāfiʿiyya li Shaykh al-Islām Zakariyya al-Anṣārī* [A gloss on Shaykh al-Islām Zakariyya al-Anṣārī's text: "The method regarding Shāfiʿī *fiqh*"], he did complete his commentary up to the chapter on the funeral prayer.[59]

Al-Bājūrī also cites al-Anṣārī on a number of occasions, including one in which he cites al-Anṣārī's opinion which goes against the relied upon position (*muʿtammad*) on a matter related to the *ʿaqīqa*, that is, the sacrifice in celebration of a newborn on the seventh day after birth. The issue at hand is whether to offer one or two sacrificial *shāh* (lamb or goat) in celebration of the birth of a child who is a hermaphrodite (one being the number offered for female infants, and two for male infants). The relied upon position, according to al-Bājūrī, is that, while given a choice, one offers two as a precaution, in case it is determined that the child is male in the future. However, al-Anṣārī's opinion is cited from his *Manhaj* as sacrificing two for a male, and one for "other than [male]." To clarify the expression of "other," al-Bājūrī cites al-Anṣārī's own commentary on the *Manhaj*, in which female infants and hermaphrodites are specified.[60]

Furthermore, despite al-Bājūrī's apparent preference for the *muʿtammad*, he cites al-Anṣārī's proof from analogizing between the issue at hand (the *ʿaqīqa*) and the issue of paying blood money (*diyya*) to the relatives of a murder or victim of unintentional manslaughter, wherein the killer, in the case of the death of a woman or hermaphrodite, pays half the *diyya* due for the death of a man. The *wajh al-qiyās*, or the basis for the analogy, is that the goal of the *ʿaqīqa* is the preservation of life, similar to the goal of paying blood money (*diyya*) in the case of accidental manslaughter, and it is one of two possible punishments meant as deterrents in the case of murder. While the *ʿaqīqa* is a celebratory expression of thankfulness and hope for a long and healthy life, the *diyya* is a deterrent punishment aimed at preserving life (i.e., by avoiding blood feuds).

Perhaps al-Bājūrī cites this evidence in order to offer the reader valid options, noting that one's individual circumstances and *taqwā* (God-conciousness) dictate one's choice (i.e., al-Anṣārī's or the relied upon opinion). Or perhaps his intent was to teach the budding jurist something of *uṣūl al-fiqh*, namely the role of *qiyās* in *ijtihād*. Regardless of intent, the latter possibility is of great importance to the subject at hand because it gives us an example of a tenth/sixteenth-century jurist practicing *ijtihād* and differing from other jurists before and after him, if in fact it is al-Anṣārī's own *ijtihād*. It is an example of an open issue in which a relied-upon opinion may have been established, yet other options remained in the *ijmāʿ–ikhtilāf* spectrum; opinions whose arguments and proofs were considered, rather than merely citing a ruling without evidence to be followed or rejected without consideration. Al-Bājūrī's preference for one opinion over another, and his consideration of the evidence of an opposing yet valid opinion show a critical assessment of the possibilities, though not as explicit as in other cases where he in fact may be exercising *ijtihād*, as discussed later in this work. It gives us further evidence of rigorous, if subtle, scholarship in contradistinction to claims of decline and mere blind following (*taqlīd*).

Al-Anṣārī, predating al-Bājūrī by three centuries, was an important precursor to al-Bājūrī's intellectual development. His scholarly corpus was similar to al-Bājūrī's, consisting of works on law, theology, logic, Sufism, and other topics. Like al-Bājūrī, he taught a number of students while also holding a government appointed position, in his case the judgeship of the Shāfiʿīs, in al-Bājūrī's, the rectorship of al-Azhar. Among al-Anṣārī's students were two extremely influential scholars whose impact on al-Bājūrī's thought is clear from his numerous references to them. The first is al-Shaʿrānī, an important scholar of Sufism (discussed later) who al-Bājūrī cites on a number of occasions. The other student whose impact on al-Bājūrī and all other later Shāfiʿī legal thought is far-reaching, was Ibn Ḥajar al-Haytamī, one of the main sources of *fatwā*s in the later Shāfiʿī school, and an important contributor to the *Minhāj* group.

The Abū Shujaʿ Group

The Abū Shujāʿ group refers to the commentaries and super-commentaries on the concise summary of Shāfiʿī *fiqh* written by Qāḍī Abū Shujāʿ (d. 590/1194). Abū Shujāʿ is Aḥmad b. al-Ḥasan b. Aḥmad al-Shāfiʿī, a *qāḍī* who was born in Baṣra (modern-day Iraq), where he taught Shāfiʿī *fiqh* for more than forty years.[61] He was appointed a *qāḍī* in Isfahan, where his father had been born. The traditional accounts narrate that he lived 160 years. His text is terse, and does not appear to have been intended as comprehensive, though it is based on *Sharḥ al-Iqnāʿ* by al-Māwārdī (d. 450/1058),[62] whom al-Bājūrī often cites. One common commentary that accompanies it is that of Ibn al-Qāsim al-Ghazzī (d. 918/1522). Al-Ghazzī's commentary often refers to other works, such as al-Nawawī's *al-Minhāj*, though it is most often an interlinear commentary, frequently filling out the statements of Abū Shujāʿ as though he is completing the sentences of the original author. Two other popular commentaries are that of al-Khaṭīb al-Shirbīnī called *al-Iqnāʿ fī ḥall alfāẓ Abī Shujāʿ*—which draws on his own commentaries on *al-Minhāj* and *al-Tanbīh*—and *Tuḥfat al-ḥabīb* by Ibn Daqīq al-ʿĪd (d. 702/1302).

According to al-Ghazzī, Abū Shujāʿ's short text (*matn*) is known by two names, the first, *al-Taqrīb* and the second, *Ghāyat al-ikhtiṣār*, though it is often referred to simply as *Matn Abī Shujāʿ*. Al-Bājūrī wrote a super-commentary (*ḥāshiya*) on al-Ghazzī's commentary, which became the standard *ḥāshiya* on this text until the present day. *Ḥāshiyas* other than al-Bājūrī's include that of al-Qalyūbī (d. 1069/1659), and that of al-Barmāwī, the latter of which serves as a foundation for al-Bājūrī's. Al-Bājūrī often refers to al-Barmāwī and al-Shirbīnī, as well as to al-Ghazzī as the commentator on *Matn Abī Shujāʿ* and on al-Nawawī's *al-Minhāj*. Al-Bājūrī, however, does not merely cite or summarize his predecessors al-Barmāwī, al-Shirbīnī, or al-Ghazzī; he often corrects what he views as their mistakes and adds significant additional details.[63]

One of many examples of al-Bājūrī's disagreement with the main text and its commentary regards the permissibility of eating meat slaughtered by a Jew or a Christian. Al-Ghazzī and Abū Shūjāʿ seem to consider the animal slaughtered by any Jew or Christian to be permissible, whereas the *muʿtammad,* which al-Bājūrī appears to favor, is that one can only eat from an animal slaughtered by a Jew or Christian who is from a community whose women are marriageable by Muslim men.[64] It also implies the dominant Shāfiʿī doctrine that the only marriageable Jewish women are from communities that are descendants of the followers of Moses before Jesus's law abrogated Mosaic law, and that the only marriageable Christian women are those who descend from the followers of Jesus before his law was abrogated by Muhammad.[65] Although the opinion stated in the original text and its commentary by al-Ghazzī is the opinion of others (*baʿdahum*), it is contrary to the *muʿtammad,* which al-Bājūrī favors in this instance.

Matn Abī Shujāʿ, with al-Ghazzī's commentary, was and is influential as an educational text, a Shāfiʿī *fiqh* primer. However, since al-Ghazzī frequently references *al-Minhāj, al-Rawḍa,* and *Tanbīh,* as does al-Bājūrī along with other sources in his *ḥāshiya,* it is probable that the *Minhāj* group, and to a lesser extent the *Tanbīh* group had a greater effect on the rulings of *qāḍīs* and *muftīs* throughout history than *Matn Abī Shujāʿ* and the commentary of al-Ghazzī. It is likely that the *ḥāshiyas* of al-Bājūrī, al-Shirbīnī, and al-Barmāwī were influential among *qāḍīs* and *muftīs* because of their advanced, detailed, and complete content. Again, these *ḥāshiyas* are deeply indebted to, but not always in agreement with, the *Minhāj* and *Tanbīh* groups, the latter to which we now turn our attention.

The *Tanbīh* Group

The *Tanbīh* group refers to a set of texts based on al-Shīrāzī's *al-Tanbīh,* discussed below. Al-Bājūrī was indebted to and influenced by al-Shīrāzī—he quotes him often, along with those who commented on his works. It is likely that with the prominence of the *Minhāj*- and

Rawḍa-based texts after al-Nawawī's time, al-Shīrāzī's direct influence was less pronounced, however, it is clearly present in al-Bājūrī's writings. Al-Shīrāzī was the leader of the Shāfiʿīs in his time, especially in Baghdad, and his *al-Tanbīh* is an important summary of the Shāfiʿī teachings, organized in accord with the traditional ordering of *fiqh* books.

Abū Isḥāq al-Shīrāzī

Abū Isḥāq al-Shīrāzī (d. 476/1083) was a scholar of Shāfiʿī *fiqh* and *uṣūl*, an Ashʿarī in theology (though this point is debated), and closely associated with prominent Sufis of his time.[66] He was an archetypal scholar whom the modern Azharī scholar ʿAlī Jumʿa, an inheritor of al-Bājūrī's teachings, calls the "shaykh of the *fuquhāʾ* of his era."[67] Al-Shīrāzī wrote the *Lumaʿ fī l-uṣūl al-fiqh*,[68] a work that was contemporaneous to major developments in post-Shāfiʿī *uṣūl*, such as the writings of al-Juwaynī, with whom he apparently differed on a number of points.[69] There is also a work of Ashʿarī creed attributed to him, *Ishāra ilā madhhab ahl al-ḥaqq*, a summary of Ashʿarī creed with *kalām* proofs. In addition to his other important work, the *Tanbīh* played a prominent role in the development of the Shāfiʿī school, as did his *Muhadhdhab*, the former receiving a commentary by al-Nawawī called *Taṣḥīḥ al-Tanbīh*, as well as commentaries by al-Rifʿa (d. 710/1310) and al-Zarkashī (d. 794/1392), and the latter having a commentary by al-Nawawī called *al-Majmūʿ*. However, as Sachau notes, by the late nineteenth century, the popularity of *al-Tanbīh* had declined and it was rarely studied.

It is unclear whether or not al-Bājūrī had read al-Shīrāzī's works directly or only as referenced in other texts. He quotes al-Shīrāzī on a number of occasions, including in his *Tuḥfat al-murīd* on the issue of the definition of the *ʿaql* (intellect), whereby al-Shīrāzī is said to have defined the intellect as "an attribute by which one discerns between the good (*ḥasn*) and the bad (*qabīḥ*)."[70] Al-Ghazzī cites al-Nawawī's *Taṣḥīḥ al-tanbīh*, but I have not yet found a direct reference to it by al-Bājūrī. He does, however, often cite al-Nawawī's *al-Majmūʿ*, which means he would have read al-Shīrāzī directly via al-Nawawī's commentary.

Al-Shīrāzī is an important early example of an archetypal scholar of the Gabrielian paradigm, being contemporaneous with al-Ghazālī and al-Juwaynī, indicating that the jurist–theologian–Sufi model did not merely reflect the result of al-Ghazālī's effort to synthesize law, theology, and Sufism, as some might believe from the popular narrative of al-Ghazālī's contributions. His affiliations with the Shāfiʿī school are well known from his own works, and his Sufi affiliations are deduced from his association with Abū Naṣr al-Qushayrī (the son of the famous Sufi Abū l-Qāsim al-Qushayrī (d. 465/1072)), and his ascetic lifestyle. Al-Nawawī says of al-Shīrāzī: "He was . . . one of the gnostic worshipers [*aḥad . . . al-ʿubād al-ʿārifīn*]."[71] Given al-Nawawī's firm grounding in Sufism, including al-Qushayrī's *Risāla*, and al-Shīrāzī's close association with al-Qushayrī's Shāfiʿī-Ashʿarī-Sufi son, discussed below, it is reasonable to interpret al-Nawawī's comment to indicate that al-Shīrāzī had realized the high spiritual states of Sufism, namely *maʿrifa* (gnosis or spiritual knowledge of Allah).

His Ashʿarī affiliation is debated, but arguably evident from his close association with and support for Abū l-Qāsim al-Qushayrī, who vexed the Ḥanbalīs of Baghdad when he preached Ashʿarī thought and criticized the Ḥanbalīs. It is also evident from his written works in *uṣūl al-fiqh*, and his *Ishāra ilā madhhab ahl al-ḥaqq*, if it can be attributed to him with certainty. Two brief examples suffice to show that he was not an anti-rationalist traditionalist, pace Makdisi. First, in his *al-Maʿūna fī l-jadal*, al-Shīrāzī discusses the technical term *ẓāhir*, defining it as "Every expression that carries two meanings (*yaḥtamilu amrayn*), wherein the first meaning is the most apparent (*aẓhar*). . . . The ruling with regard to it is that it carries the most apparent meaning, and the other meanings are not resorted to except with a proof."[72] This definition is in contradistinction to the *naṣṣ* (lit., text), which, in the technical language of *uṣūl al-fiqh*, refers to a text that can only be understood in one sense. This definition of the *ẓāhir* falls in line with al-Bājūrī and the literal–linguistic definition of many other Ashʿarīs, and in apparent opposition to Ibn Taymiyya's literal–contextual definition. Such a definition of *ẓāhir* would necessitate *taʾwīl* or *tafwīḍ* in matters pertaining to Allah's attributes, placing al-Shīrāzī again closer to the Ashʿarīs.

Second, in the *Lumaʿ*, al-Shīrāzī distinguishes between two types of rulings (*aḥkām*) with which the *mujtahid* deals: *ʿaqlī* (rational) and *sharʿī* (legal). In explanation of the *ʿaqlī* rulings, he gives as examples "the contingency of the universe, the establishment [of the existence] of a creator, the establishment of prophecy (*nubūwwa*), and other essentials of faith (*uṣūl al-diyānāt*)."[73] This is a clear affirmation that some matters of faith may be known to the intellect alone, without reference to revealed texts. The Ashʿarī *mutakallim* al-Taftazānī (d. 792/1390) says in his commentary on the Māturīdī creed of al-Nasafī: "Furthermore, the basis of *kalām* is that there is deduced from the existence of originated things (*al-muḥdathāt*) the existence of the Maker (*al-ṣāniʿ*), His unity, His attributes and His actions. . . ."[74] When comparing al-Shīrāzī's statement with al-Taftazānī's, it is clear that al-Shīrāzī's statement is an affirmation of the legitimacy of *kalām* in particular and rationalism in general.

If charged with being against the Ashʿarīs because he disagrees with some of them in the *Lumaʿ*, even referring to them as separate from his colleagues (*aṣḥāb*), this also falls short because he disagrees with some of his own colleagues (*aṣḥāb*) at times, who are not the Shāfiʿīs in exclusion of the rationalists, but rather the Shāfiʿīs of Baghdad, as opposed to those of Khurasan.[75] Indeed, in one instance where he disagrees with some of his colleagues, they have taken an opinion held by al-Ashʿarī himself.[76]

The issues discussed in the *Lumaʿ* show how al-Shīrāzī differed with a variety of groups, some within the Sunnī *madhhabs*, some within his own *madhhab*, some within his own regional sub-school of his own *madhhab*, and some outside of Sunnīsm. When he discusses the varying opinions he often cites two opinions and then declares one to be the soundest (*aṣaḥ*). This implies that both are valid, but one is more sound. At other times, he declares one to be *ṣaḥīḥ* (sound),[77] indicating that only one correct opinion exists, followed by an opinion that is deemed false (rather than valid but weak). At times, when there is a debate between his colleagues (*aṣḥāb*), he declares one to be more sound (*aṣaḥ*). In doing so, he is not *ipso facto* against anyone who holds an opinion contrary to the most sound position (*aṣaḥ*). Sometimes those who hold the opposing opinion are Muʿtazilīs, but there are also Ashʿarīs, Mālikīs, Ḥanafīs, and members of his own school, that of al-Shāfiʿī.[78]

Al-Bājūrī inherits this sort of technical terminology, declaring opinions to be soundest, relied upon, most apparent, popular, and so on. While the same terms may have taken on different implications as the Shāfiʿī school developed, their essential meanings and implications remain. Like al-Shīrāzī, al-Bājūrī entered into the discussion and debate, recognizing that there existed agreement and disagreement within his own school, and agreement and disagreement between his school and other schools. The existence of inter- and intra-affiliational agreement and disagreement was not limited to *fiqh* issues, as is apparent in the works of al-Shīrāzī and al-Bājūrī, but legitimately extended to *uṣūl al-fiqh* and theology. Just as al-Shīrāzī indicates agreement between Sunnīs and Muʿtazilīs, as mentioned above, al-Bājūrī implicitly does so when he refers to al-Zamakhsharī's (d.538/1144) opinions in his gloss on al-Ghazzī's commentary.[79]

Al-Shīrāzī was an important influence on al-Bājūrī, primarily in the realm of law. However, with his Ashʿarī affiliations apparent, and certainly the nonexistence of anti-rationalism on his part, his law-theology-Sufism paradigm further buttresses the normativity of al-Bājūrī's Shāfiʿī-Ashʿarī-Sufi paradigm, it having been prominent in al-Shīrāzī's Baghdadī tradition, al-Ghazālī and al-Juwaynī's Khurasanī tradition, as well as with the commentators between them and al-Nawawī and al-Rāfiʿī, on down to al-Bājūrī's. Though there were changes in the official positions among the Shāfiʿīs and Ashʿarīs throughout this time, such that we can talk about a late-Ashʿarī school or a late-Shāfiʿī school, these changes are certainly rooted in and connected to earlier periods, such as that of al-Shīrāzī.

Later Scholars

Al-Bājūrī cites passages and opinions from the foundational texts of the Shāfiʿī *madhhab*, including the *Umm* of al-Shāfiʿī, the abridgments of his students al-Muzanī and al-Buwayṭī, the works of al-Māwardī, al-Juwaynī, al-Ghazālī, al-Subkī, al-Ruwyānī (d. 523/1128–9), al-Anṣārī, al-Rāfiʿī, al-Nawawī, al-Shabrāmallisī, and many others. He also had significant exposure to later commentators and *muftī*s of the preceding three centuries, the era between himself and that of Ibn Ḥajar and al-Ramlī. He also references his own shaykhs from time to time, including al-Faḍālī, as well as al-Maydānī. In one important example, he mentions that his shaykh, al-Maydānī, used to order his poorer students to sacrifice a chicken at the birth of a child (*ʿaqīqa*), rather than choosing from a sheep, goat, cow, or camel, as the dominant opinion necessitates. This is particularly interesting, because al-Maydānī was analogizing (*qiyās*) from an opinion of the Prophet's Companion Ibn ʿAbbās, who permitted the ritual sacrifice (*ʿuḍḥiyya*) with a chicken or the likes, and applying this analogy to the *ʿaqīqa*. While this may not be a particularly exciting issue to many, it is meaningful in practice for Muslims, and more importantly, it is a practical example of *ijtihād* in al-Bājūrī's time, that is, the use of analogy to produce a derived ruling.

Al-Bājūrī and his Shāfiʿī predecessors further demonstrate the simultaneous diversity of thought and method over time and place, the continued normativity of the jurist–theologian–Sufi archetype in general, and the Shāfiʿī-Ashʿarī-Sufi in particular. That the chain of ever expanding and contracting commentaries and abridgments, especially those from al-Shīrāzī, al-Juwaynī, and al-Ghazālī's time onward, are primarily at the hands of Ashʿarīs, pace Makdisi, combined with the institutional history of *madrasas* discussed previously, further buttresses the traditional orientalist and Sunnī view of intellectual history, namely that from at least the sixth/twelfth century onward, the Sunnī standard bearers were primarily Ashʿarīs, among the Shāfiʿīs (and Mālikīs) and Māturīdī among the Ḥanafīs. Whether these were Ashʿarīs actively engaged in *kalām*, such as al-Juwaynī or al-Bājūrī, or primarily jurist-Sufis, such as al-Nawawī, shows mainly the diversity of intellectual inclinations among archetypal scholars, rather than exhibiting any evidence of a defeat of rationalism by so-called traditionalists.

Furthermore, the common narrative of decline, which presumably begins with al-Shāfiʿī's independent scholarship, followed by his slightly restricted early students, to the more restricted, yet still somewhat independent scholarship of al-Shīrāzī, al-Juwaynī, and al-Ghazālī, to the now more restricted al-Nawawī and al-Rāfiʿī, until either the very restricted or wholly derivative scholarship of Ibn Ḥajar and al-Ramlī, followed by the total absence of independent scholarship, seems like a believable compromise to the popular orientalist narrative of decline which, in the realm of law, is said to have occurred rather abruptly after the third/ninth century. However, even this theory of a more gradual decline, though backed by somewhat convincing evidence from one angle, still seems inappropriate in light of the depth and diversity of disagreement over so many fine points of derived law (*furūʿ*), as is evidenced in al-Bājūrī's ultimately terse yet dense commentaries wherein so many opinions are expressed and judged—opinions that come from scholars across the spectrum of early foundational scholars (such as al-Shāfiʿī, al-Muzanī, and al-Buwayṭī, as well as later commentators on the *Minhāj*, Abū Shujāʿ, and other groups of Shāfiʿī texts). As Haim Gerber puts it, "If the *madhhab* was the flour in the cake of Islamic law, *ijtihād* was the leaven."[80] The question, in many ways, comes down to valuing certain topics (*masāʾil*) over others, as though the matters discussed by later scholars were mere table scraps from the meal that had already been eaten by the early *mujtahids*. This is an arbitrary assignment of value on the one hand, and denies the continued discussions in the "major issues" on the other.

Al-Bājūrī's Sufi Predecessors

Al-Bājūrī inherited a rich Sufi legacy, replete with diverse opinions and practices. While he was influenced by and exposed to a number of different scholars, here I discuss three very different Sufi predecessors. The first, al-Shaʿrānī, represents an approach to Sufism, popular among many in the Azharī tradition, with a stong interconnection with law and Ashʿarī theology. The second, Ibn Taymiyya, though not a direct influence on al-Bājūrī, is nonetheless of great importance in understanding the normativity of al-Bājūrī as a specific manifestation of the archetypal scholar, in that Ibn Taymiyya's modern followers are often the most vociferous opponents of Sufism and al-Bājūrī's legacy.[81] The third scholar is Jalāl al-Dīn al-Suyūṭī, whose brave independence combined with strict affiliation to the past masters provides us an example of the diverse combinations of possible views on law, theology, and Sufism that can occur, despite a scholar's affiliation or the degree of his opponents' vehemence.

Al-Shaʿrānī

ʿAbd al-Wahhāb b. Aḥmad al-Shaʿrānī (d. 973/1565) was a prolific writer and established jurist, but is primarily remembered for his Sufi legacy. He was born in Sāqiyat Abū Shaʿra, a village in the Manūfiyya district a bit over ten miles from al-Bājūrī's village of Bājūr. He was an archetypal scholar, being a jurist–theologian–Sufi who considered himself an expert in all four *madhhabs*, having been taught by the likes of Ibn Ḥajar al-Haytamī. Al-Shaʿrānī viewed the four *madhhabs* as essentially equal, founded by scholars with a deep religious experience of the spiritual source of the sacred law (*ʿayn al-Sharīʿa*) from which they ultimately derived their principles.[82]

He was an Ashʿarī in faith, though, like al-Ghazālī before him, he considered the ultimate truth to be attainable via spiritual vision of Allah, which he viewed as superior to what the intellect could reach. The intellect's purpose in matters of faith was to defend points of belief to critics, but it was ultimately subordinated to the spiritual faculties.[83]

A zāwiyya was built for al-Shaʿrānī, and he had his own order (ṭarīqa) which remained prominent in Egypt until the nineteenth century. Al-Shaʿrānī criticized some ṭarīqas for their laissez faire approach to the sacred law, but also criticized scholars of fiqh for burdening the common folk with too many nuanced particulars of law. He was influenced by Shādhilī thought, and had an ancestor from Tlemcen who was a follower of the Shaykh Abū Madyan. Al-Shaʿrānī was said to have been initiated into twenty-six orders, though likely for the spiritual blessings (baraka) and not because he followed each orders' methods of spiritual purification under the guidance of a Sufi shaykh.

He is also known to have been affiliated with the Badawiyya order of Sayyid Aḥmad al-Badawī, whom al-Bājūrī mentions on several occasions, though al-Bājūrī emphasized his affiliations with al-Junayd, who was a symbol of the proper balance of Sharīʿa and Sufism. Like al-Bājūrī's Sufi shaykh, Abū Ḥurayba, al-Shaʿrānī's primary Sufi teachers were ummī, that is, illiterate Sufis, or at least not part of the scholarly class.[84] The most important of al-Shaʿrānī's Sufi shaykhs was ʿAlī al-Khawwāṣ al-Burulusī (d. 939/1532–33), who worked most of his life as a merchant and was illiterate.[85]

Al-Bājūrī adopted al-Shaʿrānī's ecumenical approach to the schools of law and Sufi orders, having had teachers and students from various madhhabs, and also embraced his interpretive method of the ecstatic utterances (shaṭḥīyāt), discussed later. Like al-Suyūṭī before him, al-Shaʿrānī argued that one should consider Ibn al-ʿArabī a great saint, but avoid reading his problematic texts.[86] Despite this word of caution, "much of al-Shaʿrānī's work is dedicated to the defense of Ibn al-ʿArabī and to the popularization of his legacy."[87]

Like so many scholars cited by al-Bājūrī, al-Shaʿrānī is a source for al-Bājūrī in some matters and not in others. Via his shaykh, Abū Ḥurayba, Al-Bājūrī had affiliations with the Khalwatiyya order, whom al-Shaʿrānī criticized for their practice of solitary cloistered dhikr (khalwa).[88] Al-Shaʿrānī was a vocal supporter of Ibn al-ʿArabī, whom al-Bājūrī seems to only hint at in his assessment of ecstatic utterances (shaṭḥīyat). In any case, al-Shaʿrānī, as a student of Ibn Ḥajar al-Haytamī, is yet another Egyptian scholar from the vibrant era of Islamic scholarship between the ninth/tenth and fifteenth/sixteenth centuries to play a prominent role in al-Bājūrī's thought.

Ibn Taymiyya

Although al-Bājūrī makes no explicit reference to Ibn Taymiyya and does not pay significant attention to the theological views of the Atharīs, Ibn Taymiyya's Sufi thought is worth exploring. Ibn Taymiyya's theological thought is related to the discussion of al-Bājūrī's theology, as he represents the primary challenge to al-Bājūrī's legacy, more so than the modernists that increased in influence soon after al-Bājūrī's death.

Ibn Taymiyya (d. 728/1328) was an archetypal scholar of the Gabrielian paradigm. He was a jurist, considered capable of *ijtihād* using the methodological tools of Aḥmad b. Ḥanbal, at the same level of *ijtihād* claimed by al-Suyūṭī and attributed to al-Ghazālī in the Shāfiʿī school. He was a theologian, and used, at times, purely rational premises (*ʿaqlī*), unaided by revelatory premises (*naqlī*), thus by most definitions, a *mutakallim*. His aversion to, nuanced definition of, and desire to be disassociated with this term notwithstanding, it seems fair to say that he was a Ḥanbalī *mutakallim*, whose own method and technical lexicon determined that the outcome of his *kalām*-based reasoning differed from that of Ashʿarī *mutakallimūn* of his day and those non-Ashʿarī *mutakallimūn* of his own school, such as Ibn al-Jawzī.

As Makdisi has brought to light, Ibn Taymiyya was a Qādirī Sufi, though many of his modern-day revivers in the Wahhābī and Salafi movements bypass this unavoidable conclusion. It appears that earlier Western scholars also missed this important aspect of his identity. Yet his magnum opus, *Majmuʿat al-fatāwā* ["Collection of *fatwas*"], and other works that today are readily in print, contain numerous references to Sufism that indicate that Ibn Taymiyya was well-versed in Sufism and an ardent practitioner, though also deeply critical of certain strands of Sufism that he considered to be in conflict with "true" Sufism.

By the nineteenth century, the Shāfiʿī–Ashʿarī dominance in Egypt had been deeply entrenched for centuries. Ibn Taymiyya's thought had not yet been revived by reformers such as Muḥammad ʿAbduh (d. 1905) or Jamāl al-Dīn al-Afghānī (d. 1897), although Muḥammad ʿAlī Pasha's raid against the Wahhābīs of the Hijaz took place during al-Bājūrī's lifetime. Al-Maqrīzī (d. 845/1441–42) mentions that Ibn Taymiyya had supporters and detractors until his time (eighth/fourteenth century), but it is quite possible that his legacy waned in Egypt under Ottoman rule.[89] I have not discovered an explicit reference to Ibn Taymiyya in al-Bājūrī's works, although he does refer by name to Ibn Qayyim al-Jawziyya, the student of Ibn Taymiyya, in his commentary on the *Shamāʾil* of al-Tirmidhī.[90]

Ibn Taymiyya's Sufism also warrants attention, as it indicates his closeness to many other archetypal Sunnī scholars. As Makdisi has argued, Ibn Taymiyya was a Qādirī Sufi who claimed to have inherited the *khirqa* (mantle) of ʿAbd al-Qādir al-Jilānī (d. 561/1166).[91] Even if the sources which indicate his direct connection to the order via an *ijāza* are not sufficient to generate certainty according to the sciences of *ḥadīth* or *uṣūl al-fiqh*,[92] when coupled with his agreed upon writings, it is clear that his views of and support for Sufism in general, and some of its specific scholars in particular, are based on the teachings of great Sufis of the past, as discussed below.

Rebuttals to Ibn Taymiyya being described as a Sufi tend to focus on a particular definition of Sufism that may include practices such as *tawaṣṣul*, specific forms of audible *dhikr*, acceptance of the teachings of Ibn al-ʿArabī, and other ideas and practices whose interpretations and applications are open to much debate. His rejection of singing and dancing in *dhikr* rituals, critical interpretation of Ibn al-ʿArabī's writings, and disdain for many Sufis' actions at the graves of past masters (i.e., *tawaṣṣul*), does not weaken the claim that he was a Sufi, nor does his apparent focus on matters of law and theology in much of his writings; while he may not have been as devoted a Sufi as al-Junayd or al-Shādhilī, for example, he was nonetheless deeply imbued with Sufi piety and thought.

A number of important criticisms of Makdisi's claims are worth noting, in particular T. F. Michael's, Fritz Meir's, and Gino Shallenbergh's who focus on the texts indicating Ibn Taymiyya's silsilah in the Qādirī ṭarīqa and his inheriting of the khirqa of al-Jilānī.[93] While, as mentioned above, these challenges to Makdisi's thesis are weighty from both the insider (i.e., scholars of uṣūl al-fiqh) and the outsider (i.e., Western academia) perspective, they only challenge the designation of "Sufi" if one defines "Sufi" as one who adheres to a Sufi order. Sufism, however, is broader than this, despite the widespread association of Sufi training and scholarship with some form of membership in Sufi order. It should therefore be noted that claiming Ibn Taymiyya to be a Sufi is not to claim that he was definitely a member of a Sufi order.

Among his explicit positive references to Sufism, and the Qādirī *ṭarīqa* in particular, Ibn Taymiyya refers to al-Jilānī as "shaykhunā" (our Shaykh) and "sayyidī" (my master), and speaks highly of a great many other Sufi shaykhs, including Abū Yazīd al-Bisṭāmī and al-Junayd.[94] He goes to great lengths to state that Sufism is not a heretical innovation (*bidʿa*), but rather, in its proper form, conforms to the *Sharīʿa* and Sunna and stems from what he calls the Sufi "*ijtihād* in obedience to Allah." He also states that the Sufi emphasis on will (*irāda*) and love (*ḥubb*) is from the Sunna.

He classifies the Sufis of his day according to three types:

1. Legitimate Sufis who experience the realities and states associated with Sufism.

2. Funded Sufis who live in Sufi lodges, who do not usually experience the realities and states, which Ibn Taymiyya concedes are rare.

3. Sufis by appearance only, wearing the dress of the Sufis, but not interested in its practice.

It is important to note that Ibn Taymiyya affirms the experiential side of Sufism, and does not declare it mere asceticism. Furthermore, he affirms the unitive experience of *fanāʾ* (annihilation), with the qualifications mentioned below, and excuses those who utter *shaṭḥ* statements[95] because they do not do so consciously. Ibn Taymiyya describes *fanāʾ* as being of three types:[96]

1. That of the Prophets, Companions, and saints (*awliyāʾ*) whose wills are in conformity with Allah's will, and whose actions are in conformity with Allah's command. Ibn Taymiyya describes it as

   > the annihilation from willing that which is other than Allah, such that he loves none except Allah, and worships none except Him, and relies on none except Him, and does not seek other than Him . . . They said: It is being free from that which is other than Allah, or from that which is other than the worship of Allah, or that which is other than wanting what Allah wants, or that which is other than that which is beloved to Allah, so the meaning is one. This is its meaning, whether it is called *fanāʾ* or not, and it is the beginning of Islam and the end of it, and it is the inner of the religion and its outer.

2. That of some of the Sufi shaykhs and *sālikīn* (travelers on the Sufi path), as well as some of the early Basran proto-Sufis of the *tābiʿīn* (the generation after the Companions). This state is imperfect, but is not considered blameworthy by Ibn Taymiyya. He describes it as

   > the annhiliation from witnessing other than Allah, and this happens to many *sālikīn*. This is a result of the excess of attraction of their hearts toward remembrance of Allah, worship of Him, and love of Him. Their hearts are too weak to witness other than that which they worship, and to see that which they seek. Nothing occurs to their hearts other than Allah. . . .

   Ibn Taymiyya attributes this experience to a weakness in the hearts of those who experience it, claiming that the Prophet and his Companions did not experience this because of the strength of their faith. This does not mean that he condemns it, however, as he attributes this state to several Sufis of whom he is supportive, such as al-Bisṭāmī (d. ca. 261/875) or al-Shiblī. (d. 334/946) He also warns against the confusion that may arise from the experience, or the *shaṭḥ* statements that are uttered by some in this state, reminding his reader that the Creator and creation are different, regardless of the unitive experience of *fanāʾ*. He also states that he does not consider the *shaṭḥ* statements to be sinful, as those who say them are like those who are insane, and thus not held accountable.[97]

3. The third type of *fanāʾ* is that of the anthropomorphists and pantheists who see the Creator and the creation as one. It is in this category that he places al-Ḥallāj and Ibn al-ʿArabī, yet he did excuse the *shaṭḥ* statement (of al-Ḥallāj) "anā al-Ḥaqq" when stated by one in an ecstatic spiritual state.[98] It seems that he considered the concept of *waḥdat al-wujūd* to mean the union of Creator and creation, whereas some defenders of Ibn al-ʿArabī have merely defined it as a description of the experience that falls under category 2 above.

While Ibn Taymiyya rejected certain Sufi practices (such as singing and dancing) on legal (*fiqh*) grounds, and others (such as his understanding of *waḥdat al-wujūd*) on theological grounds, he did not reject the science of Sufism or its resultant states. In fact, he praised them and associated himself with them.[99]

While these points help clarify Ibn Taymiyya's identity as a Sufi, they also indicate something of the overall education of a medieval scholar. A large volume of his multivolume compendium of *fatwā*s is devoted to Sufism, and is one of a number of volumes related to the core and supporting sciences of Islam (*ʿaqīda, manṭiq, tafsīr, uṣūl al-fiqh, fiqh*, etc.); this indicates that Sufism was a core part of the overall education of the scholar, regardless of whether or not it occurred in a *madrasa* college. It also tells us that not all sciences associated with the perfection of a scholar were necessarily taught in the *madrasa*s, rather, the *madrasa* was but one of many locations of learning.[100]

In summary, Ibn Taymiyya was an archetypal scholar with a thorough mastery of the core sciences of Islam. He was a jurist, theologian, and mystic. While his rejection of *manṭiq* and his harshness toward those he called Ahl al-Kalām (the people of *kalām*) indicate that he was a pure "traditionalist," he was in fact a *mutakallim* in his use of purely rational proofs in matters of creed, and at times he even gave opinions that were similar to those held by some Greek philosophers.[101] While many scholars criticized his views that ostensibly implied anthropomorphism, further research is required to determine whether or not his problematic statements could be better understood through the lens of his literal–contextual definition of *ẓāhir*, discussed later. Since he did have some supporters among the Ashʿarīs, such as al-Suyūṭī and Ṣāfī l-Dīn al-Hindī[102] (d. 715/1315) his case may be more suitably treated as similar to Ibn al-ʿArabī's, whose statements are interpreted in many different ways. For such scholars, adopting one interpretation as the only correct one is not overly useful to a study of their views. In short, his case is relegated to the *ijmāʿ–ikhtilāf* spectrum, where it falls under *ikhtilāf*.

The Independent Jurist–Theologian–Sufis and Their Affiliations

Jalāl al-Dīn al-Suyūṭī

Al-Bājūrī cites al-Jalāl al-Dīn al-Suyūṭī (d. 911/1505) in matters of *fiqh*, grammar, theology, Sufism, and, ironically, in a work on logic, albeit on a peripheral matter. Al-Suyūṭī is an extremely important archetypal predecessor to al-Bājūrī, as he is a prominent example of an independant scholar who nonetheless remains affiliated to the past masters of law, theology, and Sufism. Like al-Bājūrī, al-Suyūṭī often cites previous scholars, or comments on their works; he was known to agree with a scholar on one issue and vehemently disagree on another. He offers us a classic example of the inter-affiliational agreement and intra-affiliational disagreement so characteristic of the Islamic sciences, and so often overlooked or downplayed.

Jalāl al-Dīn al-Suyūṭī[103] was an Egyptian scholar of the Shāfiʿī school of law, Ashʿarī school of theology (though averse to *manṭiq*), and most probably of the Shādhilī Sufi *ṭarīqa*.[104] He is said to have authored many hundreds of books and treatises, with estimates ranging from 600 to 981 works.[105] The subjects of his writings cover the gamut of religious and literary topics from law to theology, exegesis to *ḥadīth*, belle-lettres to erotica.

Al-Suyūṭī was an archetypal scholar with substantial training in law, theology, and mysticism. He was a master of the legal sciences, even declaring himself an unrestricted *mujtahid*[106] in the Shāfiʿī school. He was also a *ḥāfiẓ* of *ḥadīth* (having reportedly memorized over 100,000 *ḥadīth*s), and a scholar of Qurʾānic studies; he authored the *Itqān fī ʿulūm al-Qurʾān* ["Thorough mastery of the Qurʾānic sciences"], which remains a standard reference to this day. He studied logic (and *kalām*) during his early years, then opposed his teachers and declared these subjects to be forbidden (*ḥarām*). Yet he remained an Ashʿarī, in that he opted for *tafwīḍ* in matters pertaining to apparently anthropomorphic terms in the Qurʾān and *ḥadīth*, and he openly supported al-Ashʿarī and his school on other issues, such as the salvation of the Prophet's parents. Despite having edited and abridged Ibn Taymiyya's *Radd ʿala al-manṭiqiyīn* (*Refutation of the Greek Logicians*) and having spoken out against *manṭiq* and *kalām*,[107] he remained Ashʿarī in his theological views:

> Our Ashʿarī imams among the people of *kalām*, and *uṣūl*, as well as [our imams among the] Shāfiʿī scholars of *fiqh* agree that whoever dies while not having been reached by the message of Islam (*daʿwa*) is saved.[108]

This position on the *bulūgh al-daʿwa* (being reached by the invitation to Islam) remained a standard Ashʿarī opinion down to al-Bājūrī's time.[109]

Al-Suyūṭī also wrote extensively on Sufism, including a work praising the Shādhilī *ṭarīqa*.[110] He devoted the latter part of his life to a Sufi lifestyle, but even earlier in his career he had received the *khirqa* (mantle) from a number of Sufi scholars who also authorized him to bestow the *khirqa* upon his own students.

Al-Suyūṭī is crucial to the discussion at hand because of his apparent affiliations (Shāfiʿī, Ashʿarī, Shādhilī) and their relation to his individual views as stated in his monumental corpus of works. He is a source for al-Bājūrī, being quoted in the latter's *Tuḥfat al-murīd*, a commentary on al-Laqānī's (d. 1041/1631) *Jawharat al-tawḥīd*, under verses 91 and 92 of poetry pertaining to those things that are exempted from the destruction of all things at the end of time.[111] Al-Suyūṭī versified eight things that have been exempted, namely the *ʿarsh* (throne), the *kursī* (footstool),[112] hell, heaven, the tailbone of all humans (*ʿujb al-dhanab*),[113] human souls, the preserved tablet (*al-lawḥ al-maḥfūẓ*), and the pen (*al-qalam*).[114]

In addition to being cited in a theological matter, al-Suyūṭī is referenced with regard to the interpretation of the Arabic letter *fa* ("and so") in the fifth line of al-Laqānī's poem (wa-l-baʿdu *fa* al-ʿilm bi aṣl al-dīn . . .). Al-Bājūrī interprets "and so" to mean "and so I say to you" and rejects the idea that the *fa* indicates the *jawāb al-sharṭ* (answer to a conditional sentence: *idhā* X *fa* Y, if X then Y), but he accepts that this is a matter of disagreement (*khilāf*) between the grammarians, referencing al-Suyūṭī's work on grammar, *Hamʿ al-hawāmiʿ fī sharḥ jamʿ al-jawāmiʿ fī ʿilm al-naḥw* ["The rushing floodgates in the commentary on the collection of collections in the science of syntax"].

Al-Bājūrī also cites al-Suyūṭī on a legal issue with implications for Sufi practice, namely the permissibility of using prayer beads in reciting one's litanies. In his *al-Musalsalāt*, a compendium of *ḥadīths*, al-Bājūrī argues that the use of prayer beads and/or other means of counting one's recitations was present in the time of the Companions of the Prophet, if not in the time of the Prophet, and thus ought not to be considered a heretical innovation (*bidaʿa madhmūma*).[115]

Al-Suyūṭī is important with regard to the *ijmāʿ–ikhtilāf* spectrum that characterizes the core sciences of Sunnī Islam because of his positions on a number of issues, which for some are dividing lines between various groups. He tends to fall on one side on a given matter, then on the other for another matter; he also cites as authoritative sources scholars who often oppose each other on major issues.

One salient issue was the orthodoxy[116] of Ibn al-ʿArabī, whose Sufi writings contained many controversial stories and ideas, and Ibn Taymiyya, whose legal and theological positions on a number of issues were hotly contested. It is possible to find scholars who viewed both Ibn al-ʿArabī and Ibn Taymiyya as heretics, such as the Ḥanafī scholar ʿAlā l-Dīn Muḥammad b. Muḥammad al-Bukhārī.[117] Likewise, one can find supporters of Ibn al-ʿArabī, such as al-Subkī, who consider Ibn Taymiyya a heretic.[118] The reverse is also possible, such as Ibn Qayyim al-Jawziyya, who considered his teacher Ibn Taymiyya to be Shaykh al-Islam while he considered Ibn al-ʿArabī to be a *kāfir* (disbeliever). The only other logical possibility, that of both being believers, was apparently held by a group of Ḥanbalī Sufis[119] as well as by al-Suyūṭī.

Al-Suyūṭī wrote an abridgment of Ibn Taymiyya's *Radd ʿalā al-manṭiqiyīn* ["Against the logicians"] entitled *Jahd al-qarīḥa fī l-tajrīd al-naṣīḥa*, and cited him as an authoritative source in his *fatwā* declaring logic impermissible, entitled *Ṣawn al-manṭiq wa-l-kalām ʿan fann al-manṭiq wa-l-kalām* ["Preservation of discourse and speech from the subject of logic and dialectical theology"]. But he also wrote a short treatise entitled *Tanbīh al-ghabī fī takhṭiʾat Ibn al-ʿArabī* ["Warning the ignoramus who finds fault with Ibn al-ʿArabī"], wherein he defends Ibn al-ʿArabī from his detractors, and rules that none should read

Ibn al-ʿArabī's works except those who understand the lexicon of technical terminology unique to his works.[120]

Al-Suyūṭī also defended the Sufi Ibn al-Fāriḍ (d. 632/1235), whose poetry contained controversial statements that could be considered heretical or as expressions of sound belief and experience, depending on one's interpretation. As the *fatwā* below indicates, al-Suyūṭī applied the same rules to Ibn al-Fāriḍ as he did to Ibn al-ʿArabī's writings.

> Issue 1: In that which was related by the Ḥāfiẓ Abū Nuʿaym from Abī ʿAbdullāh Muḥammad b. al Warāq . . . he said: whoever is content with *fiqh* without *zuhd* [abstinence from worldly things] then he has gone astray. And what is the meaning of that? And what is the type of *zuhd* that one contented with *fiqh* refrains from? And the *faqīh*, if he is contented with *fiqh* and leaves the debates and disagreements, does one count this as *zuhd* that the Shaykh had in mind here?
>
> The Answer: This is the speech of a Sufi speaking according to his station. The elect (*khawāṣ*) divorce the sayings of disbelief and heresy (*fisq*) from that which the scholars of *fiqh* do not divorce [i.e., the Sufis use these terms with different meanings than their legal usage]. In the same way as some of the *salaf* [predecessors] have said: The good actions of the pious are the bad actions of those who are close to Allah. They applied the meaning of bad actions to good actions with regard to their station. Likewise, this is similar to Ibn al-Fāriḍ's statement (may Allah be pleased with him): "Even if a desire of my own accord inadvertently came to my mind in *siwāk* [brushing the teeth], I ruled/decided on my apostasy." It is known that this is not apostasy in reality [rather it is figurative], and in this manner is the saying of the Sufis: Verily the *ghība* (backbiting) breaks the fast of the one fasting. So all of this is from the way of the elect, making obligatory on themselves that which is not obligatory on the common person.[121]

In his defense of Ibn al-Fāriḍ, al-Suyūṭī also indicates his continued affiliation and support of the Ashʿarīs, despite his opposition to *manṭiq* and *kalām*:

> Do not be misled by al-Dhahabī's mutterings, for he muttered against Imam Fakhr al-Dīn b. al-Khaṭīb [al-Rāzī] and against one greater than the Imam, that is, Abū Ṭālib al-Makkī the author of *Qut al-qulūb*, and against one who is greater than Abū Ṭālib, namely, Shaykh Abū l-Ḥasan al-Ashʿarī, whose mention still circulates and traverses the firmaments. His [al-Dhahabī's] books, such as *al-Mīzān*, *al-Tārīkh*, and *Siyar al-nubalāʾ*, are laden with such statements. Are you going to accept his words in these matters? By no means! By Allah, we do not accept his words regarding them, rather, we give them their due right and render it to them in full.[122]

Despite al-Suyūṭī's clear affiliation with the Ashʿarīs, both early (anti-*manṭiq* scholars such as al-Ashʿarī) and late (pro-*manṭiq* scholars such as al-Rāzī), he still maintained the opinion that *manṭiq* was not permissible. This opinion conflicts with the opinion of some of his own teachers and certainly many of the scholars (*ʿulamāʾ*) of the day, who even considered that logic was a necessary condition of the *ijtihād* that al-Suyūṭī claimed for himself.[123] Yet his disdain for these rational sciences did not exclude him from the ranks of the Ashʿarīs, as he still followed them on many issues, and did not denounce his Ashʿarī *mutakallim* teachers and colleagues as heretics.

Furthermore, al-Suyūṭī "bitterly criticized" Sultan Baybars's appointment (in the seventh/thirteenth century) of "four chief *qāḍīs* [judges], one for each of the four Sunnī *madhāhib*."[124] He did so with the opinion that Ṣalāḥ al-Dīn's "restorative work . . . had been based upon the primacy of the Shāfiʿī school."[125] Ṣalāḥ al-Dīn had also included Ashʿarī thought as central in his restorative work, as he made it a requirement that all "those appointed to *madrasa*s be Ash'arite in doctrine."[126] It could be that al-Suyūṭī cited this point only to boost the position of the Shāfiʿīs, in an environment whose unity he felt had been compromised by too much diversity of opinion. However, given his close discipleship with Ashʿarīs during his studies, his promotion of many Ashʿarī adherents, such as al-Shādhilī,[127] his following of Ashʿarī opinions on certain theological issues, his rendering al-Ashʿarī's right over him,[128] and the dominance of Shāfiʿī–Ashʿarī methodology in *uṣūl*, it is very unlikely that he would consider himself anything other than Ashʿarī despite his objection to *manṭiq*.

Another issue that indicates the scope of intra-affiliational disagreement and inter-affiliational agreement is the use of singing and dancing in Sufi rituals. While the early Shādhilīs, including al-Shādhilī and Aḥmad al-Zarrūq (d. 899/1493), apparently did not participate in the *ḥadra*—a particular Sufi dance consisting of rhythmic bowing and jumping by participants standing in a circle—later Shādhilīs did, to the extent that it is considered an integral part of many Shādhilī orders down to the present day. Al-Suyūṭī issued a *fatwā* that the singing and dancing included in the *ḥadra* is permissible.

> How can one condemn invoking Allah (*dhikr*) while standing, or standing while invoking Allah, when Allah Most High has said ". . . those who invoke Allah standing, sitting, and on their sides."[129] And ʿĀʾisha said, "The Prophet used to invoke Allah at all times." And if dancing and the likes (*wa naḥuhu*) is added to this standing, do not condemn it, for it is from the joy of spiritual witnessing (*shuhūd*) or ecstasy, and it has been narrated in the *ḥadīth* that Jaʿfar b. Abī Ṭālib danced before the Prophet when the Prophet told him, "You resemble me in appearance and in character," and that (dancing) was from the happiness of being addressed in that way, and the Prophet did not condemn him for that. And this is a basis (of permissibility) for the dancing of the Sufis from the ecstatic joys that they experience.[130]

Ibn Taymiyya, on the other hand, whom al-Suyūṭī (in his *al-Radd ʿalā man akhlada ilā l-arḍ wa jahila anna al-ijtihād fī kull ʿaṣr farḍ* ["Refutation of those who cling to the earth and ignore that independent juridical reasoning is a religious obligation in every age"]),[131] cited in support for his anti-*manṭiq fatwā* and cited as an example of a latter-day *mujtahid*, held that singing was not permissible for men and only permissible for women at restricted times.[132]

In this case, we see al-Suyūṭī differing with the early founders of the Shādhilī *ṭarīqa*, if not over its legality then at least over the inclusion of the *ḥadra* in the Sufi method, and also disagreeing with Ibn Taymiyya, whom he considered a valid source in other matters. It is important to note that al-Suyūṭī paid no attention to the harsh language of Ibn Taymiyya with regard to the issue of singing, nor to his declaration that Ibn al-ʿArabī was an apostate, but, rather, ruled according to what he believed was the soundest.

Likewise, when al-Bājūrī cites a scholar such as al-Suyūṭī, with whom he may disagree regarding certain important issues—such as the permissibility of *manṭiq*—he accepts his overall orthodoxy when quoting him in the context of creed (as in his commentary on Laqānī's

Jawharat al-tawḥīd).[133] Thus, al-Bājūrī may disagree strongly with Ibn Taymiyya in creedal matters, such as the permissibility of *taʾwīl*, yet he does not consider al-Suyūṭī to be heretical for accepting Ibn Taymiyya as a legitimate source and *mujtahid*.

The scholars mentioned above come from different intellectual traditions within the Sunnī scholarly community; they are either mentioned by al-Bājūrī, or their thought (e.g., Ibn Taymiyya) affected the discourse in which al-Bājūrī was engaged. An examination of their thought indicates the clear existence of intra-affiliational disagreement and inter-affiliational agreement in the three core Islamic sciences. Each scholar associated with Sufism, yet may have disagreed with other scholars over legal issues associated with it, such as the use of singing and dancing, or over the belief or apostasy of a given controversial figure, such as Ibn al-ʿArabī. In the case of al-Sanūsī and al-Suyūṭī, they were Ashʿarīs, yet disagreed over the permissibility of *manṭiq*, or the general methodology of the *taḥqīqī* tradition.

In the cases of al-Shīrāzī, al-Suyūṭī, and Ibn Taymiyya, we see that they disagreed with the founders of their individual schools, or others from within their schools. Al-Shīrāzī differed with those of his own colleagues (*aṣḥāb*) at times, and with some of the Ashʿarīs as well. Yet his writings, especially the *Lumaʿ* and the *Ishāra*, indicate that he was an Ashʿarī, regardless of disagreements with his colleagues (*aṣḥāb*) among the Shāfiʿīs and Ashʿarīs.

Ibn Taymiyya, though he proclaimed that he was not a *mutakallim*, indeed delves into *kalām* frequently and in great depth. While he rejects *manṭiq*, it is not so much his *kalām* methodology that dictated his opinions against the Ashʿarīs, but, with regard to the ostensibly anthropomorphic primary texts, it was rather his definition of literal (*ẓāhir*). As a Sufi, he readily accepted the Sufi scholars' "*ijtihād* in obedience" and description of spiritual states and experiences, as long as these acts of obedience or descriptions did not contradict the *Sharīʿa*.

The various authors of commentaries or abridgments on the various Shāfiʿī texts discussed above agreed to stay within the methodological framework of their founder, yet they did not hesitate to disagree with each other or their founder. They continued to offer their own views, whether by supporting a previous precedent over another, or offering juristic proofs for their own opinions. They, along with the Mālikī Ashʿarīs who so influenced al-Bājūrī's thought (such as al-Laqānī and al-Sanūsī, and al-Akhḍarī), represent important links in the biographical layers of Sunnī theological history; it is their thought that reached al-Bājūrī and was accepted as the normative majority, along with that of the Māturīdīs.

From this analysis, it becomes clear that these three core sciences indeed allowed for substantial disagreement, and the scholars of these sciences themselves were comfortable questioning those who came before them. Regardless of the harshness of their speech and the occasional (often politically motivated) imprisonments, it is evident that such disagreement was tolerated and commonplace.

It also becomes clear that the rational (*ʿaqlī*) sciences have had a long and varied history in Islam, and that their use was by no means exclusive to a group of "rationalists," nor was their discouragement restricted to a group of "traditionalists." Thus, as Abrahamov notes, it is more useful to speak in terms of "rationalist" or "traditionalist" tendencies, as it is next to impossible, in my opinion, to find a Sunnī scholar who is wholly one and not the other. In fact, I argue, as others before me have, that it is time to reject the "rationalist" versus "traditionalist" categories as a false dialectic and as artificially constructed categories that do not, at all, accurately depict the reality of Sunnī theological and legal history.

Al-Shīrāzī's placement squarely in the Ashʿarī school, and Ibn Taymiyya's open declarations of Sufism also indicate something about the education of the pre-modern scholar. It seems clear that the rational (*ʿaqlī*) sciences were very much a part of the intellectual upbringing of the premodern Sunnī scholar: the Baghdad Niẓāmiyya was founded for an openly Ashʿarī scholar, the other Ashʿarīs who used *kalām* played prominent roles throughout Niẓāmiyya history, and there was a significant geographical spread of Ashʿarī institutions, as discussed previously. However, voices such as al-Suyūṭī's indicate that their rejection, at least in the case of *manṭiq*, was tolerated, if not always heeded.

As for Ibn Taymiyya's Sufism, its prominence in his works and those of so many other scholars (that cannot all be mentioned here), indicates that it was considered a core aspect of the spiritual and intellectual upbringing of scholars. Whether or not it was taught as part of the *madrasa* curriculum in every time and place says something about education, not Sufism. That is to say, if, in certain times and places, Sufism was not part of the core *madrasa* curriculum, its being studied through a master–disciple relationship indicates that the *madrasa* was neither the sole nor ultimate place of one's requisite education.[134] Additionally, just as *kalām* worked its way into *uṣūl al-fiqh* (and thus its *furūʿ*, or derived rulings), Sufism likely also worked its way into *ḥadīth*, and Qurʾānic and legal studies, as the Sufis linked so many of their practices and so much of their thought to these sources, and indeed often taught these subjects.

This examination of al-Bājūrī's predecessors illustrates well the legacy he inherited of consensus and disagreement over a variety of issues within the various core sciences of Islam. Far from blindly repeating the words of his predecessors, as Western and reformist voices often accuse the commentators of his time, he, like al-Shīrāzī, Ibn Taymiyya, al-Sanūsī, al-Anṣārī, al-Laqānī, al-Suyūṭī, and others before him, delved into the discussion, weighed and measured different opinions, and put forth his own opinions as to what was the soundest, both methodologically and contextually.

The following chapter investigates al-Bājūrī's thought in greater detail, specifically holding it up to the light of the *ijmāʿ–ikhtilāf* spectrum in the three core sciences of Islam, the role of the *ʿaqlī* sciences therein, the role and acceptance of Sufism in the intellectual upbringing of the pre-modern scholar, and the overall normativeness of the jurist–theologian–mystic archetype.

4

Al-Bājūrī's Legal, Theological, and Mystical Thought

Al-Bājūrī on Law: *Ijtihād* and *Taqlīd*

An investigation into some of al-Bājūrī's writings on topics relevant to the development, normativity, and influence of the archetypal scholar engenders a great appreciation for the nuance, depth, and variety of views held by pre-modern scholars. It also helps to problematize many incorrect generalizations about Islamic intellectual history, and offers more accurate representations. Al-Bājūrī's opinions on *ijtihād* (independent juridical ruling) and *taqlīd* (following another's opinion) can be found in several places throughout a number of his books. This is the first topic which, when interpreted in light of the variety of opinions held by various scholars over time, helps to refute the myth of intellectual decline in the Muslim world.

Ijtihād

Al-Bājūrī's opinions on *ijtihād* have played an interesting and important role in the history of Western scholarship. Snouck Hurgronje[1] discusses al-Bājūrī's views on *ijtihād* in response to the writings of Eduard Sachau, with whose interpretation of al-Bājūrī's views he disagreed. Snouck Hurgronje, who held the popular view that the doors of *ijtihād* were closed after the third/ninth century, is considered the source for many later Western scholars, most significantly his student Joseph Schacht. While the view that the doors of *ijtihād* were closed after the third/ninth century has come under attack in recent years by scholars such as Hallaq,[2] the notion that independent, creative scholarship came to a halt long ago in the Muslim world remains popular in many Western circles.[3]

Although Snouck Hurgronje had an intimate knowledge of al-Bājūrī's works, and indeed some of al-Bājūrī's statements appear to justify the notion that *ijtihād* ceased long ago, a closer reading and contextualization of al-Bājūrī's ideas with regard to previous archetypal scholars indicates that the subject is far more nuanced than often assumed.

Snouck Hurgronje quotes a passage from al-Bājūrī's gloss of Ibn al-Qāsim al-Ghazzī's commentary on the *Matn Abī Shujāʿ*—a standard Shāfiʿī legal text to this day—that appears to indicate that al-Bājūrī believed that *ijtihād* had come to an end around the third/ninth century.[4] Commenting on Abū Shujāʿ's statement "[I was asked] to write a short work on *fiqh* according to the *madhhab* of Imam Shāfiʿī,"[5] al-Ghazzī explains the word "Imam" with two adjectives to further explicate al-Shāfiʿī's status: "al-Aʿẓam al-Mujtahid."

After al-Bājūrī explains in his gloss that *al-aʿẓam* is not intended to mean the greatest of all *mujtahid*s, but rather, from among the greatest *mujtahid*s, he then expounds on the linguistic and technical meaning of *mujtahid* and *ijtihād*. Snouck Hurgronje truncates al-Bājūrī's statement on *ijtihād*—which he translates in the main text and quotes in the original Arabic in a footnote—and begins immediately with the technical usage of the term *ijtihād*.

The deleted phrase is, however, important for current discussions of *ijtihād*, as this is where al-Bājūrī mentions the original (*aṣlī*) meaning of *ijtihād*, that is, "expending effort in the search for the intended meaning, and what is meant [by this] is investigation and striving." In many current discussions of *ijtihād*, especially in less academic or pseudo-academic settings, *ijtihād* is thrown around as a synonym for "interpretation," much like the *aṣlī* meaning mentioned by al-Bājūrī and deleted by Snouck Hurgronje. However, al-Bājūrī's discussion of its technical meaning, that of "deducing rulings from the Qurʾān and Sunna," indicates that this general (*aṣlī*) meaning is incomplete, and must be further qualified. "In this sense [deducing rulings directly from the Qurʾān and Sunna] had ceased" says al-Bājūrī "around the third [ninth] century."[6] He then mentions al-Suyūṭī's claim that "it [*ijtihād*] remains until the end of time." Echoing al-Āmidī (d. 632/1234),[7] al-Bājūrī rejects al-Suyūṭī's apparent insistence on the existence of *mujtahid*s in every age.

Al-Suyūṭī's view, which is stated in a number of his works, especially in his *al-Radd ʿalā man akhlada ilā l-arḍ wa jahila anna al-ijtihād fī kull ʿaṣr farḍ* ["The refutation of those who are alive today and are ignorant of the fact that independent juridical reasoning is a religious obligation in every age"], indicates at first glance an intra-affiliational disagreement within the Egyptian Shāfiʿī–Ashʿarī tradition. However, Hallaq has shown that the disagreement (*ikhtilāf*) over *ijtihād* is largely due to differing usages of the term *ijtihād*, and is thus more complex than a debate over the possibility or impossibility of *ijtihād* after the third/ninth century.[8]

Snouck Hurgronje, however, appears to have felt that by al-Bājūrī's time, all types of *ijtihād* had gradually ceased, although he was aware of disagreements among the scholars regarding the possibility of both absolute *mujtahid*s and non-absolute *mujtahids*.[9] Additionally, Snouck Hurgronje did give ample voice to the existence of *ikhtilāf* between the scholars of Islam regarding whether or not the *mujtahid al-muṭlaq* and the lesser *mujtahid*s could, in principle, exist. Snouck Hurgronje appears to be speaking only of the Shāfiʿī world, specifically in Egypt, with regard to the apparent decline of *ijtihād*; however, in another work, he states that Islamic law sought to "remain stationary since the year 1000 [AH],"[10] indicating that, despite opinions to the contrary, Snouck Hurgronje tended to accept that the doors of *ijtihād* had been closed.

Al-Bājūrī, like many of the scholars of al-Suyūṭī's time, appears to have understood al-Suyūṭī's use of the word *ijtihād* to imply the *ijtihād* of the *mujtahid muṭlaq mustaqill* (the absolute, independent *mujtahid*), who could develop his own derivational principles (*uṣūl*), or the "master architect" as Hallaq calls them, rather than that of the various types of lesser *mujtahid*s that are discussed below. Al-Suyūṭī responds to his critics:

> People of our century have erred because they think that *muṭlaq*, unrestricted, and *mustaqill*, independent, are synonymous, whereas this is not so . . . That which we claim is unrestricted [*muṭlaq*], not independent [*mustaqill*]; we follow Imam Shāfiʿī, may God be pleased with him, and adopt his method in *ijtihād* . . . and we are counted among his adherents. . . .[11]

Indeed, al-Bājūrī uses the term *muṭlaq* to describe the founders of the four *madhhab*s, although, as discussed below, he was aware of the use of the term *mustaqill* in the sense of the master architect. This is not surprising, as different terms have been used for the various levels of *ijtihād*. Some scholars, such as al-Ghazālī, divided *ijtihād* into only two classes, *muṭlaq* (in this sense meaning independent and unrestricted) and *muqayyad* (restricted).[12] Al-Suyūṭī, on the other hand, divides the unrestricted *mujtahid* into independent (*mustaqill*), and affiliated (*muṭlaq muntasib*), and similarly divides the *muqayyad* into three subcategories.[13]

As al-Suyūṭī mentions his claims to *ijtihād* in several sources, it is possible that al-Bājūrī had not read *al-Radd ʿalā man akhlada ilā l-arḍ*, and was perhaps relying on less complete references in al-Suyūṭī's other works, or other mentions of al-Suyūṭī in secondary sources, that is, previous commentaries. Al-Bājūrī says, regarding al-Suyūṭī's proof of unending *ijtihād* (the *ḥadīth* about the centennial renewer),[14] that it can only apply to one who confirms and establishes (*yuqarrir*) the prescriptions of the *Sharīʿa* (*sharāʾiʿ*) and the legal rulings (*aḥkām*), and not to "*al-mujtahid al-muṭlaq*." Thus, it appears that al-Bājūrī is using the term *al-mujtahid al-muṭlaq* in the same sense that al-Suyūṭī uses *al-mujtahid al-mustaqill*.[15]

This is evidenced by the fact that al-Bājūrī primarily uses only three terms for the types of *mujtahid*s:

1. *Mujtahid muṭlaq* (unrestricted and independent *mujtahid*)
2. *Mujtahid al-madhhab* (*mujtahid* within the *madhhab*)
3. *Mujtahid al-fatwā* (*mujtahid* capable of giving *fatwā*s).

The *ijtihād* of the first class is described as "deriving the legal rulings from the Qurʾān and Sunna"[16] and is the type that has ceased to exist, according al-Bājūrī, since the third/ninth century, that is, the *ijtihād* of the founders of the four schools of law as well as the now defunct schools of those additional early *mujtahid*s, whom al-Bājūrī lists and honors in his *Tuḥfat al-murīd*.[17]

The second class of *mujtahids*, *mujtahid al-madhhab*, refers to one who deduces the legal rulings using the methods (*qawāʿid*) of an imam.[18] As an example, he lists al-Muzanī, the companion of al-Shāfiʿī and one of the principle transmitters of the Shāfiʿī school. Al-Bājūrī's *mujtahid al-madhhab* would seem to be synonymous with al-Suyūṭī's *mujtahid muṭlaq muntasib*,[19] al-Zuhaylī's *mujtahid muṭlaq ghayr al-mustaqill*,[20] and al-Subkī's *mujtahid fī l-madhhab*.[21]

The third class of *mujtahid*s in al-Bājūrī's system of classification, the *mujtahid al-fatwā*, is one who is capable of giving preponderance to one opinion over another from the various opinions within the school. As examples he cites al-Rāfiʿī and al-Nawawī, but excludes al-Ramlī and Ibn Ḥajar. The works of the latter two scholars, interestingly enough, when in agreement, constitute the *muʿtammad* (relied upon) opinion of the later Shāfiʿī school. They were, however, according to al-Bājūrī, *muqallid*s, that is, mere followers of *mujtahid*s and not capable of any type of *ijtihād*, neither unrestricted (class 1 above) nor restricted (classes 2 and 3). However, he mentions the opinions of others who said that al-Ramlī and Ibn Ḥajar reached the level of *tarjīḥ*[22] in certain issues.

Al-Ramlī and Ibn Ḥajar's limited *ijtihād* in certain issues hints at another type of *mujtahid* that is mentioned in some texts;[23] it refers to those who are able to practice *ijtihād* with regard to certain issues, but not for all issues of a given *madhhab* (sometimes called *ijtihād fī l-masāʾil*). For example, it is conceivable that one could be a *mujtahid* in the realm of inheritance, but not commerce. A few hundred pages later, al-Bājūrī recognizes the concept of *ijtihād fī l-masāʾil* in his discussion of the qualifications of a judge, when he says that a *mujtahid muṭlaq* can derive rulings directly from the Qurʾān and Sunna in all the chapters of *fiqh* or just some of them.[24]

Not only can the *mujtahid muṭlaq* be qualified in only some of the matters on which *ijtihād* is performed, but also, with regard to al-Ramlī and Ibn Ḥajar, al-Bājūrī says that the two scholars may have been able to do *tarjīḥ* in some issues, *implying ijtihād fī l-masāʾil can be a subcategory of mujtahid al-fatwā*. It is obviously also conceivable that one could learn to use the methodological principles of the founder of the *madhhab* in only one area, and thus *ijtihād fī l-masāʾil* could also be a subcategory of *mujtahid al-madhhab.*

In his discussion of the qualifications of a judge, al-Bājūrī gives a standard account of the necessary qualifications of the *mujtahid*, mentioning details of the core and supporting sciences studied by the archetypal scholar discussed in Chapter 2. He then quotes Ibn Daqīq al-ʿĪd as opining that no era is devoid of a *mujtahid* except as the end of time nears, this being in opposition to "those who say that there are no more *mujtahid*s since *ijtihād* had ceased, such as al-Ghazālī, for he said that the age was devoid of the *mujtahid mustaqill*."[25] What is important in this passage is that al-Bājūrī understands al-Ghazālī's opinion to refer to the master archetect's level of *ijtihād*, and even uses the term that al-Suyūṭī prefers for this level. He contrasts al-Ghazālī's opinion with Ibn Daqīq al-ʿĪd's position which is understood in this context to refer to the master architects, like the founders of the four *madhhab*s. Therefore, even if al-Bājūrī seems to favor the opinion that only founder-level *ijtihād* came to an end, he does not hide from the reader that there is disagreement on this and cites a reputable and respected source, Ibn Daqīq al-ʿĪd. He also cites several scholars from about fifth/eleventh century who denied being *muqallid*s of al-Shāfiʿī, their opinions rather corresponding with al-Shāfiʿī's, for "how is it possible to judge in these times if they are devoid of a *mujtahid*?"[26] This claim harkens back to al-Suyūṭī's claim that as he reached higher levels of *ijtihād* he did not differ with al-Nawawī nor eventually with al-Shāfiʿī, though still restricted to al-Shāfiʿī's method.[27]

Thus far, despite having listed only three main categories of *ijtihād*, al-Bājūrī has referenced the additional phenomena of *tarjīḥ* and *ijtihād fī l-masāʾil* (though not by this name), and used the term *mustaqill* which is synonymous with his usage of *muṭlaq*, indicating familiarity with the various terms and concepts. Despite this familiarity, I am not yet convinced that the confusion over technical terms whose existence al-Suyūṭī lamented was absent from al-Bājūrī's time.

Taqlīd

Al-Bājūrī's use and definition of the term *taqlīd* also indicates the importance of properly understanding and contextualizing technical terms. Among its nontechnical usages are imitation, blind following, and adorning someone with a necklace. In his discussion of al-Laqānī's line of poetry, "Whomever does *taqlīd* in *tawḥid* [matters of faith, especially those covered in *kalām*], his faith (*īmān*) is not safe from wavering," al-Bājūrī defines *taqlīd* as belief in the sayings, actions, and tacit approval (*taqrīr*) of another without knowing their proofs.[28] Technically, in matters of law, it usually means to follow the scholarship of a *mujtahid muṭlaq* if one is not capable of that level of *ijtihād*.

Al-Laqānī says in a line of poetry in *Jawharat al-tawḥīd*: "It is obligatory to follow [practice *taqlīd*] the wisest of them, as the scholars (*al-qawm*) have clearly stated." Al-Bājūrī explains:

> . . . [H]e mentions here that it is obligatory for all who are incapable of *al-ijtihād al-muṭlaq* [*ijtihād* at the level of the founders of the *madhhabs*], even if they are at the level of *mujtahid al-madhhab*, or *mujtahid al-fatwā*, to do *taqlīd* of the four Imams regarding the *fiqh* rulings [*al-aḥkām al-furuʿiyya*].[29]

At face value, this statement could be construed to imply that *taqlīd* was all that was left to the Muslim scholar, there was no more originality of thought, critical thinking, or *ijtihād*. It could also seem contradictory, in that he labels those *mujtahids* who are restricted in their *ijtihād* as *muqallids* (those who follow, or practice *taqlīd*). However, since he mentions in his gloss on al-Ghazzī's commentary on *Matn Abī Shujāʿ* that *ijtihād* was of at least three types (*muṭlaq*, *madh-*

hab, and *fatwā*), and in that he denied the *mujtahid* status of Ibn Ḥajar and al-Ramlī—calling them mere *muqallids*—he apparently has a more nuanced definition of *taqlīd* in mind.

I can thus deduce from his gloss on al-Ghazzī and his commentary on al-Laqānī's *Jawharat al-tawḥīd* at least three types of *fiqh*-related *taqlīd* that al-Bājūrī has in mind:

1. The *taqlīd* of the *mujtahid al-madhhab*
2. The *taqlīd* of the *mujtahid al-fatwā*
3. The *taqlīd* of those incapable of any type of *ijtihād* (*muṭlaq*, *madhhab*, or *fatwā*).

The first class, *mujtahid al-madhhab*, refers to one who is apparently only required to do *taqlīd* of the derivational principles (which al-Bājūrī refers to as *qawāʿid*) developed by the founder of his given *madhhab*.[30] Thus al-Ghazālī or al-Muzanī could differ with al-Shāfiʿī, while still using the same derivational principles, as could al-Shaybānī and Abū Yūsuf with regard to Abū Ḥanīfa. They were not required to do *taqlīd* of the results of al-Shāfiʿī's *ijtihād*, rather, they were required to do *taqlīd* only of his methodology.[31]

The *mujtahid al-fatwā*, class 2 above, was more restricted than the *mujtahid al-madhhab*, in that he could only do *tarjīḥ*, that is, determine which opinions within the *madhhab* preponderate in correctness over another, as well as determine what the specific contextual variables necessitated. He was thus required to practice *taqlīd* in the sense that he was restricted to a specific pool of differing opinions—presumably those produced by scholars at the level of *mujtahid al-muṭlaq* and *mujtahid al-madhhab*—from which to draw his possible preferred opinion.

As for the *taqlīd* of those incapable of any type of *ijtihād*, that of the common folk and some scholars, this is the *taqlīd* usually referred to, that is, following the opinion of a scholar without knowing its proofs, or at least not having the ability to weigh and gauge the correctness of its proofs. This sort of *taqlīd* is only one type of *taqlīd*, and not the *taqlīd* of the three classes of *mujtahids*. The *mujtahid muṭlaq* was forbidden from this or any other type of *taqlīd*, whereas it is not clear to me whether or not the lesser *mujtahids* were forbidden from this type of *taqlīd*.

Al-Bājūrī's discussion of the qualifications of the judge confirms the above classification of levels of *taqlīd*. Regarding the judge who is a *muqallid* of his Imam, al-Bājūrī writes that he must know the methods and principles (*qawāʿid*) of his Imam, these *qawāʿid* being in relation to the *muqallid* like the sacred texts are to the founder-*mujtahid*.[32] That is, the *muqallid* judge refers to his Imam's methods and rulings in the same way that the Imam refers to the sacred texts. It is clear that he is not talking about one incapable of any type of *ijtihād*.

Here al-Bājūrī recognizes two possibilities in a judge. One is that he is an absolute *mujtahid muṭlaq*, the second possibility being that one does a limited form of *ijtihād*, relying on the *qawāʿid* of his Imam, thus indicating that one does *ijtihād al-madhhab* or *ijtihād al-fatwā* if not at the level of *mujtahid al-muṭlaq* or *mujtahid al-madhhab*.

Following Another *Madhhab*

Al-Bājūrī raises the issue of whether or not one could adhere to different *madhhab*s for different issues. To this he responds that there are three opinions, one that prohibits it absolutely, one that permits it absolutely, and one that permits it on the condition that one does not mix and match within a single action, such that one's action is rendered invalid by consensus.[33] He offers as an example of the latter, a marriage that takes place without (the specification of) a dowry (*ṣadāq*),[34] guardian (*walī*), or witnesses (*shuhūd*), in reference to the fact that some schools require the presence of the bride's guardian and the specification of the dowry amount, but not the immediate presence of witnesses—as in the Mālikī school that allows for the informing of witnesses to be delayed[35]—or vice versa, as in the Ḥanafī school that requires witnesses but not a guardian (except under certain conditions) nor the specification of the dowry amount.[36] He also mentions that some scholars consider it permissible to follow any of the four schools at any time, such that one could pray their noon prayer according to the requirements of the Shāfiʿī school, and their afternoon prayer according to the requirements of the Mālikī school.[37]

Other scholars made following multiple *madhhab*s conditional, that is, taking dispensations (*rukhaṣ*), with the prerequisite of the existence of hardship. An example would be a Shāfiʿī following the Ḥanafī school in the realm of purification on a crowded hajj, because in the Shāfiʿī school, one's ablutions are nullified by touching a member of the opposite sex, and this is something unavoidable on a crowded hajj, whereas in the Ḥanafī school, one's ablutions are not nullified by such.

Another issue that al-Bājūrī raises with regard to *taqlīd* is that of following other than the four schools. Some scholars did not permit this after the demise of the other schools, whereas others permitted Muslims to follow rulings from defunct schools or opinions of the

Companions that differed with the four schools, provided such *rukhaṣ* (dispensations) were taken in one's private life, and not in issuing *fatwā*s. Al-Bājūrī returns to this issue close to a hundred pages later in his discussion of al-Laqānī's verse, "Every good is from following the early Muslims (*salaf*), and every bad is from following those who came later (*khalaf*)."[38] He states that every good comes from following the early Muslims; this includes the four *mujtahid* Imams, and that consensus (*ijmāʿ*) has occurred regarding the prohibition of issuing *fatwā*s and deriving laws (*ḥukm*) from other than the four schools. However, he states, in what is apparently his own opinion, that "as for a person's individual practice, he is permitted to follow other than [the four schools]."[39] It is interesting to note that a certain amount of freedom is granted to the individual to follow whomever he or she prefers in private life (i.e., issues that do not have a major effect on others in society), thus lessening the apparent control of the jurists over the common folk, although the non-scholar would still need to rely on a scholar to narrate such opinions and indicate their authenticity.

This discussion of the various, nuanced, and at times differing understandings of the terms *ijtihād*, *mujtahid*, and *taqlīd* clearly indicates that the view that *ijtihād* ended after the third/ninth century is an oversimplification, if not simply incorrect. From al-Bājūrī's discussion of the types of *ijtihād*, it is clear that he only considered that *ijtihād* at the level of *mujtahid al-muṭlaq* (in the sense of the founders or 'architects') had come to an end, and that the other restricted forms of *ijtihād* were still possible. As to whether or not this was still practiced, Snouck Hurgronje appears to have believed that even *ijtihād* at these levels had ended, as, in the late nineteenth and early twentieth centuries, he saw that scholars in Egypt restricted themselves to the later recensions of the Shāfiʿī school. However, Shāfiʿīs did not necessarily refer to recensions uniformly—some preferred Ibn Ḥajar, while others preferred al-Ramlī, for example.

In addition, a *muʿtammad* opinion was not always reached; sometimes one had a choice between valid rulings that differed, as there is often a diverse pool of differing opinions from which jurists may choose, if in fact they are merely following another's opinion and not supporting their own with a previous precedent. Therefore, a certain degree of freedom of thought and ability to exercise juridical autonomy existed. This is very clear from al-Bājūrī's writings, wherein he often mentions multiple opinions within his *madhhab* and others, giving validity to the various opinions in the pool of *ikhtilāf*.

Beyond choosing from a pool of opinions in issuing *fatwā*s, there are also opinions (not considered *fatwā*s) that can be indicated by a mufti as valid to follow. The indication of these opinions is called *ishāra*. In many cases, between the varying pool of *fatwā* opinions and *ishāra* opinions there are a number of possible rulings for a particular action. Furthermore, a *muʿtammad* opinion was not always reached, giving one a choice between valid differing rulings; this, and the fact that unprecedented issues necessarily require *ijtihād* all indicate that it is unlikely that Snouck Hurgronje's observation meant all *ijtihād* had ceased, even if it was rare among Egyptian Shāfiʿīs.

We may also note that if Snouck Hurgronje's observations about al-Bājūrī's Egypt are correct, this would only have been true for a specific geographic and chronological manifestation of Shāfiʿism, and certainly not representative of all *madhhab*s or centers of scholarship. El-Rouayheb has shown that al-Bājūrī's Maghribi *taḥqīqī* contemporaries proclaimed *ijtihād* for themselves—presumably *ijtihād al-madhhab* or *ijtihād al-fatwā*.[40] Also, within the Mālikī school, there were fewer restrictions on issuing *fatwā*s from opinions that were not dominant opinions, indicating that the impulse toward *ijtihād*, as others have claimed, was channeled into the confines of the *madhhab*.[41]

Furthermore, Haim Gerber's study of Ḥanafī *fatwā* collections from the seventeenth through nineteenth centuries indicates that *muftīs* were actively engaging with the law and judges, exercising autonomy and being involved in the real-life application of legal rules, from both the "formative period" of Islamic law, and in relation to later developments.[42] They were clearly involved in *ijtihād* within the *madhhab*, which provided a "substantial measure of openness and adaptability," and they also had recourse to other legal "mechanisms . . . that allowed innovation and flexibility" such as "*istiḥsān, ḍarūra, maṣlaḥa and ʿurf*."[43] Despite these additional legal mechanisms, Gerber argues that the Ḥanafī *muftī* whose *fatwā*s he is studying, those of Khayr al-Dīn al-Ramlī, discusses cases in which *ijtihād* is possible, and cases in which it is not. Al-Ramlī also mentions different types of *ijtihād*, though without reference to the levels of *ijtihād*.

Snouck Hurgronje has been cited as possibly the first Western scholar to write about the closing of the doors of *ijtihād*.[44] His discussion of *ijtihād* occurs in his treatment of al-Bājūrī's comments on it. However, he was preceded by Sachau (Hurgronje's article was a critical review of Sachau's work on al-Bājūrī), who held that al-Bājūrī's opinion indicated that "general *ijtihād*" (to use Snouck Hurgronje terminology) still existed. Many subsequent scholars appear to have followed Snouck Hurgronje's views, then narrowed them and projected them onto the entirety of Islamic scholarship, even though some Islamicists, such as Schacht, note a continued debate over the subject of *ijtihād*.[45] The above analysis of al-Bājūrī's discussion of *ijtihād*, as found in his gloss on al-Ghazzī and his commentary on *Jawharat al-tawḥīd,* indicates that he did not believe all *ijtihād* had ceased, only what he termed the *ijtihād* of the *mujtahid al-muṭlaq*. The absence of a *muʿtammad* ruling in some issues, even total silence on an issue within the *madhhab,* when understood in combination with the methodological realities of the Mālikī school and the *taḥqīqī* tradition in the Maghrib, mean that the notion that the gates of *ijtihād* had closed in the Muslim world is patently false.

The way in which the issue of *ijtihād* is presented in many post nineteenth-century texts draws our attention to the problem that arises when one projects his or her understanding of an issue based on the views of one or more scholars restricted to a specific time and place, without contextualizing them in the historical continuum of scholarship. When al-Bājūrī's views on *ijtihād* are contextualized with the works of the scholars mentioned above, and others, it becomes clear that there was no final word on the rankings of *ijtihād,* nor on the possibility of scholars achieving the varying ranks of *ijtihād*. Rather, the evidence seems to indicate a continued, if limited, practice of *ijtihād*.

Al-Bājūrī on Sufism: Its Goals, Methods, and Explanations or Exclamations

When approaching the science of Sufism (*taṣawwūf*), it is helpful to keep in mind three core aspects: the goals of *taṣawwūf*, the methods of achieving these goals, and the explanations of the experiences given by those who have achieved these goals or their exclamations in the course of experiencing the goals. Al-Bājūrī's definition of Sufism and his discussion of these three aspects, whether mentioned directly or indirectly, are examined below.

Unfortunately, in many treatments of Sufism, both by claimed practitioners from Muslim cultures, and by certain Western writers and scholars, Sufism is presented as a separate sect within Islam, or even a separate practice disconnected entirely from Islam. The Sufism of the archetypal scholars of Sunnī Islam was fully integrated into their legal and theological traditions, albeit with some disagreement (*ikhtilāf*) over the methods of achieving the goals of Sufism or the explanations of specific Sufi experiences.

Sufism, as mentioned previously, was well-integrated into Egyptian society long before al-Bājūrī's time. Ṣalāḥ al-Dīn al-Ayyūbī had opened *zāwiyya*s as part of his Sunnī reclamation of Egypt from the Fāṭimids in the sixth/twelfth century. Jalāl al-Dīn al-Suyūṭī in the eighth–ninth/fourteenth–fifteenth centuries, himself a Sufi, was officially appointed to administer an endowment (*waqf*) for the Baybarsiyya Sufis and their *zāwiyya*.[46] The Azharīs of al-Bājūrī's time were often Sufis; the institution had an official role in the administration of the various *ṭuruq*.[47]

Definition and Goals of Sufism

Al-Bājūrī lays out his understanding of Sufism in Tuḥfat al-murīd, following al-Laqānī's ordering of topics; he first comments on the base traits which Sufis attempt to eliminate in an effort to purify the aspirant's limbs and soul.[48] These include those traits listed in standard treatments of Sufism, such as ghība (backbiting), namīma (talebearing), ḥasad (envy), and others. He lays out their definitions and primary text proofs for their prohibition, and offers cures for these diseases of the heart.

The following line of al-Laqānī's poem, "and be like the best of creation, of sworn perseverance, following the truth," is explained by al-Bājūrī as a reference to the movement of ridding oneself of the base traits mentioned in the previous line, to adorning oneself with the meritorious traits (*faḍā'il*) of Sufism. Here two distinct goals of Sufism are indicated, namely, purification and adornment. At this point, al-Bājūrī begins to give a formal definition of the science of Sufism, and thereby expound on its goals.

The Ten Points of Departure for the Science of Sufism (*al-mabādī l-ʿashara*)

Al-Bājūrī does not outline the *mabādī* (points of departure) of Sufism in the same formal manner in which he outlines the *mabādī* of *uṣūl al-dīn*. Presumably, since the ten classes had already been mentioned, the reader should be able to discern that al-Bājūrī is outlining some of them without needing to announce his intention, as he did at the beginning of his commentary on *Jawharat al-tawḥīd*. The ten *mabādī* are:

1. *al-ḥadd*: definition
2. *al-mawḍūʿ*: subject matter
3. *al-thamara*: benefit
4. *al-faḍl*: merit
5. *al-nisba*: relative position to other fields of knowledge

6. *al-wāḍiʿ*: founder of the field
7. *al-ism*: name
8. *al-istimdād*: sources of support
9. *ḥukm al-shāriʿ*: Sharīʿa ruling
10. *al-masāʾil*: problems discussed therein.

In order to better understand al-Bājūrī's views on Sufism with regard to these foundational issues, I have attempted to fill in this list by relying on what al-Bājūrī mentions of them, whether all together in the section at hand, or from other sections of *Tuḥfat al-murīd*. In doing so, I compare these ten points of departure, stated or implied, with those explicitly mentioned by the Naqshbandī Sufi of Cairo, Muḥammad Amīn al-Kurdī (d. 1332/1914) in his *Tanwīr al-qulūb fī muʿāmalat ʿallām al-ghuyūb*.[49] The result of such a comparison is the recognition of commonalities and differences between two Egyptian Naqshbandī Sufis, indicating a certain individuality and diversity of thought with regard to each scholar.

Al-Bājūrī gives as a definition (*ḥadd*) of Sufism: "A knowledge of principles through which the rectification of the heart (*qalb*) and the rest of the senses (*ḥiwās*) are known."[50] He includes other definitions, such as that given by al-Ghazālī. He also relies on al-Ghazālī in the previously mentioned section, that of defining the base traits (i.e., *ghība, namīma*), indicating that al-Ghazālī's Shāfiʿī–Ashʿarī–Sufi paradigm remained an important model throughout the centuries.

The subject matter (*mawḍūʿ*) of Sufism, though not specifically stated as such, appears to be the abandonment of base traits or vices and the adornment of oneself with the meritorious qualities (*faḍāʾil*) of Sufism.[51] This, then, hearkens back to the two notions of *muraqaba* (guarding over one's actions) and *maʿrifa* (experiential knowledge of Allah), the former being the efforts (*ʿamal*) at the beginning of the Sufi path, and the latter being the resultant state (*ḥāl*). In support of this assumption, al-Kurdī states its subject matter to be the purification of the heart and senses, similar to al-Bājūrī's definition above, or achieving the ultimate victory, namely Allah's pleasure.

Al-Bājūrī seems to refer to the benefit (*thamara*) of Sufism when he says "Its *fāʾida* (useful benefit) is to make proper and good the states (*aḥwāl*) of the person, for it has within it the incitement toward purification of beliefs (*iʿtiqād*) and perfection and rightness of actions."[52] This pithy statement has packed within it three important aspects of Sufism: the attainment of spiritual states, the purification of beliefs, and the correction of actions. As discussed earlier, Sufism can be said to have a face turned toward *īmān* (belief) and another turned toward *islām* (law, that is, the rules and regulations governing the actions of the limbs). The benefit listed by al-Bājūrī with regard to making proper and good the states of the person seems to relate to Ibn Taymiyya's statement that legitimate Sufis are those who experience the realities and states associated with Sufism. Al-Kurdī similarly states that its benefit (*thamara*) is the rectification of hearts, and adds knowledge of the unseen worlds via direct experience (*dhawq*), experiential witnessing of Allah, and so on. These additional points, perhaps, fall under "purification of the beliefs."

Al-Kurdī mentions that one of the merits of Sufism is that it is the noblest of sciences (*ashraf al-ʿulūm*), because it pertains to experiential knowledge of Allah. Al-Bājūrī does not mention the merit (*faḍl*) of Sufism in this section, as opposed to his earlier discussion of *uṣūl al-dīn*, where he states its merit to be the highest of sciences. This may be because he perceived of Sufism as necessarily linked to the other sciences; there is an element pertaining to belief, particularly what I term experiential *tawḥīd* (unity of Allah), and an element pertaining to *fiqh* or law, in that core vices must be eliminated (*ghība* and others).

Al-Kurdī considers Sufism to be the root (*aṣl*) of the other sciences. Al-Bājūrī, on the other hand, says regarding its position relative to other fields of knowledge (*nisba*): "The truth is, *taṣawwūf* is a fruit of the rest of the *Sharīʿa* sciences. It does not have its own specific set of canonized laws."[53] This is, in a sense, similar to al-Kalbī's statement, mentioned previously, that Sufism is the inner *fiqh*.

Al-Bājūrī's metaphor is especially important, as he views Sufism to be the fruit of the other sciences, thus necessarily connected to them, and indeed results from putting them into practice. The fact that he does not view Sufism as having "its own specific set of canonized laws" is especially significant, as al-Bājūrī would deem Sufism without law, theology, Qurʾān, or *ḥadīth* as a ludicrous impossibility. He would find it especially absurd to suggest that Sufism could exist independently of Islam. This was the view of the major figures of Sufism before him, including Rūmī, Junayd, and others.[54]

While al-Bājūrī does not mention the founder of the field (*wāḍiʿ*) in this section, he does refer elsewhere to al-Junayd as the "master of the Sufis, in knowledge and action."[55] He mentions this in the context of the Imams of *fiqh*, as the guides of the *umma* (Islamic nation), to which he adds al-Ashʿarī and al-Māturīdī as guides from among the scholars of theology, as well as al-Junayd and the rest of the major Sufi figures.[56] Regarding al-Ashʿarī and al-Māturīdī, al-Bājūrī notes that they are the founders of the field of *uṣūl al-dīn* only in the sense that they wrote the earliest books on the subject and defended the faith against the Muʿtazila; the actual founders were the prophets themselves.[57] Presumably, the same logic would apply to Sufism, in that al-Junayd was, like the founders of the *madhhab*s and schools of theology, one of those who began a process of systematization. Al-Kurdī lists the founder of the field as Allah Himself, who revealed the subject matter of Sufism (despite it not being formally called Sufism) to the Prophet and those prophets before him, it being the "soul" of the religions and their laws. This is similar to al-Bājūrī's statement about the founders of the schools of theology.

Al-Bājūrī tells us that the name of this science (*fann*) is *taṣawwūf*, which he deems to be derived from *ṣūf* (wool), because the early practitioners, according to al-Shaʿrāni whom he cites, wore the only thing their wages could afford them, patched wool garments. He rejects the other possibilities as being weak derivations, such as the idea that it was derived from their similarity to *ahl al-ṣuffa* (the poor Companions living on the porch of the Prophet's mosque), or that it was derived from *ṣafāʾ* (*purity*). Al-Kurdī again disagrees and opts for *ṣafāʾ*, because the Sufi is one who purifies his heart from turbidity.

The supporting sources (*al-istimdād*) are not mentioned specifically here, although al-Bājūrī does discuss the importance of taking a guide from the gnostics (*shaykh min al-ʿārifīn*),[58] whose spiritual state (*ḥāl*) is "more useful than a thousand sermons." The supporting sources of *uṣūl al-dīn* are the rational (*ʿaqlī*) and textual (*naqlī*) proofs,[59] whereas the supporting sources of *uṣūl al-fiqh* include various sciences (linguistic, *kalām*, and legal principles).[60] Since al-Bājūrī also mentions that Sufism is a fruit of all the *Sharīʿa* sciences, certain aspects of these sciences, especially *naqlī* issues, could also be considered its sources. Not surprisingly then, al-Kurdī includes in the supporting sources the Qurʾān, Sunna, and the established narrations (*athār*) regarding the elect of the Muslims (*khawāṣ al-umma*).

As al-Bājūrī indicates, the *Sharīʿa* ruling (*ḥukm al-shāriʿ*) associated with Sufism could differ according to which aspect is being considered: the aspect of self-purification and adorning oneself with the noble traits and states of Sufism.[61] Al-Bājūrī deems the first aspect obligatory, as the avoidance of sins is an obligation.[62] It is likely this aspect that is being considered when some Sufis, along with al-Kurdī, say that Sufism is a personal obligation (*farḍ ʿayn*). As for acquiring the spiritual states, or the higher degrees of Sufism, this may not be considered an obligation, as these states are, as Ibn Taymiyya says, in fact quite rare.

The problems discussed within the science (*al-masā'il*) are not indicated formally, as al-Bājūrī only hints at the ten points of departure; however, from his statements we might deduce that these are the diseases of the heart and their cures, and the means of acquiring the spiritual states and traits of the Sufis. This assumption is supported by al-Kurdī's description of the problems discussed within Sufism as "an examination into the attributes of the hearts." He adds to this the explanation of the technical terminology used by the Sufis, such as *zuhd* (abstinence), *wara'* (scrupulousness), *maḥaba* (love), *fanā'* (anhillation), and *baqā'* (subsistence), these being terms discussed in al-Qushayrī's *Risāla* [Epistle (on Sufism)].

All in all, al-Bājūrī's outline is thus far a standard representation of Sufism. He does not present the Sufis as a separate group, in conflict with the *'ulamā'*, rather he presents the *'ulamā'* themselves as Sufis, in line with the Ghazālian explanation of the three-dimensional Gabrielian paradigm. His is nonetheless a sub-branch of multiple possible derivations of the archetypal model. In addition, he is of the branch of Sufis that found no conflict inherent in engaging in *kalām* while seeking knowledge of Allah through experience (i.e., *kashf*),[63] unlike others, such as al-Nawawī or al-Ghazālī, who recommended against the common folk engaging in *kalām*.

Al-Bājūrī on the Methods of Sufism

Having deduced a general picture of al-Bājūrī's view of Sufism, and setting forth the basic goals of Sufism—purifying the heart and limbs from base traits, and adorning oneself with the meritorious states and traits of the Sufi gnostics (*'ārifīn*)—it is now possible to move on to a discussion of the second core aspect that indicates a given scholar's views on Sufism, namely, the methods used in achieving the goals of Sufism. Al-Bājūrī's view regarding the importance of the teacher–disciple model, that is, of taking an experienced gnostic (*'ārif*) as one's guide, has been discussed above. It may be said that this is the most important aspect of the Sufi method, that is, learning from merely observing the state (*ḥal*) of one's teacher. It is, as noted, of greater importance than a thousand sermons. Al-Bājūrī's views on the practices of *dhikr* (remembrance of Allah, specifically through recitation of litanies or specific formulas), *samā'* (listening to beautifully recited Qur'ān or spiritual odes), and the issue of *bid'a* (innovation) are also important aspects of the Sufi method.

While I have not yet discovered a direct reference in the books of al-Bājūrī to the topics of *samā'* and audible *dhikr*, we can note that the former is approved of by Ibn Ḥajar al-Haytamī, and the latter by al-Nawawī. Given that al-Bājūrī tends to follow these two representatives of the latter Shāfiʿī school in many issues, I presume that he might also follow them in these issues. More useful to our current study, however, are the legal principles that informed al-Bājūrī and his predecessors in determining the ruling for these means of achieving the states and traits of the Sufis. Al-Bājūrī's treatment of the subject of *bidʿa* (innovation) is thus of great interest.

There have long been legal disagreements over the permissibility of some Sufi practices. The issue of *bidʿa* (innovation) is relevant to the topic of the means of achieving the desired goals of Sufism, as some of these means were not practiced in the time of the Prophet, or did not exist in the specific forms that took shape later. Thus, some of the debate around the authenticity or "Islamic" nature of Sufism is illuminated by an investigation into al-Bājūrī's conception of *bidʿa*.

Bidʿa (Innovation)

Al-Bājūrī, like ʿIzz b. ʿAbd al-Salam (d. 660/1262) and al-Nawawī before him, determined that all innovations fell under one of five categories. These five categories are the same five categories of Islamic law under which all actions fall, that is, obligatory (*wājib*/*farḍ*), recommended (*mandūb*), neutral (*mubāḥ*), prohibitively disliked (*makrūh*), or forbidden (*ḥarām*). He cites examples for each:

1. Obligatory innovation: The collecting of the Qurʾān into one codex (*maṣḥaf*) and codification of the laws.
2. Recommended innovation: Praying the *tarāwīḥ* (additional nightly prayers in Ramadan) prayers in congregation.[64]
3. Neutral innovation: Using a sieve, which al-Bājūrī reports was the first newly begun matter to appear after the death of the Prophet.
4. Prohibitively disliked innovation: Decorating mosques and Qurʾāns.
5. Forbidden innovation: Those taxes (*al-makūs*) which Islam does not sanction and all innovations which oppose the guidelines of the *Sharīʿa*.[65]

He summarizes his view of the subject of *bidʿa* a few pages later, by stating that anything in harmony with the Qurʾān, Sunna, *ijmāʿ*, and *qiyās* is considered of the Sunna, while anything which is in opposition to these is considered a *bidʿa madhmūma*, that is, a reprehensible innovation.

This conception of *bidʿa* relates to Sufi practices that fall under the category of actions (thus being matters of *fiqh*), because various Sufis disagreed over the permissibility and utility of given practices, be it listening to mystical odes, reciting litanies silently or aloud in groups, or participating in mystical dances. These were, above all, *fiqh* disagreements. They also relate to the issue of incorporating practices found in other cultures—if in fact there are such borrowings—in that if a given action is deemed permissible by the *Sharīʿa*, regardless of who else does that action, then it is considered a permissible innovation. Therefore, according to al-Bājūrī's system, and that of his predecessors, the incorporation of certain Sufi practices not found at the time of the Prophet does not, in and of itself, separate Sufism from the Qurʾānic and Sunnaic teachings, which he viewed as being amply accepting of new matters.

Explanations of the Unexplainable: The Problematic Sayings of the Sufis

The third core aspect that I believe is an important indicator of a given scholar's view of Sufism is his approach to the descriptions of one's spiritual experiences, or the unintentional statements pronounced in states of spiritual ecstasy; these theopathic or ecstatic utterances are called *shaṭḥiyāt*.

There are a few statements from al-Bājūrī that help to explain his view on the issues that arise from the *shaṭḥiyāt* of various Sufis while in a state of annihilation in Allah (*fanāʾ*). Al-Bājūrī quotes al-Shaʿranī, who is reported to have asked his shaykh, ʿAlī al-Khawwāṣ al-Burulusī (d. 939/1532–33): "Why do the scholars metaphorically interpret (*taʾwīl*) the statements of the lawgiver (in this case, the Prophet) that could be erroneously interpreted to imply something problematic (*al-muhim al-wāqiʿ*), yet not do the same for the *walī*?"[66] Al-Shaʿranī's shaykh affirms that a metaphorical interpretation (*taʾwīl*) of the sayings of the *awliyāʾ* (s. *walī*) may be more just, since they are excused because of their "debilitation in the states of the presence [of Allah], unlike the lawgiver who possesses the station of unshakable establishment."[67] However, he explains that this more generous interpretation is not given because the prophets are followed in whatever they say and do, whereas the *awliyāʾ* are not. Thus, if the *awliyāʾ* state something that can be erroneously interpreted to imply something problematic, their statement is considered invalid.

Al-Bājūrī, like many before him, adopted the opinion that the theopathic utterances of the Sufis were excused; that is, Sufis were not held accountable for these statements because they were not in possession of their intellects while in the debilitating state that occurs when in the presence of Allah. Ibn Taymiyya also adopts this opinion in his discussion of *fanāʾ*, as does al-Ghazālī.

While discussing the issue of Allah's attribute of existence (*wujūd*) and its relation to other existent things, al-Bājūrī addresses the issue of *waḥdat al-wujūd* (the unity of being) and the case of al-Ḥallāj. Al-Bājūrī states that as for our existence "it is by His creative power [lit. His actions]," thus affirming some sort of existence for something other than Allah, albeit contingent upon Allah's existence.[68] He then mentions that

> some have witnessed (*yushāhidūn*) that there is no existence except the existence of Allah, they call this the unity of being (*waḥdat al-wujūd*). Some of the *awliyāʾ* have plunged into it to the extent that they have stated things that could be erroneously interpreted to mean indwelling (*ḥulūl*) and union (*ittiḥād*).[69]

As an example of these statements that could erroneously be interpreted to imply indwelling and union, al-Bājūrī gives the example of al-Ḥallāj, whom he misquotes or interprets as having said "anā Allāh" (I am Allah) rather than "anā al-Ḥaqq" (I am the Truth).[70] This sort of statement is not permissible (*la yajūz*) according to al-Bājūrī, due to the delusory and misguiding suggestions contained within it (*li īhāmihi*). However, such statements can be metaphorically interpreted (*yuʾawwil*) to have an appropriate meaning once such people regain mastery of their states.[71] Al-Shaʿranī's teacher, as noted earlier, seems to imply that such metaphorical interpretation is not permissible and such statements should be rejected, yet excused. Here we find an apparent intra-Sufi disagreement over the permissibility of accepting metaphorical interpretations of theopathic utterances, thus indicating that there was not a universal approach to such statements.

Al-Bājūrī does not mention why this principle was not extended to al-Ḥallāj, only that al-Junayd was one of those who gave the *fatwā* that al-Ḥallāj should be executed for his statements. According to Massignon's research on al-Ḥallāj's case, however, the official cause for al-Ḥallāj's execution was his opinion that the hajj could be substituted with a similar ritual done in one's own house.[72] In addition, al-Junayd died twelve years before al-Ḥallāj's execution, though two years after Ibn Dāwūd's first efforts to have al-Ḥallāj condemned. Massignon has shown[73] that a number of apocryphal accounts about al-Junayd and al-Ḥallāj have been disseminated, and in the absence of any concrete proof of al-Junayd's actual condemnation of al-Ḥallāj, al-Bājūrī's view appears to be based on a repetition of statements from secondary sources.

Indeed, al-Bājūrī relied on al-Sanūsī's *Sharḥ al-kubrā* for the information on al-Ḥallāj, so it is likely that his information came from secondary sources, as he does not devote too much time to al-Ḥallāj in general. Interestingly, Ibn Ḥajar al-Haytamī's opinion on al-Ḥallāj, with which al-Bājūrī would presumably be familiar, appears to lean toward interpreting al-Ḥallāj's statement "anā al-Ḥaqq" to mean "(God says) 'anā al-Ḥaqq,'" and is forgivable because it was spoken in a state of mystical ecstasy.[74]

Ibn Taymiyya also stresses that al-Ḥallāj's statements that imply indwelling (*ḥulūl*) and unification (*ittiḥād*) were the reason for his execution, thus perhaps al-Ḥallāj's case was a traditional, almost expected, subject of discussion in writings on creed, yet not one that a scholar felt required to delve into too deeply. In other words, the historicity of the account may not have been as crucial as the actual subject of *ḥulūl* and *ittiḥād*.

While Ibn Taymiyya does not consider it a sin to say "Glory to me" (*subḥānī*), "I am the Truth" (*anā al-Ḥaqq*), or "There is no one in this cloak except Allah" (*mā fī l-jubba illā-Llāh*), while one is in a state of spiritual drunkenness caused by the extreme love of Allah, he nonetheless condemns al-Ḥallāj for the very same statement while excusing al-Bisṭāmī (who said "subḥānī"). Ibn Taymiyya held the view that al-Ḥallāj was blamed for saying these sorts of things because he was not in a state of spiritual drunkenness, rather he believed that al-Ḥallāj "spoke with full presence of mind."[75] He also cites al-Ḥallāj's alleged involvement in sorcery and his statement about there being a God in heaven and one on earth as further justification for his execution.[76]

Al-Bājūrī, on the other hand, merely quotes al-Ḥallāj's purported statement "anā Allāh," as well as the statement of another Sufi "mā fī l-jubba illā-Llāh," claiming these statements impermissible yet excusable, and (potentially) open to metaphorical interpretation. While al-Bājūrī clearly leans away from these notions of *waḥdat al-wujūd* (oneness of being), and apparently inclines toward an anti-Ḥallājian view—according to his understanding of al-Ḥallāj—his actual view remains elusive.[77] While a later authority in the Shāfiʿī school, al-Haytamī, sided with al-Ḥallāj, al-Sanūsī, a later authority in the Ashʿarī school, apparently sided against al-Ḥallāj's sanctity. Al-Bājūrī, then, seems somewhere in between.

Al-Bājūrī's presentation of *waḥdat al-wujūd* seems to indicate that he viewed it as having pantheistic implications. This was also the view of Ibn Taymiyya and indeed a number of other scholars.[78] However, some of al-Bājūrī's contemporaries were Sufis of the Shādhilī order,[79] some of whose adherents, past and present, held good opinions of both al-Ḥallāj and Ibn al-ʿArabī. Among the former, for example, Abū l-ʿAbbās al-Mursī is said to have approved of al-Ḥallāj, and the contemporary Damascene Shādhilī Shaykh, ʿAbd al-Raḥmān al-Shāghūrī (d. 2004) taught and defended Ibn al-ʿArabī as an orthodox Sufi.[80] Shaykh al-Shāghūrī,[81] whose training included traditional Ashʿarī texts, divided *waḥdat al-wujūd* into two categories, one which was pure pantheism (i.e., the creator and the creation are one) and the other which was in conformity to Ashʿarī teachings, that is, that all existent things other than Allah are ontologically connected to Allah's creative power and thus only exist through His creation of them.

It is perhaps because of this apparent disagreement over the definition of *waḥdat al-wujūd*, as well as over the permissibility or appropriateness of metaphorically interpreting theopathic utterances, that al-Bājūrī does not treat the subject in detail or harshly. Al-Bājūrī's treatment, in comparison to Ibn Taymiyya and al-Suyūṭī, also indicates that the almost wholesale acceptance of *waḥdat al-wujūd* as pantheism is again a case of Western scholars adopting, as true and monolithic, one possible interpretation offered by pre-modern scholars. Just as the scholars had a number of disagreements over the subject of *ijtihād*, which were sometimes a result of misunderstanding how others interpreted the term *ijtihād*, disagreements over the orthodoxy of a given Sufi or his statements often arose over interpretations of technical terms or the permissibility or appropriateness of metaphorical interpretations of theopathic utterances.

Al-Bājūrī's Sufism is the Sufism of the jurists and theologians, not a separate practice in conflict with jurisprudence and theology. It is the Sufism of the archetypal Sunnī scholar, and not a tradition that can be extracted and practiced without its other two necessary components (law and theology). This does not exclude the existence of disagreement over certain legal and theological issues in relation to Sufism, but since so many of the *ʿulamāʾ* were themselves Sufis, so, too, many legal and theological debates about Sufism can really be considered intra-Sufi disagreements over law and theology, just as al-Junayd's and al-Ḥallāj's disagreement was legal (if over the issue of the hajj) or theological (if over the statement "anā al-Ḥaqq").

Al-Bājūrī on the Rational Sciences

There are two principle subjects related to the rational sciences that I have sought to relate to the broader topics of the Gabrielian paradigm and its characteristic spectrum of consensus and disagreement. These are, first, the discussion of the classification and interpretation of Allah's attributes, specifically with regard to metaphorical or literal interpretation; and second, the definition of *kalām*, and whether or not the purported antagonists of the rational sciences in general are necessarily excluded from the ranks of *kalām* practitioners.

In the section that follows, I explore al-Bājūrī's thought with regard to these two subjects, with an additional focus on his opinions on the study of syllogistic logic (*manṭiq*).

Al-Bājūrī on *Ta*ʾ*wīl*, *Tafwīḍ*, and *Ẓāhir*

The issue of how to interpret texts in which the literal (linguistic) meaning contradicts established principles laid down in the Qurʾān is quite possibly the main issue of contention between the general body of Ashʿarīs and Atharīs. Each of the three possibilities for interpretation—*ta*ʾ*wīl* (metaphorical interpretation), *tafwīḍ* (entrusting the actual intended meaning of a word to its speaker), or *ʿalā ẓāhirrihā bi lā takyīf* (literally without ascribing modality)—have their proponents and critics. Often the subject of *ta*ʾ*wīl* is considered to be rooted in the issue of rationalism, that is, a rationalist, based on his rationalist theories, would deny that a given word can be taken literally, and therefore it must be interpreted metaphorically. From this assumption, the issue of rationalism has been considered the main dividing line between Ashʿarīs and Atharīs. Rationalism, though related to *ta*ʾ*wīl*, was not, in and of itself, the core difference between the two camps, as both were involved in rationalist dialectics in some form.

The following section seeks to better understand the issue of *ta*ʾ*wīl* and the interpretation of primary texts that imply anthropomorphism, and the relationship of this interpretive problem to the issue of rationalism. *Ta*ʾ*wīl* is often understood to mean metaphorical interpretation. Al-Bājūrī's treatment of the topic, however, indicates that the term can have more nuanced meanings and implications.

His discussion of how *ta'wīl* relates to the Ashʿarī conception of *ẓāhir* (literal linguistic meaning), in comparison to other definitions, helps to enhance our understanding of this core issue of debate between the Ashʿarīs and Atharīs.

Al-Bājūrī's discussion of *ta'wīl* begins with his commentary on al-Laqānī's verse, "And every primary text (*naṣṣ*) that gives the erroneous impression of anthropomorphism, metaphorically interpret it or entrust its actual meaning (practice *tafwīḍ*), and betake yourself to purification."[82] After a grammatical analysis, he begins to define the terms so that al-Laqānī's verse is comprehensible. This is necessary, as the term *naṣṣ* has both a linguistic meaning and a technical meaning. Its linguistic meaning is a text whose meaning is not derived via "analogy (*qiyās*), deduction (*istinbāṭ*), or consensus (*ijmāʿ*)."[83] Specifically, he says, it is a proof (*dalīl*) from the Qur'ān and Sunna, a primary text. An example of this type of text would be the term *dābba*, whose usage in modern Arabic can refer to any animal that is ridden or used as a "beast of burden." Its linguistic meaning however is "anything which crawls or walks on the earth."[84]

Naṣṣ can also have a technical meaning in the science of *uṣūl al-fiqh*, wherein it means, as al-Bājūrī defines it, "that which conveys a complete, self-contained meaning that does not imply other than it."[85] It is a *qaṭʿī* (unequivocal, decisive) statement, one that does not accept multiple interpretations.

Al-Bājūrī explains that it is the former—*naṣṣ* in the general linguistic sense of being a primary text—that is intended by al-Laqānī, as the latter *uṣūlī* technical meaning would not be open to *ta'wīl* because it admits no other possible meaning. While it may seem a digression, this discussion opens up an important area of linguistics that constitutes a major area of disagreement between the Ashʿarīs and some Atharīs, such as Ibn Taymiyya.

Specifically, the discussion brings us to the issue of the actual definition of the term *ẓāhir*, as the Ashʿarī conception of *ẓāhir* admits that there can be a root meaning and a number of possible derived meanings, and thus it does not apply to a *naṣṣ* in the technical sense of the word, which only admits one meaning. The *ẓāhir* is, as al-Bājūrī explains in the same passage, in opposition to the *naṣṣ* in its technical sense, that is, it accepts multiple meanings.[86] Al-Bājūrī also gives a brief description of the term *ẓāhir* in his discussion of the qualifications of the judge capable of *ijtihād*: "The *ẓāhir* is that which indicates an apparent meaning (*dalālah ẓāhirah*) for something while also permitting other than it (i.e., other meanings)."[87] Furthermore, the term *ẓāhir* has been explained by Ashʿarīs as being a word with an original root linguistic meaning, as well as additional meanings that were derived later.[88]

In all cases discussed above, what can be understood is that, according to Ashʿarīs like al-Bājūrī, a word which has an apparent (*ẓāhir*) meaning, and other meanings as well, is therefore eligible for *taʾwīl*, under certain circumstances. According to a maxim given by Arab linguists, "Predominance in speech is given to the literal sense [*ẓāhir*]."[89] Thus, a word is not taken on other than its *ẓāhir* meaning, unless the context indicates that it must be (i.e., either by the express intention of the author, or from context).

Ibn Taymiyya, who offers another perspective on the predominant Ashʿarī stance, appears to deny that the term *ẓāhir* must necessarily contain a root linguistic meaning; he claims that the meanings of words are what come to the mind of those who speak the language, as defined by convention and context.[90] He even goes to the extent of agreeing that those meanings that the Ashʿarīs claim to be the root literal linguistic meanings are certainly not the intended meanings of these words.[91] Thus, *yad* does not mean a hand like the limbs of the creation. He commends whoever disassociates these terms from meanings that imply anthropomorphism.[92] His main point of contention with the Ashʿarīs then is their claim that the *ẓāhir* meaning can *only* be those anthropomorphic meanings, whereas the *ẓāhir* meaning in Ibn Taymiyya's mind is what is derived from the context of the Qurʾān and *Ḥadīth*. Thus, Allah's being dissimilar from creation, as stated clearly in the Qurʾān, should indicate that the terms *yad* or *wajh* do not carry the same meaning as when applied to created things. Their meanings, however, are still considered literal (*ẓāhir*) to Ibn Taymiyya. It is this latter point, however, which is difficult to grasp, and thus, Ibn Taymiyya faced great criticism for having made it.

When returning to the issues of *taʾwīl* and *tafwīḍ*, discussed earlier, it becomes clear that Ibn Taymiyya's ambiguity on the actual *ẓāhir* meaning of the words in question reflects a disagreement with both the Ashʿarīs and other fellow Atharīs. Al-Bājūrī has an extremely useful bipartite definition of *taʾwīl*, connected to *tafwīḍ*, which in some ways illustrates often overlooked points of similarity between Ashʿarīs and Atharīs. The two types of *taʾwīl* according to al-Bājūrī are:

- *al-taʾwīl al-ijmālī* (general): which diverts the expression from its *ẓāhir* meaning, and
- *al-taʾwīl al-tafṣīlī* (particular, detailed): which, after engaging in *al-taʾwīl al-ijmālī*, gives a particular interpretation and elucidates the intended meaning.[93]

The first class of *ta'wīl*, as shown above, is actually done by Ash'arīs and Atharīs alike, regardless of how they define the term *ẓāhir*, as both camps deny that the anthropomorphic meanings, which the Ash'arīs consider to be the *ẓāhir*, have any relation to Allah.

The second type of *ta'wīl* is the actual *ta'wīl* over which controversy arose. According to the Ash'arīs, one elucidates a possible intended meaning by choosing a meaning from among the derived, figurative meanings that harmonize with the core Qur'ānic principles of Allah's dissimilarity from creation. Often this is done by choosing a meaning that is related to one of the *ṣifāt al-ma'ānī* (attributes of meaning).[94] For example, since *yad* is figuratively used to mean power, al-Bājūrī says that the phrase "Allah's *yad* is over their hands" is interpreted to mean Allah's power.[95]

Al-Bājūrī's definition of *tafwīḍ* includes the first type of *ta'wīl*. He says that *tafwīḍ* means that "after *al-ta'wīl al-ijmālī*, one consigns the intended meaning to Him [Allah]."[96] He lists in his *Tuḥfat al-murīd* a number of Qur'ānic verses and *ḥadīth*s that contain terms which could be misunderstood to imply anthropomorphism, many of which are found in Ibn al-Jawzī's *Kitāb akhbār al-ṣifāt* and *Daf' shuba al-tashbīh bi-akaff al-tanzīh*. In each case al-Bājūrī gives the opinion of the *salaf*, whom he defines as being those who lived before 500 AH [1107].[97] Their method, *tafwīḍ*, is always to say "[hand, form, face, establishing (*istawā'*), etc.] we do not know it [i.e., its intended meaning]," all the while diverting it from its *ẓāhir* meaning and affirming its status as revelation or a truthful statement from the Prophet.[98] Al-Bājūrī also offers, in each case, the opinion of the *khalaf* (those who came after the *salaf*) and their *ta'wīl*.

This method of *tafwīḍ* is also that of Ibn Qudāma, al-Suyūṭī, Aḥmad b. Ḥanbal, al-Ash'arī, and Ibn Kathīr. The latter appears to offer a definition similar to that of al-Bājūrī when he discusses *tafwīḍ* in his exegesis of the Qur'ānic verse pertaining to Allah's *istiwā'*. Ibn Kathīr says,[99]

> People have said a great deal on this topic, and this is not the place to expound on what they have said. On this matter, we follow the early Muslims (*salaf*): Mālik, Awzā'ī, Thawrī, Layth b. Sa'd, Shāfi'ī, Aḥmad b. Ḥanbal, Isḥāq b. Rāhawayh, and others among the imams of the Muslims, both ancient and modern—that is: *[A] to let it (the verse in question) pass as it has come, without saying how it is meant (min ghayr takyīf)*, without likening it to created things (*wa lā tashbīh*), and without nullifying it (*wa lā ta'ṭīl*). *[B] The*

> *literal meaning (ẓāhir) that occurs to the minds of anthropomorphists (al-mushabbihīn) is negated of Allah,* for nothing from His creation resembles Him: "There is nothing whatsoever like unto Him, and He is the All-Hearing, the All-Seeing (Qurʾān 42:11).[100]

The underlined text marked [A] above is essentially al-Bājūrī's description of the *salaf*'s statement "we do not know it," while the underlined text marked [B] above is al-Bājūrī's description of *al-taʾwīl al-ijmālī,* in that Ibn Kathīr is diverting the meaning of the text from its *ẓāhir* meaning. Here Ibn Kathīr is implicitly affirming that one valid definition of the term *ẓāhir* is its literal linguistic meaning, which is anthropomorphic.[101] Some modern followers of Ibn Taymiyya claim that *bi lā takyīf* would only mean *tafwīḍ* of modality[102] not of meaning (*maʿnā*), but as discussed below, *kayfiyya* is a part of meaning and without detailing which aspect of meaning remains after de-anthropomorphizing a term, one ends up with *tafwīḍ*.

Ibn Taymiyya's main objection then is to the Ashʿarī and fellow Atharī claim that the *salaf* said they did not know the meaning (*maʿnā*) of the words, which he understood to mean that they let them pass as orthographic symbols recited by the reader, but with no intelligible meaning. This is somewhat understandable, as statements such as al-Bājūrī's were common (i.e., "we do not know it['s meaning]," "letting it pass without asking how it was meant," etc.). Ibn Taymiyya's solution, however, as noted earlier, does not offer any concrete meaning to the terms in question.

Rather, Ibn Taymiyya claims them to be literal, but says the literal sense does not mean the same as the anthropomorphic meanings usually ascribed to them. Thus, this view does not actually, positively assign any meaning to the words, as all previous meanings—whether linguistic root meanings or metaphorical usages—have been canceled. For example, if Ibn Taymiyya denies the anthropomorphic meanings—the Ashʿarī *ẓāhir*—usually associated with terms like hand and face, and also denies any of the metaphorical usages—which otherwise would be *taʾwīl*—he has essentially erased the dictionary entry for the word, adding instead a new word, derived contextually from the Qurʾān, or *ḥadīth*. The Qurʾān and *ḥadīth*, however, mention the words without further definition of them, and only qualify them as unlike created things. Thus, Ibn Taymiyya is essentially doing *tafwīḍ*, as he leaves them uninterpreted, only claiming that they are literal, and attributes to be added to a list of attributes.

If he instead says that there is a meaning that is comprehensible to one who speaks the language, and if he has already erased the dictionary entry as mentioned above, then its meaning is a new meaning, derived from the Qurʾān and *ḥadīth*, which did not have an effect on the Arabic language until the Prophet entered his prophetic office. This is, in a sense, a form of *taʾwīl* by Ashʿarī standards, because diverting from the literal linguistic meaning and choosing a word that was introduced later is *taʾwīl*.

In order for the meaning of *yad Allāh* to be known, regardless of "bi lā takyīf," there would have to be a common denominator between all usages of the term *yad*, otherwise it would be a homonym. If the term "*yad*" in "yad Allāh" and "yad al-khalq" were homonyms, the Qurʾān and *ḥadīth* offer no definition of the term *yad Allāh* other than the qualification that it is unlike the *yad*s of creation. If it is a homonym, whose literal meaning is known from context and convention, and context and convention have nothing to offer other than dissimilarity and grammatical attribution to Allah, then the only thing one can understand is that Allah has an attribute called *yad* and it is unlike any homonyms attributed to creation. This would imply that Allah revealed these terms so that Sunnīs could add them to their lists of attributes for later disputes with Muʿtazilīs, that is, to make a list of grammatical ascriptions.

Al-Bājūrī's definition of *tafwīḍ*, that is, employing *al-taʾwīl al-ijmālī*, followed by not assigning a derived, metaphorical meaning to the texts provides us with a demonstration of the method of many Ashʿarī and Atharī scholars. Even Ibn Taymiyya's thought agrees up to this point, but he adds the conditions that one declare that the word is *ẓāhir* and its meaning (*maʿnā*) is known, but without modality. However, as mentioned above, he apparently does not explain what a hand that is not a limb, or a hand that is not bound by the six directions might be, or of what it informs the reader regarding his or her creator.

We might glean from al-Bājūrī's bipartite division of *taʾwīl*, and how it relates to *tafwīḍ*, that it is not always accurate to declare Atharīs to be literalists or anthropomorphists. While some of them may indeed have gone to that extent—al-Bājūrī refers to them as "those who call themselves Ḥanbalī"—many of them merely denied the ascription of metaphorical meanings to primary texts, opting instead to divert its meanings from any anthropomorphic definition and then opt out of applying a definition to the word.[103] Ascribing modality (*kayfiyya*) is an aspect of defining a term, thus, leaving a word whose meaning is thought to resemble no other usage of the term without any modality ascribed to it is to leave it uninterpreted.[104] When some Atharīs claimed these words to be *ẓāhir*, but indicate something dissimilar to creation, they may have ultimately only meant that they were nonmetaphorical.

While it is possible to consider the classification systems of attributes derived by Muʿtazilīs and Ashʿarīs as entering into the realm of rationalism,[105] I believe the crux of the issue is mostly linguistic. That is, regardless of how many types of attributes there are, and how they relate to the essences that they describe, ultimately one must begin with the issue of how words are classified; do there exist root literal–linguistic meanings (the Ashʿarī *ẓāhir*) and later derived meanings, or are there simply literal words whose meanings are derived by context and convention (the Ibn Taymiyya *ẓāhir*)? Many of the Ashʿarīs limited the meanings of words to their literal root–linguistic meanings, and derived meanings. Their denial of a third category, linguistic-contextual (Ibn Taymiyya's *ẓāhir*), is not an issue of rationality, rather it is an issue of linguistics, specifically regarding the origins of words.

Ibn Taymiyya's stance on attributes is that they have real, extramental existence, and they include that which is attributed to Allah by Himself or His Prophet, which is not a separate corporeal thing (i.e., the she-camel of Allah, the house of Allah, etc.). The Ashʿarī stance, when an Ashʿarī chooses to do *taʾwīl* rather than *tafwīḍ*, includes these points, but also excludes, in addition to separate corporeal things, descriptions that could be interpreted to imply anthropomorphism. Thus, Ibn Taymiyya and those Atharīs who follow him deny only one category of things attributed to Allah as being real attributes (i.e., separate corporeal things), while the Ashʿarīs (and non-Ashʿarīs such as Ibn al-Jawzī) deny a second category, namely those terms that could imply anthropomorphism. Thus, some words, through the process of *taʾwīl*, are denied the status of being an essential attribute, while those Atharīs who oppose *taʾwīl* find fault in this, claiming that the one who has done so has denied an actual, extra-mental existing attribute. There is, at this point, an irreconcilable difference, one that cannot be considered a merely semantic difference.

However, even within the category of *tafwīḍ*, one might not affirm or deny that a given term is meant to be classified as an attribute. We can therefore distinguish two classes of practitioners of *tafwīḍ*, the first being those who do not delve into the meanings of the words, or discuss whether or not these are real existent attributes subsisting in Allah's entity,[106] and the second group being those that do not delve into meanings but nonetheless classify these terms as attributes, as is reported of al-Ashʿarī.

It appears to me that the issue of rationality enters into the subject of the classification of attributes, which itself is reached only after the linguistic issue of root meanings and metaphorical usages is dealt with. Thus, the issue of *taʾwīl* and *tafwīḍ* is not entirely an issue of rationality, and the aspect of this issue that deals with rationality—classifying attributes—is in fact secondary. Thus, regardless of how one classifies attributes, the issue of *taʾwīl, tafwīḍ,* and the definition of the term *ẓāhir* will nonetheless arise, as all Sunnīs (Ashʿarī, Māturīdī, and Atharī) agree that the anthropomorphic meanings—the Ashʿarī *ẓāhir*—are not intended.[107] However, it would be useful to know whether or not grammarians constructed this division—root linguistic and derived metaphorical—after their system of classifying attributes made it necessary. Regardless, the effort to determine the nature of language and meaning to such a degree of meticulousness is evidence of one of the many instances of pre-modern textual criticism in Muslim scholarship, brought about by the demands of the revealed text.

The Permissibility of *Manṭiq*

The permissibility of the use of *manṭiq,* that is, syllogistic logic, was debated within both Ashʿarī and Atharī circles. While some objections surfaced among the Ashʿarīs after al-Ghazālī's time, it appears to have been accepted in many institutions of Ashʿarī learning. Indeed, many of the classic manuals of logic were written, studied, and commented upon between the seventh and ninth/thirteenth and fifteenth centuries, a period during which the science of logic underwent significant development. From the ninth/fifteenth century until the beginning of the twentieth century, it was a standard subject in many scholars' education.[108]

However, prior to becoming an almost universally accepted subject of study for scholars, *manṭiq* first sustained a number of critiques and attacks. One of the most detailed critiques of logic is Ibn Taymiyya's *Radd ʿalā al-manṭiqiyīn,* in which he challenges many aspects of *manṭiq,* especially the inability of the syllogism to produce certain knowledge of the reality of anything actually existent. Another salient point in his critique is the logician's theory of definitions, which, according to Ibn Taymiyya, does not provide any information that could not have otherwise been learned through sensory perception by those ignorant of *manṭiq*.

Ibn Taymiyya's essential contention was that the Greek philosophers' philosophical realism—the belief that universals had actual existence[109]—was built into many of the fundamental bases of *manṭiq*.[110] Thus, he considered al-Ghazālī and those who followed him to be incorrect in considering *manṭiq* a mere tool, free of the errors of the heretical philosophers who had wielded it.[111]

Al-Bājūrī indirectly addresses the problem of extreme realism in his denial of the Platonic forms (such as 'chairness')[112] and the Muʿtazilīs' belief that non-existent things exist in veiled form prior to being brought into existence as we know it. Al-Bājūrī rejects these opinions in his discussion of atomism and al-Laqānī's verse "wa ʿindanā al-shayʾ huwa l-mawjūd, thābitun fī l-khāriji l-muwjūdu"[113] [And with us (the Ashʿarīs) the "thing" (shayʾ) is existent, and the existent is that which is established in the extra-mental world (khārijan)].

Al-Bājūrī's place in the spectrum between Ibn Taymiyya's nominalism and Plato's extreme realism, would be conclusively decided were he to have explicitly expressed an opinion on the existence of physical universals (a position that was contested even among Ashʿarīs). Nonetheless, al-Bājūrī's study of *manṭiq* did not cause him to adopt extreme realist opinions, nor the emanationist theories found in Ibn Sīnā's works, on which many later *manṭiq* texts were originally based.[114] Thus, Ibn Taymiyya's charge that *manṭiq* leads to the heretical ideas of the philosophers did not hold true in all instances, as in al-Bājūrī's treatment of the abovementioned subjects. In addition, al-Kātibī (d. 675/1277), author of the popular handbook on logic entitled *al-Shamsiyya*, did not consider the discussion of the existence or nonexistence of universals as being part of the science of logic, further distancing logic from the potential heresies that Ibn Taymiyya claimed were inherent therein.[115]

Al-Bājūrī's perspective on *manṭiq* is interesting, as it appears to differ from presentations of *manṭiq* in the works of Ibn Taymiyya and al-Suyūṭī. While Ibn Taymiyya and al-Suyūṭī appear to lump all *manṭiq* into the same category (i.e., heretical), al-Bājūrī, along with a number of important scholars before him, divides *manṭiq* into two classes. The first is that of the *mutaʾakhkhirūn*, a group of later scholars whose works include the *Mukhtaṣar* of al-Sanūsī, the *Īsāghūjī* by Athīr al-Dīn al-Abharī (d. 663/1264–65),[116] the *Mukhtaṣar* of Ibn ʿArafa, and others that he lists in his commentary on al-Akhḍarī's *Sullam al-manṭiq*.[117] These are later scholars, those whom Ibn Khaldūn mentions as having developed the science of *manṭiq* into its own subject, to the extent that the works of the earlier scholars (*mutaqaddimūn*) were no longer mentioned.

According to al-Bājūrī, the defining characteristic of this class of *manṭiq*, that of the *mutaʾakhkhirūn*, is its being devoid of the heretical ideas of the philosophers.[118] Its purpose is to guide one to correctness of belief. Al-Bājūrī held that there is no disagreement over the permissibility of this class of *manṭiq*. In fact, he claims that this class of *manṭiq* is *farḍ kifāya*—a communal obligation—on the people of every province.[119] However, if one is not in need of the *manṭiq* of the later logicians (*muta'akhkhirūn*), because a person possesses a strong and sound intellect, they may do without it.[120] Thus the Companions (*ṣaḥāba*), Followers, (*tābi'īn*), and the *mujtahid* imams were not in any need of this class of *manṭiq*, nor under any obligation to use it, because of the strength of their intellects. This latter point was probably mentioned to justify how these aforementioned scholars could function properly without access to a later development (i.e., a purified form of logic) that would become communally obligatory after their time. But it is also important as it relates to the critiques of *manṭiq* of Ibn Taymiyya and al-Suyūṭī, as some of the absolute claims that they make are not necessarily applicable. Al-Bājūrī's point that one of sound intellect can dispense with *manṭiq* indicates that he does not hold that concepts can be formed only via definition (*ḥadd*), or that judgments (*taṣdīqāt*) can be known only via the syllogism (these being two key points of Ibn Taymiyya's contention with *manṭiq*).[121]

Al-Bājūrī justifies ruling *manṭiq* as *farḍ kifāya* (a communal obligation) by claiming that it is a necessary supporting science which *kalām* depends upon in the refutation of doubts. The science of *kalām* is, according to al-Bājūrī, also *farḍ kifāya*. Whatever science is necessary to another *farḍ kifāya* science, its becomes *farḍ kifāya*.[122] That is, since *kalām*, which is a communal obligation, depends on *manṭiq*, then *manṭiq* is also a communal obligation, as *kalām* could not properly function without it. Al-Bājūrī makes it very clear that any debate over the permissibility of *kalām* or non-heretical *manṭiq* is hardly worth mentioning. In fact, he speaks as though there really are no opposing opinions. The only disagreement over the permissibility of *manṭiq* regards the second class of *manṭiq*.

In al-Bājūrī's system the second class of *manṭiq* is that of the *mutaqaddimūn*, those earlier scholars, presumably Aristotle and those ancients who preceded and proceeded him, as well as their Arab translators and interpreters, presumably including Ibn Sīnā and al-Farābī.[123] The defining characteristic of this class is that they are not devoid of the heretical ideas of the philosophers. Thus, scholars were in disagreement as to the permissibility of engaging in this science.[124]

Al-Akhḍarī presents three opinions (*aqwāl*) regarding this type of *manṭiq*. The first is that of al-Nawawī and Ibn al-Ṣalāḥ (c. sixth/twelfth century), both mentioned by name in the poem, who held that engaging in this type of *manṭiq* is prohibited (*ḥarām*). Al-Suyūṭī also held this opinion, using al-Nawawī as his source, although he held that al-Nawawī's opinion applied to all classes of *manṭiq*, because al-Nawawī had studied the *Isogoge* (presumably al-Kātibī's, rather than Porphery's text by the same name), which al-Bājūrī considers to be from the first class of agreed-upon permissible *manṭiq*, and then ruled it was *ḥarām*.[125]

Thus, the classification of the *manṭiq*—not just the ruling related to it—is another prominent case of disagreement between al-Bājūrī and al-Suyūṭī, both Shāfiʿī–Ashʿarī–Sufis. In the case of *ijtihād*, they differed on the number and descriptions of the classes of *mujtahids*. In the case of *manṭiq*, al-Suyūṭī apparently only sees one type of *manṭiq*, whereas al-Bājūrī sees two. I am tempted to postulate that in al-Suyūṭī's time, the works of al-Sanūsī and al-Akhḍarī may not have been as widespread as they were by al-Bājūrī's time, as these two scholars were contemporaries of al-Suyūṭī. Perhaps, as their works came to dominate the subject of logic in the coming years, the division between the two classes of logicians became more pronounced, and voices such as al-Suyūṭī's, already an apparent minority in his time, further waned.[126] It is also possible, indeed probable, that Ibn Taymiyya and al-Suyūṭī unfairly treated all classes of logic as a monolithic whole.[127]

The second opinion offered by al-Akhḍarī and explained by al-Bājūrī, is that *manṭiq* of the second class is necessarily studied. This was the opinion of al-Bājūrī, al-Ghazālī and others; however, there was some disagreement as to whether they considered it necessary at the level of being a communal obligation (*farḍ kifāya*), or considered it to be strongly recommended.[128] Al-Ghazālī's view was that *manṭiq*, like math, astronomy, and physics, was a useful tool that did not necessarily lead to the heretical metaphysical conclusions of the philosophers.[129]

The third opinion, which al-Akhḍarī calls *mashhūr* (popular) and *ṣaḥīḥ* (sound), is that the study of *manṭiq* is permissible for one of sound intellect who knows the true creed of the Qurʾān and Sunna.[130] Al-Bājūrī then discusses the implications of al-Akhḍarī's describing this opinion as the "popular opinion." According to al-Bājūrī, it is described as such because of the large number of people who held this opinion.

However, it may be that al-Akhḍarī, being a Mālikī and having authored works on Mālikī *fiqh*, intended his statement to reflect that it was the dominant opinion in the Mālikī school, and thus held more weight than the other two opinions. In the Mālikī school, *mashhūr* is a technical term that generally implies that an opinion is considered the strongest in terms of proofs; or it is the opinion of Ibn al-Qāsim stated in his *al-Mudawwana*;[131] or it is the opinion that has been stated by the greatest number of qualified scholars.[132] The assumption that al-Akhḍarī may have intended the term *mashhūr* as a technical term is supported by al-Bājūrī's declaration that the popular ruling is the *aṣaḥ* (the most sound), which in the Shāfiʿī school technically means that it is the strongest opinion, though there are sound (*ṣaḥīḥ*) opinions that are less strong. As for al-Akhḍarī's calling this opinion *ṣaḥīḥ*, al-Bājūrī explains that it is because of the strength of the arguments used to prove its soundness (*quwwatu dalīlihā*).

Al-Bājūrī stresses, however, that the popularity of the other two opinions is not negated by al-Akhḍarī's ascription of *mashhūr* to the third opinion, as both opinions have a large number of proponents. Thus, if all debates over the permissibility of logic were lumped under the second category of *manṭiq*—that which is not free of heretical ideas of the philosophers—then all views on the matter would be considered acceptable, and al-Nawawī, al-Ghazālī, and al-Bājūrī would be representatives of the three acceptable opinions. Ibn Taymiyya's view, however, may be slightly less acceptable, as he uses it as proof for declaring the Ashʿarīs to be Ahl al-Bidʿa (heretical innovators), an idea which al-Nawawī, while declaring the second class of *manṭiq* to be *ḥarām*, did not, however, share.

Reviewing al-Bājūrī's comments on the subject of *manṭiq*, it is clear that no consensus regarding its permissibility or impermissibility ever occurred among the jurists, neither among the Ashʿarīs,[133] nor the Atharīs. While al-Bājūrī claims that there was no disagreement over the *manṭiq* that was devoid of heretical philosophical views (that of the later logicians (*mutaʾakhkhirūn*)), it appears that there may still have been a few opponents. As for the disagreement over the second type of *manṭiq*—that of the early logicians (*mutaqaddimūn*)—the disagreement was of three types and all three were considered acceptable opinions, even if the *mashhūr* opinion stated by al-Akhḍarī came to dominate many of the institutions of Muslim learning after the ninth/fifteenth century. Thus, even if al-Suyūṭī and Ibn Taymiyya were correct that no form of logic could be free of the heretical ideas of the philosophers, the three varying opinions mentioned by al-Akhḍarī would still apply, that is, the disagreement over the permissibility of *manṭiq* was considered an acceptable disagreement.

Al-Bājūrī on *Kalām*

Al-Bājūrī's opinion that *kalām* was a communal obligation—such that if no one from a given area practiced it, all of its inhabitants would be sinful—has already been mentioned above.[134] In his *Tuḥfat al-murīd*, he discusses the various different views regarding the necessity for each Muslim to know the *kalām* proofs for the attributes of Allah and the prophets, and gives preponderance to the opinion that it is an obligation to know general proofs—though not detailed proofs—and that one is sinful, yet still a Muslim, if he or she does not know them.[135]

While he follows his predecessors—especially al-Sanūsī and al-Taftazānī—very closely, al-Bājūrī's works on *ʿaqīda* offer an expansive view into the multifarious issues pertaining to the field. Although it is a lengthy topic, worthy of more comprehensive treatment elsewhere, al-Bājūrī's recension of later Ashʿarī thought offers us a different perspective on some of the common subjects of theology, particularly on the cosmological proof for the existence of God. Further examination of his thought also gives additional weight to the role of disagreement within theology.

Regarding the cosmological proof for the existence of God, al-Bājūrī addresses the issue of whether or not the attribute of existence is the entity of the thing itself, or other than it, in his discussion of the term *wujūd* (existence) in his commentary on al-Sanūsī's *Muqaddima*. After discussing al-Ashʿarī's view that existence and the *dhāt* (entity)—the thing itself—are the same, and al-Rāzī's view that the attribute (*ṣifa*) and the thing to which it is attributed (*mawṣūf*) are distinct and separate, he then mentions that some scholars claim that it is not necessary for a person to choose a particular side, as it is a matter of a difference of opinion among the *mutakallimūn*.[136]

Indeed, later *mutakallimūn* were not entirely uniform in the presentation of their ideas on the difference, or lack thereof, between existence (*wujūd*) and entity (*dhāt*), a matter that had been framed by Ibn Sīnā's analysis and challenge of the opinions earlier *mutakallimūn* who had originally conceived the issue as a distinction between thing (*shayʾ*) and existence.[137] Scholars such as al-Rāzī, al-Taftazānī, al-Bayḍāwī, and al-Iṣfahānī (d. 749/1348), all differed with al-Ashʿarī on this matter, and expressed their analyses of the difference between existence and entity from varying angles, though they were unified in doing so within the framework provided by Ibn Sīnā. Their doing so indicates a further development in the science of *kalām*, as Ibn Sīnā himself had left some "loose ends" surrounding the issue.[138]

The recognition of development between the early Ashʿarīs and later post-Ghazālī Ashʿarīs—who should have ceased to philosophize and reason according to proponents of theory of decline—as well as al-Bājūrī's recognition that no final verdict had been reached, indicates that theologians in his time were free to determine their own position on the matter based on their own reasoning. Al-Bājūrī clearly states that when there is legitimate *ikhtilāf* within the Ashʿarī school, due to the lack of definitive proof and the fact that such an issue does not impinge on anything fundamental, one is not required to follow one opinion over the other, just as one can choose between various opinions within the schools of *fiqh*. The difference, at least in principle, was that one should not blindly follow (i.e., practice *taqlīd*) in matters of theology, and therefore, should one feel compelled to determine the difference between existence and entity; one's own scholarly judgment of the discourse is to be the fruit of his independent investigation and assessment of the issue. Though focused on a highly specific issue of philosophical and theological concern, the issue of existence and entity indicates a development in *kalām* that is more complex and involved than the work of the earlier *mutakallimūn*, and one that required the budding theologian to consider, investigate, and possibly advance his own conclusion.

Regarding his discussion of the rational proofs for the existence of God, I believe al-Bājūrī and his intellectual predecessors contribute something to the discussion—a perspective or approach that is rarely, if ever, found elsewhere. The argument begins with the traditional cosmological proof of God's existence, namely, the existence of the universe. It then departs from the usual course of the cosmological argument—the discussion of the causal dependency of a given thing on a previous cause. Al-Bājūrī says in his *Risāla fī ʿilm al-tawḥīd*: "Necessary with regard to Him most high is existence (*wujūd*). Its opposite [which is impossible] is non-existence (*ʿadam*). The proof for that is the existence of these originated things (*makhluqāt*)."

Al-Bājūrī notes (in *Tuḥfat al-murīd*) that the obligation is for one to know, in a general way, the proofs for the core points of *tawḥīd*, thus what he offers in the *Risāla* is this general proof—the bare minimum one should know. He goes into an explanation of the detailed proofs in *Tuḥfat al-murīd* and in his commentary on al-Sanūsī's *Muqaddima*, where he comments,

> The proof of His existence is the createdness of the world (*ʿālam*). For if it had no creator, rather it came into existence by itself, that would necessitate that one of two equal states be equivalent to the other and simultaneously preponderant over it without any cause, and such would be impossible.[139]

Here al-Sanūsī begins the argument for the necessity of a creator by indicating that *since* the universe had a beginning, it either had a cause or it was uncaused. If it were uncaused, that would lead to a union of opposites. The two opposites are the state of preponderance and equality, as Ibn ʿĀshir says in his versified summary of the

Muqaddima.[140] What is intended is that there are, by default, two equal states—represented by two balanced scale pans[141]—that is, the possibility of existence or nonexistence for the universe. Since we witness that the universe exists, there must have been a preponderance on the side of existence. However, to claim that this preponderance occurred without cause is to claim that the possibility of existence was both equal and preponderant, a claim that entails a union of opposites.

Al-Bājūrī says, regarding the above perspective, "This is when you regard it [al-Sanūsī's statement above] based on the notion that existence and non-existence are equal with regard to their essential possibility."[142] He also adds that while this is the popular (*mashhūr*) interpretation, there is another valid reading that indicates the impossibility of preponderance occurring without a cause. In either interpretation, the argument for a creator due to the origination of the universe is proved first on rational grounds without reference to a chain of causality. In other words, one reading proves the impossibility of the universe coming into existence without a prior cause, arguing that such a claim entails the union of opposites, that is, the simultaneous equivalence and preponderance of the scale pans. The other reading proves the impossibility of the universe coming into existence without a prior cause by arguing that the movement of the scale pan from a state of equilibrium to a state of preponderance would entail an effect occurring without a prior cause. The usual approach to the cosmological proof is to argue that the universe had a beginning, and therefore a creator, due to the impossibility of an infinite regress, that is, a chain of causes and effects, each effect being dependent on a previous cause. With no first cause, there could be no chain of effects.

As for the proof that the universe had a beginning, upon which the aforementioned proof depends, it is the necessary connection between the universe (al-Bājūrī specifies that what is intended are the celestial bodies (*ajrām*), the component parts of the universe) and its contingent attributes (*aʿrāḍ*)[143] such as motion and stillness, which are seen coming into existence and going out of existence. In other words, since one witnesses that the attribute of movement begins for a particular thing, and then comes to an end when it takes on the attribute of stillness, one reasons that they are created (as whatever has a beginning is created, and whatever comes to an end, necessarily had a beginning).[144] Therefore the various bodies in the universe must have had a beginning, as they are necessarily connected to their attributes. And furthermore, the entire universe must have had a beginning, if its constituent parts had beginnings.

The necessary connection of the universe's constituent parts to their attributes is fascinating, as al-Bājūrī eventually discusses the impossibility of an infinite regress of initiator creators with regard to the *aʿrāḍ* themselves. In doing so, however, he does not refer to the causal dependency of effects on their causes, leading back to a first cause; rather, he proves the rational absurdity of an infinite regress by proving that two infinite quantities of finite units can be considered both equal and unequal simultaneously, a concept that the intellect should find absurd.[145] He begins his demonstration of the absurdity of this idea by giving as an example two different points in time, the flood[146] and the present moment. If one then imagines two timelines—one beginning with the flood, and the other beginning with the present moment—extending back into infinity, both lines are said to be infinite, and thus equal. However, since there is a finite duration between now and the flood, the timeline of the present moment is finitely greater than the timeline beginning at the flood, thus making it both equal and greater.[147]

Thus, al-Bājūrī and his intellectual predecessors attempt to prove the necessity of the universe having a beginning, and needing a cause, without reference to a chain of causality, rather, by purely mathematical logic (in both cases the impossibility of simultaneously ascribing both equality and preponderance).[148] I believe that al-Bājūrī and his predecessors did this because at some point later in the scheme of arguments, causality is denied for everything except God. This occurs when treating the subject of *kasb*—man's acquisition of responsibility for his chosen actions, the effects of which were created by Allah.[149]

Proving the need for a creator without referencing the chain of causality is important, as modern popular arguments against God often claim that God does not "[provide] a natural terminator to the regresses."[150] This is because God is often conceived of in terms with which the Ashʿarīs do not agree, as physical being, undergoing changes in state, place, thought, and so forth. All of these are impossible from the Ashʿarī perspective, as all of them would lead to an actual infinite number of finite things (i.e., changes), which, according to the Ashʿarīs, is absurd.[151] A god as such would, by Ashʿarī definitions, be *muḥdath*, created or originated, and thus just another link in the regress, certainly not the necessarily existent (*wājib al-wujūd*) God who does not present any problem as the logical terminator of the regresses. Thus, the Ashʿarī perspective, which has only been touched upon in the contemporary English language discourse on the cosmological proof, would offer a significant variation to the discussion.[152]

Al-Bājūrī, in *Risāla fī ʿilm al-tawḥīd*, and his predecessors from among the later Ashʿarīs[153] ordered their arguments in a deliberate manner; this is a point that is often missed. They do not begin with the proof for Allah's being endlessly eternal (*baqāʾ*), rather they begin with the proof for His existence. This proof often rests on sub-proofs, some of which were discussed above. The initial proofs and sub-proofs for existence are then referred back to as proofs for the attributes listed thereafter.

1. Existence (*wujūd*)
    a. The impossibility of the universe coming into existence without a cause (union of opposites—preponderance and equality).
    b. The impossibility of a beginningless universe/infinite regress (union of opposites—equality of two infinite lines, one of which is also greater in length).
2. Beginningless eternality (*qidam*)
    a. The impossibility of having a beginning, as that would lead to the infinite regress of previous creators (1b above).[154]
3. Endless eternality (*baqāʾ*)
    a. The impossibility of coming to an end, as that also leads to an infinite regress (1b above).[155]
4. Dissimilarity from creation (*al-mukhālifa li-l-ḥawādith*)
    a. The impossibility of having a beginning (2a above), as all created things have beginnings to their existence, by definition.

Once 1 and 2 above have been proven, the remaining *ṣifāt al-salbiyya* can refer back to them, though sometimes through multiple steps. It is this relationship that deserves further exploration by Western scholars if the *kalām* arguments are to be accurately addressed in the Western philosophical discourse.[156]

Opponents to al-Bājūrī's *Kalām*

One of the common critiques of al-Bājūrī and his Ashʿarī inheritors is that they were engaged in *kalām*, a science their critics claim is prohibited. There is clearly a striking difference in rulings between al-Bājūrī, who considers *kalām* a communal obligation, and his modern-day critics, who consider it a heretical innovation (*bid'a*). Despite the potential differences in the outcome of their reasoning, al-Bājūrī's opponents among historical and modern-day Atharīs are clearly engaged *kalām*, as I show below. Demonstrating their involvement in *kalām* further buttresses the normativity of al-Bājūrī's model of the archetypal scholar of the Gabrielian paradigm, just as demonstrating Atharī connections to Sufism further strengthens the claim that the Gabrielian paradigm is a normative view of Islam, despite its diverse manifestions.

If *kalām* is the discussion of those propositions, especially those that are not mentioned in the Qur'ān or *Ḥadīth*, whose premises return to rational rather than empirical or revealed sources, then by necessity, as I demonstrate below, Atharīs such as Aḥmad b. Ḥanbal, Ibn Taymiyya, al-Lālakā'ī (d. 418/1027), and others must be included among those who engage in *kalām* (the *mutakallimūn*).

What then is the difference between Ash'arī *kalām* and Atharī *kalām*? To answer this, we must first look at examples of Atharī *kalām* to determine whether or not they contain:

- Premises which return to rational (*'aqlī*) sources rather than revelatory (*naqlī*) sources
- Discussions of issues pertaining to physics, metaphysics, or any other issues not explicitly stated in the Qur'ān
- Discussions of the nature of Allah and His attributes.

By way of example, Ibn Taymiyya's *al-Jawāb al-ṣaḥīḥ li man baddala dīn al-masīḥ* [The correct response to whomever changed the religion of Christ][157] contains numerous arguments that openly refer to rational proofs for their validity. Below are two examples:

1. Among the evidence that affirms His attributes of perfection is that if He was not described as being Ever-Living, All-Knowing, All-Powerful, All-Hearing, All-Seeing, and Speaker, He must be described with the opposite of that, by (the attributes of) death, ignorance, impotence, deafness, muteness, and voicelessness. But, He is exalted above all these deficiencies by necessity of reason. It is impossible that the most perfect of all beings . . . should be impotent, ignorant, deaf, mute, and voiceless.[158]

2. It is necessary to know that the occurrence of things must be caused by an originator, for it is essential, inherent knowledge. That is why Allah, the exalted, says, "Were they created by nothing, or were they themselves the creators?" [Qurʾān 52:35]. It is known both by natural disposition and by reason that an occurrence does not occur without an occasioner to occasion it and that it is impossible for an occurrence to occur without an occasioner to occasion it. . . .[159]

Ibn Taymiyya's refutation of *manṭiq* is a third example of a work replete with rational argumentation.

> The third consideration. Universal, general propositions do not exist in the extra-mental world as such. They are universal in the mind, not in particulars. Matters existing in the extra-mental world are particulars; every existing thing has a reality particular to it, a reality which distinguishes it from other existing things that share no such reality with it. Therefore, it is not possible to infer the particularity of an individual existent through a syllogism.[160]

Restated:

- All universals are only existent in the mind.
- All things existing in the extra-mental world are particulars.
- All existent things (particulars) have their own distinguishing reality, unshared with another existent thing.
- The syllogism [whose premises are universal and general] cannot produce certain knowledge of the reality of a specific particular.

These three arguments, from different sources and aimed at different audiences, are based on premises that are (a) purely rational, (b) pertain to subjects not mentioned in the Qurʾān and Sunna, and/or (c) relate to the contemplation of Allah's attributes.[161] Examples one and two are basic Ashʿarī premises, namely that whatever has a beginning must have an originator/maker, and that the opposites of Allah's necessary attributes are rationally impossible. The third example contains a conclusion based on premises not found in the primary texts.

The Atharī scholar al-Lālakāʾī is also noted to have used *kalām*. In defending the Sunnī position that the Qurʾān is Allah's uncreated speech, al-Lālakāʾī claims that if Allah's attribute of speech were created, that would mean that it was created by Allah's creative fiat "*kun*" (be!). But since Allah's speech is created, His saying *kun* would also have been created. This *kun* would also have been created, as would the preceding one, and so on, leading to an infinite regress. To prove the falsity of a claim by indicating that it leads to an infinite regress is a purely rational statement, as in (a) above.[162]

Al-Bukhārī (d. 256/870), the compiler of the most relied upon collection of *ḥadīths* in the Sunnī tradition, is considered by Atharīs to be among their ranks, yet he is known to have engaged in *taʾwīl* regarding the term *wajh* (lit., face), interpreting it to mean "dominion" or "domain." In his chapter on exegesis, he mentions his interpretation of Sūrat al-Qiṣaṣ, verse 88: "All things are perishing except His face [Bukhārī comments . . .], i.e., except His domain (*mulkuhu*)."[163] *Taʾwīl* is not synonymous with *kalām*, as mentioned previously, yet it falls under the category of *kalām*, in that it pertains to discussions of Allah's attributes, the rational absurdity of anthropomorphism, and choosing a metaphorical usage of a term that does not lead to rational contradiction.

Ibn Kathīr (d. 774/1373), a student of Ibn Taymiyya, affirms a similar reading as al-Bukhārī in his exegesis *Tafsīr Ibn Kathīr*, rendering the term *wajh* to mean *dhāt* (essence/entity) rather than face in its literal meaning. ". . . All essences (*dhawāt*) are annihilated, perishing, and passing, except His essence (*dhāt*)."[164]

Ibn Mufliḥ (d. 763/1361), also a student of Ibn Taymiyya, mentions in his book, *al-Ādāb al-sharʿiyya*, that Aḥmad b. Ḥanbal changed his opinion on *kalām* after refraining from it, as is evidenced by his *Radd ʿalā l-zanādiqa wa-l-jahmiyya*, which includes rational arguments.[165] That one could attribute *kalām* to Aḥmad b. Ḥanbal or other Atharīs indicates that *kalām* itself is not a core derivational method of one school to the exclusion of another.

It appears that the Atharīs did not, on the whole, necessarily disapprove of using purely rational arguments or delving into issues not mentioned in the Qurʾān—despite some of their adherents' claims to the contrary. The core issues separating Ashʿarīs from Atharīs, regardless of anti-*kalām* statements from various Atharī scholars, are not, in reality, about the permissibility of the entirety of *kalām*; the examples in the preceding paragraphs of Atharīs arguing theological positions from purely rational premises lend credence to al-Ashʿarī's charge[166]: that while his opponents declared *kalām* impermissible, they often engaged in it themselves. Rather, their core disagreements often revolved around creedal points, which at times were the *result* of *kalām*-based reasoning. In other words, both camps were engaging in *kalām*, but the results of their *kalām*-based reasoning sometimes differed. At other times, their differences were ultimately over the rules of language, as discussed above regarding the definition of the technical term *ẓāhir*.

Al-Bājūrī's discussion of theological hermeneutics and the rational sciences indicates a number of nuances, often ignored by those who focus exclusively on the early stages of Islamic intellectual history. His discussion of a bipartite approach to metaphorical interpretation, when coupled with disagreements over the technical definition of the literal meaning (*ẓāhir*), indicates that few on either side of the debate, or among Western scholars of Islamic theology, have fully realized the heart of the disagreement. His discussion of the two schools of logic, that of the early and later logicians, as well as his discussion of the varying opinions on logic's permissibility, indicate that efforts to declare a preponderance of opposition or support for logic in the pre-modern Muslim world fall short. His discussion of what is commonly called the cosmological proof for God's existence, though rooted in al-Sanūsī's thought, calls our attention to approaches to the discussion that are all but absent in the Western philosophical discourse.

Finally, al-Bājūrī's explicit recognition of legitimate disagreement in theological matters, coupled with his support for the opinion that belief ought not be founded upon following the opinions of others without knowing their (general) proofs (i.e., *taqlīd*), indicates that al-Bājūrī saw each believer as possessing the right to parse the *ijmāʿ–ikhtilāf* spectrum within theology to the best of their ability, and believing what they concluded to be soundest, or to even suspend judgment, as in the case of the difference between existence and entity. Al-Bājūrī's greatest contribution to Ashʿarī theology may have been to frame the discourse within a *taḥqīqī* framework that permits scholars to view multiple possibilities in determining the truth of matters that were not unquestionably established (*qatʿī*). This, in addition to his framing and critiquing each individual topic in his own way.

Al-Bājūrī, as a Shāfiʿī–Ashʿarī–Naqshabandī *muḥaqqiq* in the later traditions of the three core sciences, was an archetypal scholar from a long tradition of scholarly predecessors; yet he differed from other earlier scholars in significant ways. He was a post-Sanūsī Ashʿarī who considered *kalām* and logic (*manṭiq*) to be communally obligatory (*farḍ kifāya*). He was a Shāfiʿī who followed the narrating if not weighing of various opinions (*tarjīḥ*) by Ibn Ḥajar and al-Ramlī, yet still ruled otherwise when the times necessitated that he do so. He was a Sufi of the master–disciple model in the organizational structure of the *ṭarīqa*. While the legal and theological schools, and *ṭarīqa*s had changed along with the times, a connection to the early masters was still sought, and often, I believe, attained.

Through the commentary, explanations, interpretations, judgments, comparisons, and contrasts in his many commentaries, al-Bājūrī joined the communal conversation carried out by the *ʿulamāʾ* over many centuries and across the many lands of the Muslims. One does not form the impression that he saw himself as being outside the tradition, looking back, or reconstructing, but was, rather, firmly planted in it and connected to it. A current Azhar graduate mentioned that, through his education in this tradition, he could easily have entered into a conversation with any of the past masters at any point in history. I believe al-Bājūrī, too, felt that this was the case, and that he was in fact engaged in just such a conversation.

5

Legacy and Conclusion

Al-Bājūrī's Legacy

While al-Bājūrī has not attracted much attention from Western scholars in recent times,[1] there have been occasional references to his legal, theological, and Sufi views. Majid Fakhry, in his *History of Islamic Philosophy*, mentions him briefly in the context of a decline of Islamic theology starting from Fakhr al-Dīn al-Rāzī, ending with al-Bājūrī, and followed by Muḥammad ʿAbduh.[2] J. N. D. Anderson mentions a ruling of al-Bājūrī cited in a legal dispute regarding the permissibility of building a wall that blocks one's neighbors' windows.[3] Suzanne Pinckney Stetkevych quotes extensively from his commentary on al-Busayrī's *Qaṣīda al-Burda* ["Poem of the Mantle"].[4] Frank Griffel mentions al-Bājūrī's views with regard to reason and revelation in his article "The Harmony of Natural Law and Shari'a in Islamist Theology," wherein al-Bājūrī's views are represented as one of the final expressions of the Ashʿarī tradition, which he states was popular until al-Bājūrī's time and waned dramatically after the reformist efforts of Muḥammad ʿAbduh.[5]

The most important recent work I have found thus far on al-Bājūrī is Peter Gran's short essay—buried in a volume of mostly Arabic-language articles on Muḥammad ʿAlī Pasha—entitled "The Quest for a Historical Interpretation of the Life of Shaykh al-Azhar, Ibrāhīm al-Bājūrī." Gran laments the "relative under-development of the study of modern Egyptian cultural history" and attributes the emphasis on nineteenth-century liberals to the exclusion of traditional scholars to the prevalance of the "Oriental Despot"[6] approach to the study of modern Egypt. Although Gran offers an excellent glimpse into al-Bājūrī's Egypt, due to the nature of the volume in which the article appears, it focuses mainly on religion and political power, which is, regrettably, outside the focus of this work. It is an important article, however, as it is a rare expression of appreciation for al-Bājūrī's legal and theological scholarship; one that does not dismiss al-Bājūrī as a mere reporter of past opinions.

Gardet and Anawati rely heavily on al-Bājūrī's *Tuḥfat al-murīd* as a source for the study of Islamic theological doctrines in a number of their works. They devote some attention to al-Sanūsī, al-Laqānī, and al-Bājūrī, indicating the importance of this chain of thinkers, though they view al-Bājūrī's time as one in which "fixed conservatism" reigns, and *kalām* is a purely scholarly matter, rather than being of use to the greater community.

Gilbert Delanoue's *Moralistes et Polotiques Musulmans dans l'Egypt du XIXeme Siecle (1798–1882)* provides excellent information about al-Bājūrī and his teachers, much of which is gleaned from ʿAlī Mubārak's *Khiṭaṭ*. Despite their regard for al-Bājūrī, Delanoue, along with Gardet and Anawati, situate al-Bājūrī in a context of decline, thus detracting from their ability to sufficiently emphasize al-Bājūrī's contributions and strengths.

Most of the works written in European languages produced in the twentieth and twenty-first centuries that address al-Bājūrī usually tend to focus on his prominent role as a nineteenth-century premodern theologian and jurist who explains the long-held orthodox Shāfiʿī and Ashʿarī views. These sources do not study his unique contributions, the subtle expressions of his own views, or the greater implication of his life and thought in Sunnī Islamic intellectual history. A few nineteenth-century Orientalists did treat his life and works in some detail. Eduard Sachau translated various selections from Abū Shujāʿ's *Matn* into German—mostly from later chapters of the traditional chapters of *fiqh* (*abwāb al-fiqh*)—and provides commentary that is largely adapted from al-Bājūrī's gloss on al-Ghazzī's commentary on *Matn Abī Shujāʿ*.[7] Snouck Hurgronje also devotes a good deal of attention to al-Bājūrī and Sachau's interpretation of him in works such as "E. Sachau, Muhammedanishes Recht Nach Schafītishcher Lehre."[8]

Al-Bājūrī warranted a very short entry in the *Encyclopaedia of Islam*,[9] wherein its author lists a number of his works, though some incorrectly.[10] A more substantial entry has been included in the third edition of the *Encyclopaedia of Islam*.[11]

In the Muslim world, al-Bājūrī's works, especially *Tuḥfat al-murīd* and *Ḥāshiya ʿalā sharḥ Ibn al-Qāsim al-Ghazzī ʿalā matn Abī Shujāʿ* continue to be used in major institutions of Muslim learning today, including al-Azhar. His works are still popular in many Indonesian institutions of learning, as well as in Morocco and Syria.[12] Many of his books are in print, in multiple editions. *Tuḥfat al-murīd*, *Ḥāshiya ʿalā sharḥ Ibn al-Qāsim al-Ghazzī*, and *Sharḥ ʿalā l-Burda* are easy to come by, even through online Arabic book sites.

His works have been cited in multiple English translations and commentaries, among them, Nuh Keller's translation of Aḥmad b. Naqib al-Miṣrī's *ʿUmdat al-sālik*, translated as *Reliance of the Traveler*, and Muḥammad Bin Abdur Rahman Ebrahim's translation of the *Shamāʾil* of al-Tirmidhī, which includes a commentary that draws from al-Bājūrī's commentary.[13] Babu Sahib's *Tenets of Islam*, published by a Singapore government agency (Majlis Ugama Islam Singapora), is largely a translation and adaption of al-Bājūrī's *Tuḥfat al-murīd*.[14]

A certain Shaykh ʿAbd al-Hādī Najā al-Abyārī (d. 1888) wrote an abridgment (*mukhtaṣar*) of al-Bājūrī's *Ḥāshiya ʿalā sharḥ Ibn al-Qāsim al-Ghazzī ʿalā matn Abī Shujāʿ*; thus indicating that it was considered an important text in Egyptian Shāfiʿī pedagogy early on.[15] Sachau mentions that in his time, the late nineteenth century, al-Bājūrī's *Ḥāshiya ʿalā sharḥ Ibn al-Qāsim al-Ghazzī ʿalā matn Abī Shujāʿ* was "the dominating book of law in al-Azhar and Egypt" and that it had "also found broad distribution and appreciation outside Egypt and in the entire Mohammedan world . . . ," a rank he believed it rightly deserved.[16] Muḥammad al-Nashshār al-Shirbīnī's gloss on al-Bājūrī's *Risāla*, published in 1900, also indicates that al-Bājūrī's work was incorporated into the Ashʿarī curriculum in Egypt after his death.

As mentioned previously, several of al-Bājūrī's students, including Salīm al-Bishrī, went on to occupy the position of Shaykh al-Azhar, and another of his prominent students, al-Ṭahṭāwī, served in official government positions and is known for his travel to France. The existence of commentaries or abridgments of his works, coupled with the prominent positions of some of his students in government or in educational institutions likely contributed to his continued popularity. The introduction of lithograph and later printing technology in Egypt also may have had an influence on the dissemination of his thought.

I have endeavored to ask a number of students and scholars of Shāfiʿī *fiqh* and Ashʿarī *ʿaqīda* about their perceptions of al-Bājūrī. Those who studied at al-Azhar were all familiar with his works, and spoke very highly of him. Scholars from other parts of the Shāfiʿī world—Brunei, Singapore, Syria, Jordan, and others—had also been exposed to his gloss on Abū Shujāʿ's Shāfiʿī *fiqh* primer. The latter text was taught even recently in a study circle in the al-Azhar mosque, where *ijāza*s were granted by Shaykh ʿImād ʿIfat—known as the martyr of al-Azhar after being shot and killed in a protest in 2011—and by the *muftī* of Egypt, Shaykh ʿAlī Jumʿa, to a number of students from around the world to teach and transmit this book.[17]

Al-Bājūrī's commentary on al-Laqānī's *Jawharat al-tawḥīd* has had an even greater impact, as students from Mālikī- and Ḥanafī-dominated institutions have also had significant exposure to it. Shaykh Adīb Kallās (d. 2011)—a well-known contemporary Syrian scholar who taught al-Bājūrī's *Tuḥfat al-murīd* to his students—referred to al-Bājūrī as "Muḥaqqiq ʿaqīdat Ahl al-Sunna wa-l-Jamāʿa," that is, the verifier of Sunnī creed.[18] Shaykh Nuḥ ʿAlī Salmān (d. 2011), former *muftī* of the Jordanian armed forces, and then *muftī* of Jordan, also taught students al-Bājūrī's *Tuḥfat al-murīd*. Many scholars who studied in Morocco, Syria, Jordan, and Egypt have studied al-Bājūrī's *Tuḥfat al-murīd* with various scholars. It is a text that continues to be used as part of the required curriculum of Sunnī Islamic scholarship.

The former *muftī* of Egypt, Shaykh ʿAlī Jumʿa, has published a critical edition of al-Bājūrī's *Tuḥfat al-murīd*, and teaches and transmits al-Bājūrī's teachings to his students. I have met a number of his students who are familiar with al-Bājūrī and speak highly of his works. Al-Bājūrī's works continue to be transmitted and taught in Egypt and around the world. Other scholars have published critical editions of al-Bājūrī's *Tuḥfat al-murīd*, some with copious footnotes.

Under Khedive Saʿīd's rule (1854–1863), reform-oriented students were under pressure at al-Azhar, while traditional Azharīs had regained prominence.[19] Despite the pro-government tenure of al-ʿAṭṭār under Muḥammad ʿAlī Pasha, al-Azhar steadily maintained its traditional stance, and "quietly resisted" the ebb and flow of the secularizing impetus of the state. Al-Bājūrī was perhaps the last Shaykh al-Azhar to oversee the institution in its centuries-old form, and likely represents the last return to a pre-modern traditional Azharī worldview, that is, more politically independent and rooted in the classical tradition. After his death, secularization and reform swept over Egypt, and traditionally minded Azharīs no longer had the luxury of assuming dominance. Al-Bājūrī was not the last to write a commentary, nor the last Shaykh al-Azhar to adhere to the Gabrielian paradigm, however, in many regards, his impact on the traditional pre-modern discourse, as it has been carried on into modernity, remains unsurpassed among Shāfiʿīs and Ashʿarīs (regardless of *madhhab*). Though ignored by so many Western and Muslim scholars, al-Bājūrī's thought has framed a great deal of legal and theological discourse, primarily through the use of his texts in the training of scholars to this day.

As mentioned previously, I believe that al-Bājūrī provided his students and successors a framework that viewed tradition as a wide road of agreed-upon and debated positions that could be addressed by the informed scholar from within broad yet fixed methodological frameworks.

Conclusion

This work describes the contours and characteristics of a normative model of Sunnī Islamic scholarship that I have termed the "archetypal scholar." The archetypal scholar functioned within a methodological framework whose defining characteristics included a spectrum of views between two points, one point representing total consensus, the other representing the furthest possible bounds of acceptable disagreement that remained within the realm of Sunnī Islam. I have called this spectrum of acceptable views the *ijmāʿ–ikhtilāf* spectrum. The closer a view was to consensus, the more widely accepted it was. The closer a view was to the edge of acceptable disagreement, the more controversial it was.

The defining characteristic of the archetypal model of Sunnī scholarship is the Gabrielian paradigm: *islām* (law), *īmān* (belief), *iḥsān* (Sufism). Within the scope of law, a system developed wherein varying ranks of *mujtahid* scholars exercised different types of *ijtihād,* deriving legal rulings from various points of *uṣūl*. Those incapable of some or all types of *ijtihād* followed the *ijtihād* of those more qualified. The varying ranks of *ijtihād* produced differing ranks of *taqlīd,* ranging from partial to absolute. In all cases, one's authenticity and qualification to exercise the varying levels of *ijtihād* was based on one's command of the primary texts and the sciences associated with them, as confirmed by a teacher who granted an *ijāza* confirming one's understanding or fitness to teach.

In the realm of belief, two currents emerged within the *ijmāʿ–ikhtilāf* spectrum, one was generally distrustful of incorporating certain rational sciences into the science of determining proper beliefs, and the other was generally more accepting. In each current, there were levels of agreement and disagreement over the rational sciences. Within the three schools that evolved within Sunnī Islam, Ashʿarī, Māturīdī, and Atharī, numerous stances in relation to the rational sciences were taken, to the extent that none of the three could be claimed as wholly free of, or accepting of them. Beyond the issue of rationalism, the grammatical issue of the nature of words, and how this relates to the attributes of Allah and the Qurʾān produced the greatest gulf between the Atharīs and the Ashʿarīs (and Māturīdīs). While there were accusations of heresy and even disbelief, there were also significant ecumenical voices that viewed all three schools as being within the folds of Sunnīsm. The existence of intra-affiliational disagreement on these key issues of rationalism and interpretation, as well as the existence of inter-affiliational agreement, demonstrates that it is inappropriate for scholars in the Western academy to label one of these three Sunnī schools as representative of "orthodoxy" and exclude another.

Regarding the realm of the spiritual, mystical experience of faith, the experiential states and character traits of Sufism formed the third component in the triad of the Gabrielian paradigm. There was general agreement on the goals of Sufism—achieving most of the Sufi states and traits—however, disagreement arose over the methods used to achieve these goals, and the expressions and terms used to describe Sufi experiences, or stated while experiencing certain states. Consensus was not reached on the definitions of *waḥdat al-wujūd,* the case of al-Ḥallāj or Ibn al-ʿArabī, or the permissibility of music and dance or other practices used to express or induce the desired Sufi states.

The difference of opinion that existed within the three core components of the Gabrielian paradigm indicates that pre-modern Sunnī Islam was a wide road that defies simple categorization and description. Sunnī Islam was not a static phenomenon, nor merely the narrowly defined "traditionalist" approach of a handful of fifth/eleventh-century Baghdadī scholars. One cannot speak in terms of a single *uṣūl al-fiqh* being representative of "orthodoxy" while "rationalist" approaches to *uṣūl al-fiqh* were heterodox. Nor is it appropriate to label Sufism a separate sect in conflict with the "orthodox," or define all uses of the term *waḥdat al-wujūd* as pantheism. It is inaccurate to claim that philosophy received a death blow followed by steady intellectual decline. Similarly, one cannot say that *ʿilm al-kalām* was the sole defining characteristic of Ashʿarī thought. These overly narrow essentialist and reductive theories or descriptions of Sunnīsm in whole or in its multifaceted parts are simply incorrect.

Rather, it is more useful to describe varying views of individual phenomena within Sunnīsm, situate them in the broader continuum of scholarship and practice, and search for a variety of views across geographical and chronological boundaries. There are manuscript libraries filled with unexamined texts, entire disciplines that have been ignored until recently (such as post seventh/ thirteenth-century *manṭiq*), and centuries of tradition utterly neglected because of an excessive emphasis on the study of the origins of a phenomenon.

I have focused on a particular figure in the continuum of Sunnī intellectual history, namely Ibrāhīm al-Bājūrī, for a number of reasons. First, he was a jurist, a theologian, and a mystic who wrote on *fiqh*, *ʿaqīda*, and *taṣawwūf*, as well as subjects from the trivium, such as rhetoric and logic. He represents a later development in the Shāfiʿī school, from the post-Ibn Ḥajar and al-Ramlī era, and in the Ashʿarī school, from the post-Sanūsī era. While these developments within both the Shāfiʿī and Ashʿarī schools produced highly sophisticated and involved systems that differed from the earlier manifestations of these schools in many ways, they were also, I believe, connected to the thought and works of the early masters both in core methodology and outcome. Likewise, al-Bājūrī's Sufism was informed by developments after the formation of the *ṭarīqa*s, yet connections to the early masters are certainly to be found.

Thus, in al-Bājūrī one finds the general model of the archetypal Sunnī scholar, but also a more specific manifestation of the archetypal scholar in later Islamic scholarship, a manifestation that sheds light on earlier scholarship. Al-Bājūrī was involved in processing and interpreting more than a millennium of accumulated data that had been transmitted to him. Unlike the early scholars and founders of the various legal, theological, and Sufi schools, al-Bājūrī and his contemporaries had more data to sift through. With new times came new issues and ideas which demanded *ijtihād*, *taḥqīq*, and interpretation.

But old issues, those that had been discussed in previous generations, also demanded attention. When one studies Shāfiʿī *fiqh*, for example, one is struck by the degree to which later scholars, such Ibn Ḥajar and al-Ramlī, continued to debate and research even the minutest details of ritual purity. In terms of the variety of views among Ashʿarī scholars regarding the cosmological argument for the existence of God, the nature of attributes, the utility and permissibility of *manṭiq*, and the details of the theory of *kasb* (human acquisition of the acts Allah creates), one is exposed to multiple layers of subtle thought and ingenuity that perhaps might not be seen in some of the earlier works of theology.

Al-Bājūrī the jurist informs us that *ijtihād* in its technical and general linguistic sense did not end altogether, but rather varying levels of *ijtihād* remained. In addition to these varying levels of *ijtihād*, the individual also had recourse to rulings from other *madhhab*s, even defunct *madhhab*s, though judges were limited to the four remaining schools in issuing *fatwā*s and forming laws. While I have the sense that there is a point or result of Shāfiʿī methodology that promotes borrowing from stronger opinions across the *madhhab*s—rather than taking dispensations from the pool of weaker opinions within the Shāfiʿī *madhhab*s—other *madhhab*s, such as the Mālikī school, appear to promote a more vertical approach, that of delving into the pool of weaker opinions within the *madhhab* before resorting to dispensations from other *madhhab*s. In any case, these points of later *fiqh* methodology lead to diverse possibilities of thought and practice, rather than some narrower presentations of later Sunnī legal practice.

Al-Bājūrī the theologian tells us that *kalām* was considered a communal obligation in his day, as was its supporting science of *manṭiq*. The study of *manṭiq* and *kalām* were part of the pedagogy and curriculum of eighteenth- and nineteenth-century scholars from Cairo to Timbuktu, from the Maghrib to Java. This was not a recent development, rather it had been the case for many centuries prior to al-Bājūrī, from the eras of al-Sanūsī and al-Suyūṭī and arguably before. The proofs and methods of Ashʿarī thought changed and evolved, and disagreements on secondary and tertiary issues were accepted and normal, though the Ashʿarī school was integral to education in North Africa and elsewhere for many centuries prior to al-Bājūrī.

Al-Bājūrī the Sufi further demonstrates the centrality of Sufism in the overall production of the top scholars of Islam. While there were those who objected to certain aspects of Sufism early on, even to the term itself, on the whole, I think it safe to label the study of Sufism[20] a necessary condition—albeit insufficient in and of itself—of pre-modern Sunnī scholarship.

While the work of Massignon and Lings began the effort of determining the Qurʾānic and Sunnaic roots of Sufism, and others followed suit, more work, I believe, is necessary to further judge the multitude of practices and varying controversial sayings found in the centuries of Sufi practice. Nonetheless, al-Bājūrī, and his predecessors in the continuum of archetypal scholars present a potential mechanism for incorporating foreign or new practices (and potentially ideas) into the method of Sufism, namely the division of innovation (*bidʿa*) into necessary, recommended, neutral, disliked, and prohibited, in keeping with the division of *fiqh* rulings.

Al-Bājūrī, like his predecessors, debated the validity of certain legal and metaphysical, ecstatic, metaphorical, or technical data in Sufism, but he recognized the validity of this debate, and offered his own voice to the discussion. Most importantly, to my mind, is his emphasis on the master–disciple relationship; he believed that the mere observance of the gnostic (*ʿārif*) is more educational and useful than a thousand sermons.

The master–disciple relationship was the ideal context for the transmission of Sufi states and traits, as well as Qurʾānic recitation, legal rulings and methodology, theological teachings, and almost every other science. While some scholars learned disciplines from books alone, this came after substantial training in the master–disciple method. From the master, the disciple received his authorization, and later granted it to his students. Likewise the master had been granted his authorization from his teacher, who had received his authorization from his teacher, who was connected in a chain of authorized transmission back through the generations.

The authorized transmission of knowledge, states, and traits, from master to disciple in the three core sciences is another essential component of Sunnī methodology which al-Bājūrī fully embraced and exemplified. In each core science, authenticity in transmission and understanding was sought, as was certainty, though apart from the key areas of consensus, levels of uncertainty were accepted as inevitable because of the nature of language and the transmission of knowledge.

Al-Bājūrī parsed the *ijmāʿ–ikhtilāf* spectrum, and ruled by or narrated what he deemed correct. He emerges as his own man, in the details, even if standing on the shoulders of giants of the past. His works indicate a familiarity with variant views, and an acceptance of certain disagreements as an acceptable aspect of law, theology, and Sufism. He was the Shaykh al-Azhar, and given the title Shaykh al-Islam under Muḥammad ʿAlī Pasha. He was an authoritative voice in nineteenth-century Sunnī Islam, and continues to be to the present day. He did not merely regurgitate the ideas of those who came before him, rather he delved deeply into a multitude of subjects, offered his own views, and applied these ideas to his life.[21] He lived by the Gabrielian paradigm, and imparted its ideas, practices, and realities to his students.

His life in the context of the continuum of previous archetypal scholars teases out details of Sunnī Islam that should not be ignored; details that may help us to better understand the origins of the phenomenon of Shāfiʿī, Ashʿarī, or Naqshabandī thought and practice, as well as the thought and practice of other legal, theological, and Sufi schools. Rather than trying to apply grand theories or definitions to Sunnī law, theology, and Sufism and all its developments and manifestations, I believe a much greater effort and undertaking is called for in both the Western academy and in modern Muslim scholarship. A much more detailed and careful study of the many geographic and chronological manifestations of these Sunnī schools, practices, and ideas must be undertaken. I believe this undertaking has only just begun, and will require generations of effort as additional manuscripts and critical editions come to light. It will take humility in explanation, patience in collecting and interpreting data, and perseverance in a multi-generational effort. These are qualities that we can learn from al-Bājūrī; certainly it is an effort that al-Bājūrī, his contemporaries, predecessors, and descendants engaged in, and their insight into earlier generations of Sunnī practice is well worth hearing.

Notes

Introduction

1. The terms "mystical" and "mysticism" are potentially problematic terms, due to their multiple connotations, many of which are antithetical to their use in this work. Throughout this text, mysticism is used in the sense of being a discipline or approach to religious practice, the end goal of which is to cultivate experiences of the soul that transcend (without contradicting) physical and rational experience.

2. The exact nature of his affiliation with the Naqshbandī order is not entirely clear. His shaykh in Sufism was Abū Ḥurayba al-Naqshbandī l-Shintināwī, who had affiliations with the Shādhilī, Khalwatī, Qādirī, Rifāʿī, and Khatmī orders. Whether or not Abū Ḥurabya trained disciples according to one method, or an amalgam of methods is not known to me. Al-Bājūrī shows familiarity with multiple orders in his writings, and was certainly exposed to them in his administrative life. Based on Abū Hurayba being referred to as "al-Naqshbandī," and reports from modern scholars of al-Azhar that his *tarbiyya* (Sufi instruction) was according the Naqshbandī way, I have opted to refer to al-Bājūrī as a follower of the Naqshbandī order, despite the possibility that his training may have entailed exposure to multiple orders.

3. A number of articles and books arguing against the traditional narrative of decline continue to be published. Among those that have informed my work are: Khaled el-Rouayheb, "Opening the Gate of Verification: The Forgotten Arab-Islamic Florescence of the Seventeenth Century," *International Journal of Middle East Studies* 38, no. 2 (May 2006): 263–281. Also see A. I. Sabra, "Situating the Arabic Sciences: Locality Verses Essence," *Isis* 87 (1996): 654–70. Also Robert Wisnovsky, "Avicenna and the Avicennian Tradition," in *The Cambridge Companion to Arabic Philosophy*, ed. Peter Adamson and Richard C. Taylor, 92–136 (New York: Cambridge University Press, 2005), 113.

4. Robert Wisnovsky, "Avicenna and the Avicennian Tradition," in *The Cambridge Companion to Arabic Philosophy*, ed. Peter Adamson and Richard C. Taylor, 92–136 (New York: Cambridge University Press, 2005), 113.

5. Ibid.

6. Ibid. According to Wisnovsky, many supporters of the theory of decline failed to notice the channeling of Ibn Sīnā's thought into the science of *kalām*.

7. I am indebted to Dr. Timothy Winters for this notion, which he mentioned in a speech at MIT in 2007–8. This inability to comprehend some of the complex principles and terms is not just limited to orientalist scholars of Islam, but also to many within the Islamic tradition as well.

Chapter 1

1. Much of the biographical information in this section, unless otherwise noted, is based on ʿAlī Jumʿa's biographical notice on al-Bājūrī in his edition of *Tuḥfat al-murīd*: Ibrāhīm al-Bājūrī, *Tuḥfat al-murīd ʿalā jawharat al-tawḥīd*, critical edition by ʿAlī Muḥammad Jumʿa (Cairo: Dār al-Salām, 2006). Note that this is the edition referred to throughout this work (shortened form *Tuḥfat al-murīd*), with one exception, which is noted at its occurrence. Jumʿa was, until recently, the Grand Mufti of Egypt, and narrates a short *isnād* (chain of narration) containing few men between himself and al-Bājūrī.

2. ʿAlī Mubārak, *al-Khiṭaṭ al-Tawfīqiyya al-jadīda li-Miṣr al-Qāhira wa-muduniha wa-bilādihā al-qadīma wa-shahīra* (Cairo: Maṭbaʿat Dār al-Kutub, 1969), 9:2.

3. Ibid.

4. The sayings, deeds, and tacit approvals of the Prophet Muḥammad.

5. Timothy Mitchell, *Colonising Egypt* (New York: Cambridge University Press, 1988), 83.

6. Ibid., 133. Also, for the social implications of blindness in late nineteenth-and early twentieth-century Egyptian society and education, see Fedwa Malti-Douglas, *Blindness and Autobiography: Al-Ayyam of Ṭaha Ḥusayn* (Princeton University Press, 1988).

7. A city in northern Egypt.

8. E. M. Sartain, *Jalāl al-Dīn al-Suyūṭī: Biography and Background* (Cambridge and New York: Cambridge University Press, 1975), 29, 38.

9. Those works of al-Faḍālī upon which al-Bājūrī commented are listed below in al-Bājūrī's list of works.

10. Aḥmad b. ʿAlī Maqrīzī, *al-Mawāʿiẓ wa-l-iʿtibār fī dhikr al-khiṭaṭ wa-l-āthār* (London: Muʿassasat al-Furqān li-l-Turāth al-Islāmī, 2002), 4:48–50. (Known as *al-Khiṭaṭ al-Maqrīziyya.*)

11. Daniel Newman, *An Imam in Paris: Al-Tahtawi's Visit to France (1826–31)* (London: Saqi Books, 2009).

12. Arthur Goldschmidt, *Biographical Dictionary of Modern Egypt* (Boulder, CO: Lynne Rienner Publishers, 2000), 33.

13. David Dean Commins, *The Wahhabi mission and Saudi Arabia.* (London: I. B. Tauris, 2006), 210.

14. ʿAbd al-Raḥmān b. ʿAbd al-Laṭīf b. ʿAbdullah Āl al-Shaykh, *Mashāhir al-ʿulamāʾ najd wa ghayrihā* (Riyadh: Dār al-Yamāmah lil-Baḥth wa-al-Tarjamah wa-al-Nashr, 1974), 79–80.

15. Gilbert Delanoue, *Moralistes et politiques musulmans dans l'Egypte du XIXe siècle (1798–1882)* (Cairo: Institut français d'archéologie orientale du Caire, 1982), 99–100. However, al-Ṣāwī did criticize them in his commentary on *Tafsīr al-Jalālayn.*

16. I have thus far been able to obtain copies of several of these *ijāza*s. They are often included in a larger collection of *ijāza*s from various scholars, sometimes from different centuries. I am deeply indebted to Najah Nady and Sara Omar for obtaining these and other manuscripts of al-Bājūrī's from various libraries in Egypt.

17. R. S. Fahey, *Enigmatic Saint: Ahmad ibn Idris and the Idrisi Tradition* (Evanston, IL: Northwestern University Press, 1990), 167.

18. This poem being delivered on the occasion of al-Bājūrī's ascension to the seat of Shaykh al-Azhar, the implication of the ever rotating dynastic powers (*dawlah*) and the drawn sword of merit being that he had struggled his way to the top.

19. I read this to mean: Give the office of Shaykh al-Azhar to al-Bājūrī, because he deserves the position, as there has already been too much controversy over previous appointments or potential rival candidates.

20. Aside from the more obvious metaphor, I understand this to refer to the poem's desire to be understood by the listener.

21. Peter Gran, *Islamic Roots of Capitalism: Egypt 1760–1840* (Austin: University of Texas Press, 1979), 118. The translation of this agreement can be found in F. de Jong, *(Austin: University of Texas Press, 1979), 118. The translation of this agreement can be foizational Dimensions of Islamic Mysticism* (Leiden: Brill, 1978), 194–195.

22. al-Dhahabī, *al-Tafsīr*, 1:294. Quoted from Mohammed Zakyi Ibrahim, "Communication Models in the Holy Qur'an: God-Human Interaction" (PhD diss., McGill University, Montreal, 1997).

23. ʿAbd al-Razzāq Bayṭār and Muḥammad Bahjat Bayṭār, *Ḥilyat al-bashar fī tārīkh al-qarn al-thālith ʿashar* (Beirut: Majmaʿ al-Lugha al-ʿArabiyya, 1993; repr. of 1961), 10.

24. Peter Gran, "Quest for a Historical Interpretation of the Life of Shaykh al-Azhar Ibrahim al-Bajuri (1784–1860)—an Agenda Article," *Islāh am taḥdith Miṣr fī ʿasr Muḥammad ʿAlī* (Cairo: al-Majlis al-Aʿla, 1999), 62.

25. Mitchell, *Colonising Egypt*, 85.

26. Gran, "Quest," 66cf.

27. See Peter Gran, "Rediscovering al-Attar," *Al-Ahram Weekly Online*, no. 770 (24–30 November 2005), for a discussion of the limitations of the *nahda* paradigm in explaining nineteenth-century Egyptian culture and thought. Online: <http://weekly.ahram.org.eg/2005/770/cu4.htm> [May 30, 2012].

28. Ibid.

29. Gran, "Quest," 61.

30. Ibid.

31. *Tuḥfat al-murīd*, 41.

32. Mitchell, *Colonising Egypt*, 103.

33. Ibid., 102.

34. *Ḥāshiya*, 1:25.

35. Ibrāhīm b. Muḥammad al-Barmāwī (d. 1694), *Ḥāshiya Ibrāhīm al-Barmāwī al-Shāfiʿī ʿalā Sharḥ al-Ghāya li-Ibn Qāsim Ghazzī* (Cairo: al-Maṭbaʿa al-ʿĀmira, 1287/1870), 12

36. Ehud R. Toledano, *State and Society in mid-Nineteenth Century Egypt* (New York: Cambridge University Press, 1990), 19.

37. This assessment is supported by Gran's as well. Gran, "Quest," 62.

38. C. Snouck Hurgronje, "E Sachau: Muhammedanisches Recht nach schafiitischer Lehre," in *Verspreide Geschriften van C. Snouck Hurgronje*, vol. 2 (Bonn und Leipzig: Kurt Schroeder, 1923–27), 417–18.

39. As discussed below, others have placed his death in the year 1860, and even 1865.

40. Ibid.

41. Gran, "Quest," 63. Kenneth M. Cuno and Aaron Spevack, "al-Bājūrī, Ibrāhīm b. Muḥammad," *EI*[3].

42. Toledano, *State and Society*, 181.

43. Ibid.

44. Ibid.

45. Mitchell, *Colonising Egypt*, 85.

46. ʿAlī Mubārak, *al-Khiṭaṭ al-Tawfīqiyya al-jadīda li-Miṣr al-Qāhira wa-muduniha wa-bilādihā al-qadīma wa-shahīra* (Cairo: Maṭbaʿat Dār al-Kutub, 1969), 4:40; and Indira Falk Gesink, *Islamic Reform and Conservatism: Al-Azhar and the Evolution of Modern Sunni Islam* (London: Tauris Academic Studies, 2010), 42.

47. Gran, *Islamic Roots of Capitalism*, 118. Also, Gran, "Rediscovering al-Attar."

48. ʿAbd al-Raḥim, "Bājūrī, Shaykh Ibrahim, al- *Coptic Encyclopedia*, vol. 2. Online: <http://ccdl.libraries.claremont.edu/cdm4/item_viewer.php?CISOROOT=/cce&CISOPTR=298> [May 30, 2012].

49. ʿAbd al-Razzaq al-Bayron *SḤ ʿAbd aal-bashar fī tārīkh al-qarn al-thālith ʿashar* (Damascus, 1961–63), 1:7; al-Maqrīzī, *al-Khiaqrīzī, 61–63), 1*, 9:3–4.

50. This anecdote was related to me by Najah Nady from her teacher, Shaykh Imad ʿIfat. I mention it here not as historical fact—as such a claim, without further proof, is inadmissible by both Western academic and traditional Islamic scholarly standards—but rather to demonstrate that al-Bājūrī's legacy is a living and multifaceted subject amongst Azharīs today.

51. ʿAbdallāh b. Aḥmad Bā Sūdān, *Zaytūnat al-ilqāḥ: Sharḥ manẓūmat Ḍawʾ al-miṣbāḥ fī aḥkām al-nikāḥ* (Jedda: Dār al-Minhāj, 2002), 29.

52. A *muftī* is one who can give authoritative religious rulings.

53. He does not, however, include the *Ḥāshiya* on the *Shamāʾil* of al-Tirmidhī in the list, but references it in a footnote (*Tuḥfat al-murīd*, 11).

54. Though his works on *kalām* and *manṭiq* were refutations.

55. *Tuḥfat al-murīd*, 10–11.

56. Shaykh ʿAlī Jumʿa notes that this has been published with a commentary by Shaykh Muḥammad al-Nashshār al-Shirbīnī under the name *Khalāṣat al-tuḥfa al-saniyya ʿalā l-risālat al-Bājūriyya* (Egypt: Maṭbaʿat Muḥammad Muṣṭafā, 1318/1900).

57. Jum'a does not include this in his list of works, yet he refers to a copy that he says contains the earliest biography of al-Bājūrī. The date of completion for the *Sharḥ al-shamā'il* is found in this copy, which appears to be Jum'a's source for the first half of the biographical information he includes in his edition. See al-Bājūrī, *Ḥāshiya Ibrāhīm al-Bājūrī l-musammā bi-l-mawāhib al-laduniyya 'alā l-shamā'il al-Muḥammadiyya* (Egypt: al-Maṭba'at al-Baḥiyya, 1883).

58. al-Bājūrī, *al-Musalsalat*, manuscript in Dār al-Kutub al-Miṣriyya (Cairo), catalog no. 252, *muṣṭalaḥ ḥadīth*.

59. Al-Bājūrī commented up to the end of the author's introduction.

60. Al-Bājūrī completed over two hundred pages of commentary on this work.

61. Al-Bājūrī commented up to the chapter on the funeral prayer. From potentially as early as the second/eighth century, the chapters of books of *fiqh* have followed a common order, beginning with purification and prayer and other matters of worship, moving on to matters of commerce, social dealings, politics, and so on.

62. Abdullah Muḥammad al-Ḥibshī, *Jāmi' al-shurūḥ wa-l-ḥawāshī: mu'jam shāmil li-asmā' al-kutub al-mashrūḥa fī l-turāth al-islāmii wa-bayān shurūḥiha*. 3 vols. (Abu Dhabi: Abu Dhabi Authority for Culture and Heritage Cultural Foundation, 2004), 636.

63. Abū Madyan is mentioned in *Tuḥfat al-murīd*, 201.

64. M. H. Abd al-Raziq, "Arabic Literature Since the Beginning of the Nineteenth Century," *BSOAS* 2, no. 4 (1923), 758. This is evidenced by the numerous commentaries on these texts, however, in the absence of lists of curriculum, Abd al-Raziq's statement may need additional verification. Nonetheless, I tend to accept it as likely.

65. Ibid.

66. Gran, "Quest," 62.

67. al-Bājūrī, *Ḥāshiya al-Shaykh Ibrāhīm al-Bājūrī 'alā Sharḥ al-'Alāma Ibn al-Qāsim al-Ghazzī 'alā Matn al-Shaykh Abī Shujā'* (Beirut: Dār al-Kutub al-'Ilmiyya, 1999), 2. Hereafter referred to as *Matn Abī Shujā'*.

68. *Tuḥfat al-murīd*, 21.

69. Aḥmad b. Muḥammad al-Ṣāwī, *Ḥāshiya al-Ṣāwī 'alā Jawharat al-tawḥīd fī 'ilm al-kalām* (Beirut: Dār al-Kutub al-'Ilmiyya, 2010).

70. *Tuḥfat al-murīd*, 218.

71. See section on al-Bājūrī and *ijtihād*.

72. al-Barmāwī, *Ḥāshiya Ibrāhīm al-Barmāwī*, 337.

73. al-Bājūrī, *Matn Abī Shujā'*, 32–35.

74. See chapter 4 for more details on al-Bājūrī's views on this passage.

75. Ibid (section on al-Bājūrī and *ijtihād*). al-Barmāwī, *Ḥāshiya Ibrāhīm al-Barmāwī*, 8.

76. That is, he mentions when it is forbidden, disliked, neutral, recommended, or obligatory to mention it.

77. The *'aqīqa* refers to the ritual animal sacrifice on the seventh day after the birth of a child.

78. al-Barmāwī, *Ḥāshiya Ibrāhīm al-Barmāwī*, 335–36.

79. See al-Bājūrī, *Matn Abī Shujāʿ*, 568.

80. Ḥasan b. Darwīsh Quwaysinī, *Sharḥ naẓm al-Sullam al-munawraq fī l-manṭiq li-ʿAbd al-Raḥmān al-Akhḍarī* (al-Dār al-Bayḍāʾ: Dār al-Rashād al-Ḥadītha, 2006), 14.

81. Delanoue, *Moralistes et politiques musulmans*, 112 (unpublished translation by Gabrielle Lochard).

82. Usually done in *taqrīr* commentaries but also in the context of the *ḥāshiya* commentaries. For a distinction between *sharḥ*, *ḥāshiya*, and *taqrīr*, see Abd al-Raziq, "Arabic Literature," 758.

83. *Tuḥfat al-murīd*, 12.

84. I am indebted to Kenneth M. Cuno for bringing this point to my attention.

85. This is not to say that we cannot speak of a decline in any aspect of Islamic thought, rather, it is an objection to claiming that all Islamic thought—legal, theological, Sufi, and otherwise—declined absolutely.

Chapter 2

1. The science of properly reciting the Qurʾān.

2. Maḥmūd al-Ṭaḥḥān, professor of *ḥadīth* at the University of Kuwait, mentions five types of *ijāzas*, each being of different weight. Some are simply *ijāzas* of *baraka* (blessings)—such as granting the general masses permission to relate whatever one has related—others are full confirmation of one's understanding of a given subject or text. Maḥmūd al-Ṭaḥḥān, *Taysīr muṣṭlaḥ al-ḥadīth* (Riyadh: Maktabat al-Maʿārif, n.d.), 160–61.

3. *Ḥāshiya Taḥqīq al-maqām*, 2. *Ḥāshiya Risālat al-Faḍālī fī Lā ilāha illa-Llāh*, 2.

4. The manuscript can be found in Dār al-Kutub al-Miṣriyya (Cairo), catalog no. 511, *muṣṭalaḥ ḥadīth*, 6.

5. al-Bājūrī, *al-Musalsalat*.

6. Scholars divide the levels of *ijtihād* into a number of classes. Some divide them into three classes, as al-Bājūrī does; others divide them into four or five classes. See Chapter 4 for a detailed discussion of this issue.

7. For ʿIlīsh's views, see Indira Falk Gesink "'Chaos on the Earth': Subjective Truths versus Communal Unity in Islamic Law and the Rise of Militant Islam," *American Historical Review* 108, no. 3 (June 2003). Online: <http://www.historycooperative.org/journal/ahr/108.3/gesink.html#REF15> [Jan. 13, 2008].

8. Category 1: those who practice *kalām*, and either practice *taʾwīl* or *tafwīḍ*. Category 2: those who do not practice *kalām*, and either practice *tafwīḍ* or affirm the literal meaning without modality (*ẓāhir bi lā takyīf*).

9. The term "spiritual" can have multiple connotations in Western discourse. Throughout this work, it refers to the inward, nonrational aspect

of religious experience. The Arabic term, *ruḥānī* seems more appropriate, meaning that which pertains to the experience of the soul as opposed to the intellect and limbs.

10. Mitchell, *Colonising Egypt*, 83.

11. Examples include Ibn Juzay al-Kalbī, *al-Qawānīn al-fiqhiyya* (ʿAyn Malīla, Algeria: Dār al-Hudā, 2000), a work of comparative *fiqh* from a Mālikī perspective; Ibn ʿĀshir, *al-Murshid al-muʿīn* (Casablanca: Dār al-Furqān li-l-Nashr al-Ḥadīth, 2002); and al-Nawawī, *al-Maqasid: Nawawi's Manual of Islam*, trans. Nuh Ha Mim Keller (Beltsville, MD: Amana Publications, 2002).

12. al-Bājūrī, *Durar al-ḥisān*. Online: <http://makhtota.ksu.edu.sa/makhtota/339/5> [May 30, 2012].

13. Al-Bājūrī's discussion of the definition of *fiqh* given here is substantially more involved, venturing into matters of logic, epistemology, and rational theology. He affirms the definition above, as it is stated in the commentary of al-Ghazzī, and expands on it in his super-commentary, *Matn Abī Shujāʾ*, 1.

14. For example, the setting of the sun is the cause of making the evening prayer an obligation at that time. Without the occurrence of the setting of the sun, the evening prayer cannot be prayed and would not be valid.

15. Having done one's ablutions is a condition for one's ritual prayer being counted as valid (*ṣaḥīḥ*, as above) without which the prayer would be invalid (*fāsid*, as above).

16. A woman's menses is a preventative for her to offering the ritual prayers, as her prayers are not valid until her menses passes.

17. *Tuḥfat al-murīd*, 66.

18. Regarding the pseudo-controversy of the origins of the *madhhabs* raised by some Western scholars, these are primarily based on disagreements over definitions of the *madhhab*. I see no reason not to declare a *madhhab*, at base, to be a method of deriving legal rulings based on the core methodology of a *mujtahid* (one possessing the qualifications to independently derive legal rulings from the primary sources). Whether or not this method was explicitly stated, as in al-Shāfiʿī's case, or explained by the students of a given *mujtahid*, as in Mālik's *madhhab*, is not a necessary condition for someone to be declared a founder.

19. Islamicists are those in the Western academy who study Islam. It does not have the same associations as the term Orientalist, and can include scholars of various different persuasions. It is also not to be confused with "Islamists," a term which refers to followers of various contemporary political movements.

20. Neither Schacht's or Melchert's definition of a *madhhab* allows Abū Ḥanīfa or Mālik to be the eponymous founders of their *madhhabs*, however Schacht may have accepted that Shāfiʿī founded his school, and both Schacht and Coulson accepted that Aḥmad b. Ḥanbal was the founder of his *madhhab*. Melchert rejects all four scholars as the founders of their schools. See Christopher Melchert, *The Formation of the Sunnī Schools of Law, 9th–10th centuries C.E.* (Leiden and New York: Brill, 1997); Schacht, *An Introduction to Islamic*

Law (Oxford: Clarendon Press, 1982); and Noel J. Coulson, *A History of Islamic Law* (Edinburgh: Edinburgh University Press, 1971).

21. One can refer to Muḥammad Saʿīd al-Būṭī, *al-Lāmadhhabiyya: Akhṭar bidʿa tuhaddidu al-sharīʿa al-Islāmiyya* (Damascus: Maktabat al-Fārābī, 1985), or Tahir al-Alwani, *Source Methodology in Islamic Jurisprudence: Usul al-fiqh al Islami*, trans. Yusuf Talal DeLorenzo and A. S. al-Shaykh-ʿAlī (Herndon, VA: International Institute of Islamic Thought, 1994) for a contemporary Shāfiʿī–Ashʿarī perspective on the origins of Islamic law. See Nuh Keller, *Reliance of the Traveller* (trans. of *ʿUmdat al-sālik wa ʿuddat al-nāsik*, by Aḥmad b. al-Nāqib al-Miṣrī) (Evanston, IL: Sunna Books, 1991; 1994), 19–20, for a translation of selections from al-Būṭī's work.

22. *Tuḥfat al-murīd*, 247.

23. This being the highest rank in *ḥadīth* scholarship, a rank also attributed to Imam Mālik.

24. *Tuḥfat al-murīd*, 247–48.

25. See al-Bājūrī's commentary on al-Sanūsī's *Umm al-barāhīn*, 71–75. *Ḥāshiya al-Bājūrī*, lithographed copy at Harvard Widener Library, catalog number 2274.823.568.1861.

26. *Tasdīq* implies belief, faith, assent, and actively confirming and agreeing with something.

27. Or, "assent to everything that the Prophet brought."

28. al-Bājūrī, *Durar al-ḥisān*.

29. *Uṣūl al-dīn* translates to foundations of religion, but is commonly understood and used throughout this text as "theology." *ʿAqīda* literally means creed, but may be used as the "science of *ʿaqīda*," which means theology in the same sense as *uṣūl al-dīn*. In other words, *uṣūl al-dīn* and *ʿaqīda* are often used interchangeably.

30. That is, a Shāfiʿī among Shāfiʿī–Ashʿarīs would need to actively claim not to be from among them, or clearly disavow core Ashʿarī views in order to be considered otherwise.

31. See Harry A. Wolfson, *The Philosophy of the Kalam* (Cambridge, MA: Harvard University Press, 1976), ix.

32. According to the traditional narrative, the Muʿtazilīs were an early sect of Islam that appeared in the first/seventh century. One of their key positions was that Allah did not possess attributes (i.e., will, power, knowledge). Additionally, they claimed that the Qurʾān was created, rather than being the eternal word of Allah. They also metaphorically interpreted (*taʾwīl*) the Qurʾānic descriptions of heaven, hell, and the Day of Judgment. As for their legal affiliations, there were Sunnī jurists from the Shāfiʿī and al-Ḥanafī schools that adhered to Muʿtazilī doctrine, thus blurring the distinction between Sunnī and Muʿtazilī for some. Indeed some Shīʿīs adopted Muʿtazilī views, as did some Jews. Therefore, the traditional narrative that al-Bājūrī and many in the Western academy still accept reflects a later conception of the boundaries Sunnī thought, and may not effectively address the ambiguities of the early development of Islamic theology. Nonetheless,

I use the terms Sunnī and Muʿtazilī in this later sense of being doctrinally distinct, as the primary concern here is to understand al-Bājūrī's conception of Islamic intellectual history.

33. *Tuḥfat al-Murīd*, 160.

34. Ibid.

35. Ibid., 160–61. Regardless of the authenticity of this story, it shows the great respect that scholars had for each other, despite their differences.

36. For more on the historical spread of Ashʿarī thought, see Martin Nguyen, "The Confluence and Construction of Traditions: Al-Qushayrī (d. 465/1072) and the Intersection of Qurʾānic Exegesis, Theology, and Sufism" (PhD diss., Harvard University, 2009).

37. *Tuḥfat al-Murīd*, 40.

38. The term Atharīs is derived from *athar* (pl. *āthār*), which implies transmitted content (rather than rationally derived content).

39. Early Western scholars such as McCarthy, Gibb, Goldziher, and Elder accepted the Ashʿarī/Māturīdī dominance that was apparent into the early twentieth century and even later in many *madrasa*s across the Muslim world. Other Western scholars whose research focused on Ḥanbalism—such as George Makdisi—often reflected the tone and views of the works to whose study they devoted themselves. Makdisi's work on Ashʿarī thought and "traditionalism," which in this work is referred to as Atharism, has reclaimed some important ground for Atharīs, yet has overstated its historical importance and erroneously made it the sole standard bearer of orthodoxy.

40. Such as al-Dhahabī and Ibn Kathīr, both Shāfiʿīs.

41. Frank notes that the relationship between the later followers and the founder is often complex, at least in certain issues, however the connection is far from tenuous. R. M. Frank, *Being and their Attributes: The Teaching of the Basrian School of Mu'tazila in the Classical Period* (Albany: State University of New York Press, 1978), 7n3.

42. Eventually Sufism (*taṣawwūf*) came to refer to similar phenomena which may have been known by other names (or, in some cases, remained nameless). Sufism in this text is used to comprehensively include mystical practices that were considered acceptable to some if not all jurists. It excludes practices that entail actions or beliefs in contradiction to Islamic law or theology, such as the drinking of wine or consideration that one is not obligated to perform ritual prayer due to having reached a high station.

43. Ibn Juzay al-Kalbī (d. 741/1340) divides (what I call) the core religious sciences into only two categories—*uṣūl al-dīn* (*īmān*) and *furūʿ al-fiqh* (*islām*)—*taṣawwūf* (*iḥsān*) being viewed as the inner *fiqh* (*fiqh al-bāṭin*). This, however, appears to be little more than a disagreement on definition. See al-Kalbī, *al-Qawānīn al-fiqhiyya*, 361.

44. *Tuḥfat al-Murīd*, 340.

45. Ibid.

46. I have borrowed this notion of Sufism's two aspects or faces from Nuh Keller's writings and lectures.

47. *Tuḥfat al-murīd*, 340.

48. Nuh Keller, "The Place of Tasawwuf in Traditional Islam," online: <http://www.masud.co.uk/ISLAM/nuhsufitlk.htm> [Jan. 13, 2008]. Also, William C. Chittick, *Faith and Practice of Islam: Three Thirteenth-Century Sufi Texts* (Albany: State University of New York Press, 1992).

49. There is some skepticism over whether or not each order was "founded" by the scholar that bears his name; however, the near obsession that some scholars have with disconnecting a phenomenon from its historically accepted origins at times seems to be little more than semantic disagreement over what it means to "found" a school of thought. See J. Spencer Trimingham, *The Sufi Orders in Islam* (New York and Oxford: Oxford University Press, 1998), 14.

50. *Tuḥfat al-murīd*, 248.

51. Among the scores of Qur'ānic sciences are the science of abrogation (*nāsikh wa mansūkh*), the science of variant readings (*qira'āt*), and others. Among the *ḥadīth* sciences is the knowledge of narrators (*ʿilm al-rijāl*), or the science of verifying the reliability of narrators (*al-jarḥ wa-l-taʿdīl*).

52. *Matn Abī Shuja'*, 619.

53. The form this consensus took was, however, a matter of debate. Was a legally binding consensus only to be found among the Companions of the Prophet, or could it be found among the early scholars of Medina, or among the scholars of any given time?

54. Keller, *Reliance of the Traveller*, 20–23. Original source: Aḥmad b. al-Naqīb al-Miṣrī, *ʿUmdat al-sālik wa ʿuddat al-nāsik*, ed. Ṣāliḥ Muʿadhdhin and Muḥammad al-Ṣabbāgh (Damascus: Maktabat al-Ghazālī, 1405/1985), 11–13.

55. *Tuḥfat al-murid*, 41.

56. Ibid.

57. Sherman Jackson, "Islam(s) East and West: Clash of Imaginations?" Lecture delivered at Harvard Divinity School, March 2007. Online: <http://www.hds.harvard.edu/cswr/resources/lectures/sjackson.html> [Jan. 13, 2008].

58. Muḥammad b. Ismā'īl al-Bukhārī, *Ṣaḥīḥ al-Bukhārī*, critical edition by Jawād ʿAfānah (Amman: N.p., 2003), *ḥadīth* no. 6805.

59. According to Abū Isḥāq al-Shīrāzī, *al-Lumaʿ fī l-uṣūl al-fiqh* (printed with *Takhrīj aḥādīth al-lumaʿ fī l-uṣūl al-fiqh*, critical edition and commentary on the *ḥadīth*s found in *al-Lumaʿ* by ʿAbdallāh al-Ghumārī) (N.p.: ʿAlām al-Kutub, n.d.), 357–58.

60. Ibn Taymiyya's view, discussed later, that the early Sufis were exercising *ijtihād* in *ʿibāda* (worship) seems to implicitly recognize the possibility, and perhaps necessity, of *ikhtilāf*.

61. See al-Bājūrī's *Tuḥfat al-murīd* for numerous examples of the way he compared varying views within Ashʿarī thought, as well as among the scholars of *fiqh*. See Chapter 3 for more on al-Suyūṭī and al-Shīrāzī.

62. George Makdisi rightly notes that one of the key functions of the genre of *khilāf* literature—those works that discuss the varying opinions of scholars—is to negatively outline the actual areas of *ijmāʿ*. That is to say, if

a common legal ruling or theological belief does not find its way into the books of *khilāf*, it quite likely falls under the category of *ijmāʿ*.

63. The seventh through ninth (thirteenth through fifteenth) centuries were a key period of transition in law, theology, and Sufism that have received inadequate attention, due partly to the pernicious and persistent assumption that these sciences underwent a decline during that period.

64. Jonathan E. Brockopp, "Early Islamic Jurisprudence in Egypt: Two Scholars and their Mukhtasars," *IJMES* 30, no. 2 (May 1998): 167–82.

65. I am indebted to Ahmed el-Shamsy for drawing my attention to the continued practice of al-Shāfiʿī's legal methodology by his immediate Egyptian disciples such as al-Buwayṭī. El-Shamsy, "The First Shāfiʿīs: The Traditionalist Legal Thought of Abū Yaʿqub al-Buwayṭī," *Islamic Law and Society* 14, no. 4 (2007).

66. Ahmed El-Shamsy, "From Tradition to Law: The Origins and Early Development of the Shāfiʿī School of Law in Ninth-Century Egypt" (PhD diss., Harvard University, 2009).

67. Ibid., 151.

68. Ibid., 152.

69. Ibid., 155.

70. Sherman A. Jackson, *Islamic Law and the State: The Constitutional Jurisprudence of Shihāb al-Dīn al-Qarāfi* (Leiden and New York: E. J. Brill, 1996), 53.

71. Ibid., 54.

72. Ibid., 53.

73. Michael Winter, *Egyptian Society under Ottoman Rule, 1517–1798* (London and New York, Routledge, 1992), 114.

74. Gran, "Quest," 80–81.

75. Aḥmad b. ʿUmar al-Dayrabī was a Shafiʿī scholar who taught at al-Azhar.

76. *Matn Abī Shujaʾ*, 572.

77. Ibid.

78. Al-ʿArūsī, the reform-minded Shaykh al-Azhar under Muḥammad ʿAlī Pasha, was himself a Māturīdī.

79. This is essentially Makdisi's view as stated in many of his works, including his study of Ibn ʿAqīl, his biography of Ibn Taymiyya, and elsewhere.

80. Gary Leiser, "Hanbalism in Egypt before the Mamluks," *Studia Islamica* 54 (1981): 155–81.

81. Ibid., 166.

82. The extent to which al-Azhar was used for teaching and learning immediately following Ṣalāḥ al-Dīn's imposing Sunni creed is unclear, there being, perhaps, a delay in resuming its use as a prominent center of teaching.

83. ʿAbd al-Raḥmān b. Ismāʿīl Abū Shāmah, *Kitāb al-Rawḍatayn fī akhbār al-dawlatayn al-nūriyya wa-l-ṣalāḥiyya* (Cairo: Maṭbaʿat Wādī l-Nīl, 1287/1870–1), 10.

84. Leiser, 167.

85. However, al-Jabartī implies that Ṣalāḥ al-Dīn's reform incorporated both Ashʿarī and Māturīdī thought, though I assume that al-Jabartī thought of the two as paired in some way as representative of proper Sunni creed, as opposed to the "corrupt creed" it replaced. Al-Jabartī also makes the anachronistic claim that al-Ghazālī sent Ṣalāḥ al-Dīn a book of creed which the latter imposed, but this would have been decades after the former's death. In any case, the claim that the Ḥanafīs followed the Ashʿarī school likely needs further research. ʿAbd al-Raḥmān al-Jabartī, *ʿAjāʾib al-āthār fī al-tarājim wa-al-akhbār* (Cairo: Dār al-Kutub al-Miṣriyya, 1998), 25.

86. Ibid. However, Sherman Jackson does call attention to a report that Ṣalāḥ al-Dīn may have founded a *madrasa* for Ḥanbalīs. See Jackson, *Islamic Law and the State*, 53n8.

87. The spread of Ashʿarī thought via Ṣalāḥ al-Dīn and Ibn Tumart is also recounted in Maqrīzī's work, *al-Khiṭaṭ al-Maqriziyya*, 4:440–441.

88. H. R. Idris, "Ibn Abī Zayd al-Kayrawani, Abū Muḥammad ʿAbd Allah b. Abī Zayd ʿAbd al-Raḥmān," *EI*[2].

89. Madeleine Fletcher, "The Almohad Tawhid: Theology which Relies on Logic," *Numen* 38, Fasc. 1 (June 1991), 112.

90. See chapter 4 for al-Bājūrī on the logic of the later logicians, as well as Aaron Spevack "Apples and Oranges: The Logic of the Early and Later Logicians" *Islamic Law and Society* 17, no. 2 (2010).

91. A. L. Tibawi, "Origin and Character of al-Madrasah," *BSOAS* 25, no. 1/3 (1962): 225–38.

92. Makdisi, "Ashʿarī and the Ashʿarites," 78.

93. Abū Shāma, *Kitāb al-rawḍatayn*, 1:10.

94. Keller, *Reliance of the Traveller*, 1030.

95. Delanoue, *Moralistes et politiques musulmans*, 100.

96. The manuscript can be found in Dār al-Kutub al-Miṣriyya (Cairo), catalog no. 49, Maktabat Taymur.

97. Gran, *Islamic Roots of Capitalism*, 118. Also see de Jong, *Ṭuruq and Ṭuruq-linked Institutions*, 34, and 194 for a translation of the agreement.

98. *Fallaḥ* is often translated as peasant, with the implication of being a farmer rather than a land owner.

99. Delanoue, *Moralistes et politiques musulmans*, 324.

100. Al-Suyūṭī, *Ḥusn al-muḥāḍara fī tārīkh Miṣr wa-l-Qāhira*, ed. Muḥammad Abū l-Faḍl Ibrāhīm (Cairo: ʿĪsā l-Bābī l-Ḥalabī, 1967–68), 511.

101. The exact date being dependent on when al-Ashʿarī's thought became rooted in Egypt. It was already present in the Maghrib in the late fourth/tenth century with al-Qayrawānī (as mentioned above), and thus could quite possibly have been established in Egypt by then.

102. Hamid Algar, "The Naqshbandī Order: A Preliminary Survey of its History and Significance," *Studia Islamica* 44 (1976), 146.

103. The Ḥanbalīs received no mention by Sachau.

104. Khaled el-Rouayheb "Opening the Gate of Verification: The Forgotten Arab-Islamic Florescence of the Seventeenth Century," *IJMES* 38, no. 2 (May 2006): 263–81.

105. That is, the third/ninth century did not mark the end of discussions on matters of *fiqh*, and al-Ghazālī's supposed death blow to all things philosophical did not cause all philosophical inquiry to cease.

Chapter 3

1. al-Bājūrī, *Tuḥfat al-murīd* (Beirut: Dār al-Kutub al-ʿIlmiyya, 1995), 54 (this quotation is not taken from the ʿAlī Jumʿa edition used throughout this work).

2. Eduard Sachau, *Muhammedanisches Recht nach schafītischer Lehre* (Stuttgart: W. Spemann, 1897), xxiv. Translation by Kristina Musholt.

3. Regarding al-Bājūrī's *Tuḥfat al-murīd*, Delanoue says: "We can effectively conclude from reading this manual, that Baguri has almost no direct contact with religious literature of the classical age. The works he uses, indeed those he has at his disposal, are attributable to authors from the mamelouke and ottoman eras; these authors are mostly—but not exclusively—Egyptians and Maghrebins; some were teacher, or teachers of teachers." Delanoue, *Moralistes et politiques musulmans*, 112.

4. While the scholarship of women in Islam warrants far more than a footnote, indeed it warrants a great deal of further study, I have made the difficult decision to limit myself the scholars mentioned by al-Bājūrī, none of whom are women. However, many major archetypal scholars, such as al-Suyūṭī, Ibn Ḥajar al-ʿAsqalānī, and others listed a significant number of women among their teachers, thus indicating that gender did not play a role in defining the archetypal scholar of Islam, even if it did determine official and high profile appointments to mosques, judgeships, and such. Indeed, one finds evidence of many women studying and teaching the Islamic sciences in the biographical and historical works of Ibn ʿAsākir, al-Sakhāwī (*d.* 902/1497), and others.

5. Seyyed Hussein Nasr, "Fakhr al-Din al-Razi," in *A History of Muslim Philosophy*, ed. M. M. Sharif Wiesbaden: Harrassowitz, 1963), 642–55.

6. Spevack, "Apples and Oranges," 165. Also see Ibn Khallikān, *Wafayāt al-aʿyān wa-anbāʾ abnāʾ al-zamān* (Beirut: Dār Ṣādir, 1994), 312.

7. Nasr, "Fakhr al-Din al-Razi," 646.

8. I am indebted to Carl Sharif el-Tobgui for clarifying this principle for me, via an early draft of his dissertation. See el-Tobgui, "Reason, Revelation, and the Reconstitution of Rationality: Taqī al-Dīn Ibn Taymiyya's Darʿ Taʿārud al-ʿaql wa'l naql, or, 'The Refutation of the Contradiction of Reason and Revelation'" (PhD diss., McGill University, 2012).

9. Spevack, "Apples and Oranges," 181.

10. As al-Taftazānī wrote works relating to both *madhhabs*, his affiliations are contested. Masʿūd b. ʿUmar al-Taftazānī, *al-Talwīḥ ilā kashf ḥaqāʾīq al-tanqīḥ* (Beirut: Sharikat al-Arqām Ibn Abī l-Arqam, 1998), 11–13.

11. Although, he also adopted Māturīdī opinions. See al-Taftazānī, *A Commentary on the Creed of Islam Saʿd al-Dīn al-Taftāzānī on the Creed of Najm*

al-Dīn al-Nasafī, trans. Earl Edgar Elder (New York: Colombia University Press, 1950), xxiv–xxx. Also see Alexander Knysh, *Ibn Arabi in the Later Islamic Tradition: The Making of a Polemical Image in Medieval Islam* (Albany: State University of New York Press, 1999), 146.

12. *EI*[2], s.v. al-Taftazānī (W. Madelung).

13. al-Taftazānī, *A Commentary on the Creed,* trans. Elder, xxi.

14. Knysh, *Ibn Arabi in the Later Islamic Tradition,* 147.

15. Ibid., 150.

16. Aḥmad b. Muḥammad al-Mālikī al-Ṣāwī, *Kitāb Sharḥ al-Ṣāwī ʿalā Jawharat al-tawḥīd* (Beirut: Dār Ibn Kathīr, 1997), 10.

17. al-Bājūrī, *al-Musalsalat,* 7.

18. Bencheneb places al-Sanūsī in the tradition of Abū Madyan; given that there is an almost three-hundred-year gap between the two, I assume al-Sanūsī would be linked somehow to the Shādhilīs, who preserved Abū Madyan's teachings. This assumption, however, needs further authentication. H. Bencheneb, "al-Sanūsī, Abū ʿAbdallāh Muḥammad b. Yūsuf b. ʿUmar b. Shuʿayb," *EI*[2].

19. *Tuḥfat al-murīd,* 76.

20. Bencheneb presumably has Qarawayīn University in mind here: "logic at Fās was done through the *Mukhtaṣar.*"

21. Bencheneb, "al-Sanūsī."

22. Ibid.

23. Ibid. See Montgomery Watt, *Islamic Creeds* (Edinburgh: Edinburgh University Press, 1994).

24. Joseph P. Kenny, "Muslim theology as presented by M. b. Yusuf as-Sanusi: especially in his al-Aqida al-Wusta" (PhD diss., Edinburgh University, 1970).

25. See New York, Public Library and Public Library New York. *Bulletin of the New York Public Library.* vol 15, (New York: New York Public Library, 1911), 231.

26. Ibid.

27. For al-Sanūsī, *Umm al-barāhīn,* see <http://www.loc.gov/exhibit/mali/mali-exhibit.html> for an a scanned copy of a manuscript with the commentary of Muḥammad al-Miṣrī from a private manuscript library in Mali.

28. Bencheneb, "al-Sanūsī."

29. Ibid.

30. Khaled el-Rouayheb discusses the relation of al-Sanūsī's Persian *taḥqīqī*-inspired work to al-Suyūṭī's "method of the Arabs" in his article, "Opening the Gate of Verification: The Forgotten Arab-Islamic Florescence of the Seventeenth Century," *IJMES* 38, no. 2 (May 2006): 263–81.

31. Perhaps the most famous and widely used commentary on the *Ṣaḥīḥ Muslim* is that of al-Nawawī, wherein one finds many *ḥadīths* interpreted according to Ashʿarī *taʾwīl.*

32. *Tuḥfat al-murīd,* 56.

33. Muḥammad al-Fuḍālī, "The Sufficiency of the Commonality in the Science of Scholastic Theology," in *Development of Muslim Theology, Jurisprudence, and Constitutional Theory*, ed. Duncan B. MacDonald (Lahore: Premier Book House, 1960).

34. Further research is needed on the premise that al-Sanūsī based his beliefs on the works of al-Ghazālī and al-Juwaynī, yet Ibn Khaldūn describes al-Ghazālī as having refuted the proofs of earlier Ashʿarī *mutakallimīn*, including al-Bāqillānī's view that the proofs are themselves obligatory. So the question arises: Is there a distinction between which set of proofs al-Bāqillānī and al-Sanūsī felt were obligatory? That is to say, did they use the same proofs for the necessary points of belief, or did they have differing proofs? Al-Sanūsī's set of proofs would have incorporated the rules of *manṭiq* (see Ibn Khaldūn for this distinction) while al-Bāqillānī's proofs were of the type that al-Ghazālī refuted. Were they in agreement on the ruling of obligation but not on the details of which proof was obligatory? The nature and content of the proofs that each considered obligatory may have changed over time, thus al-Bāqillānī and al-Sanūsī may not have agreed on the exact proofs that were considered necessary to learn.

35. This obligation was only for one who had been reached by the sound message of Islam. See *Tuḥfat al-murīd*, 67.

36. According to the Ashʿarīs and Sunnīs in general, disbelief is the only unforgivable sin.

37. *Tuḥfat al-murīd*, 56

38. Ibid.

39. The *taḥqīqī* tradition can be understood as an approach to the Islamic sciences that emphasizes not mere reproduction of past knowledge, but a deep engagement in the sources and proofs for various rulings and opinions, as well as a willingness to express one's own opinions on the issues in question.

40. El-Rouayheb, "Opening the Gate," 269.

41. Ibid., 268.

42. I am indebted to Jawad Qureshi for bringing this work to my attention. See Muḥammad Bakrī al-Dimyāṭī, *Iʿānat al-ṭālibīn ʿalā ḥall alfāẓ fatḥ al-muʿīn.* (Cairo: al-Maṭba'ah al-Khayrīyah, 1903).

43. Sachau, *Muhammedanisches*, xxiv. Also see Barbara Daly Metcalf, *Islam in South Asia in Practice* (Princeton, NJ: Princeton University Press, 2009), 404.

44. This brief biography of al-Rāfiʿī is excerpted and edited from an earlier biography written for Hamza Yusuf's "Content of Character." See Hamza Yusuf, *The Content of Character: Ethical Sayings of the Prophet Muhammad* (San Francisco: Sandala, 2005).

45. Keller, *Reliance of the Traveller*, 1090.

46. Muḥyī l-Dīn b. Sharaf al-Nawawī, *al-Majmūʿ sharḥ al-muhadhdhab* (Cairo: Maṭbaʿat al-ʿĀṣima, 1966–69), 1:13.

47. Delanoue, *Moralistes et politiques musulmans*, 112.

48. al-Barmāwī, *Ḥāshiya Ibrāhīm al-Barmāwī*, 330.

49. ʿAlī b. Aḥmad Bāṣabrayn, *Ithmid al-ʿaynayn fī baʿḍ ikhtilāf al-shaykhayn* (Beirut: Dār al-Fikr al-Muʿāṣir; Damascus: Dār al-Fikr, 1996).

50. "Standing and dancing during gatherings of remembrance (*dhikr*) and audition (*samāʾ*) is permissible according to a group of great scholars, among them ʿIzz al-Dīn Shaykh al-Islam Ibn ʿAbd al-Salam" (Ibn Ḥajar al-Haytamī, *al-Fatāwā al-ḥadithiyya* [Egypt: Muṣṭafā l-Bābī l-Ḥalabī, 1970], 298).

51. A copy exists in manuscript form in Dār al-Kutub al-Miṣriyya.

52. El-Rouayheb, "Sunnī Muslim Scholars on the Status of Logic," *Islamic Law and Society* 11, no. 2 (2004): 213–32. Online: <http://www.jstor.org/stable/3399304>.

53. See ʿAbd al-Raḥmān Ibn al-Jawzī, *The Attributes of God: Ibn al-Jawzī's dafʿshuba al-tashbih bi-akaff al-tanzih*, trans. Abdullah bin Hamid Ali (Bristol, UK: Amal Press, 2006).

54. Ibn Ḥajar al-Haytamī, *al-Fatāwā al-ḥadithiyya*, 143–44.

55. *Ḥāshiya*, 556.

56. Abū l-Ḥasan Aḥmad b. Muḥammad al-Maḥāmilī, *al-Lubbāb fī fiqh al-Shafiʿī* (Medina: Dār al-Bukhārī, 1416/1996), 34.

57. Zakariyya al-Anṣārī, *Ghāyat al-wuṣūl fī sharḥ lubb al-uṣūl* (Egypt: Dār al-Kutub al-ʿArabiyya, n.d.), 180.

58. Al-Subkī and possibly al-Anṣārī, then, may be sources for al-Bājūrī's commentary on *Jawharat al-tawḥīd*, wherein he mentions and honors the founders of the *madhhabs*, al-Ashʿarī (and al-Māturīdī), and al-Junayd, but as is often the case, al-Bājūrī goes beyond what is mentioned by al-Ansārī. See Chapter 2 for al-Bājūrī's discussion of the founders of the *madhhabs* and schools of theology.

59. Although I have not yet found a copy of this work, based on his gloss on al-Ghazzī's work and the standard ordering of chapters and discussions, I presume this to consist of a significant amount of commentary.

60. *Ḥāshiya*, 570.

61. ʿAbd al-Wahhāb b. ʿAlī l-Subkī, *Ṭabaqāt al-Shāfiʿiyya al-kubrā*, ed. Muṣṭafā ʿAbd al-Qādir Aḥmad ʿAṭā (Beirut: Manshūrāt Muḥammad ʿAlī Bayḍūn, Dār al-Kutub al-ʿIlmiyya, 1999), 6:15 (no. 567).

62. Ibid.

63. See *Ḥāshiya al-Bājūrī*, 564 where al-Bājūrī declares one of al-Barmāwī's opinions weak (*ḍaʿīf*). Al-Barmāwī is usually referred to as al-Muḥashī, the super-commentator.

64. *Matn Abī Shujāʾ*, 543.

65. See ʿImād al-Dīn Abī Hijla, *al-Najjūm al-lāmiʿa fī thaqāfat al-Muslim al-jāmīʿa* (Amman: Dār al-Rāzī, 1999), 521.

66. Sufism in al-Shīrāzī's time was of the master–disciple type, prior to the founding of *ṭarīqas*. The biographical literature includes several narrations about al-Shīrāzī's close association with Abū Naṣr al-Qushayrī (the son of the famous Sufi Abū l-Qāsim al-Qushayrī (d. 465/1072)), as well as his being known as a *zāhid* (one who lives an ascetic lifestyle) and an *ʿārif* (gnostic). I am not yet aware of his having taken on a master–disciple relationship. For some narrations of al-Shīrāzī's association with Abū Naṣr al-Qushayrī,

in addition to those mentioned below, see Ibn al-Ṣalāḥ, *Ṭabaqāt al-fuqahāʾ al-Shāfiʿiyya* (Beirut: Dār al-Bashāʾir al-Islāmiyya, 1992), 1:302–10.

67. *Tuḥfat al-murīd*, 273. This may not in fact be Shaykh Jumʿa's words, rather, it may be an earlier annotator of al-Bājūrī's text.

68. al-Shīrazī, *al-Lumaʿ*.

69. Al-Subkī mentions these in his *Ṭabaqāt al-Shāfiʿiyya al-kubrā*.

70. *Tuḥfat al-murīd*, 273.

71. Abū Isḥāq Ibrāhīm b. ʿAlī b. Yūsuf Fīrūzābādī l-Shīrāzī, *al-Muhadhdhab fī fiqh al-Imām al-Shāfiʿī*, ed. Muḥammad al-Zuḥaylī (Damascus: Dār al-Qalam; Beruit: al-Dār al-Shāmiyya, 1992–96), 1:12.

72. al-Shīrāzī, *Kitāb al-maʿūna fī l-jadl* (Kuwait: Jamʿīyat Iḥyāʾ al-Turāth al-Islāmī, Markaz al-Makhṭūṭāt wa-l-Turāth, 1987), 27–28.

73. al-Shīrāzī, *al-Lumaʿ*, 357.

74. al-Taftazānī, *A Commentary on the Creed*, trans. Elder, 10.

75. While Khurasan was a hotbed of Ashʿarī activity in al-Shīrāzī's day, the regional division of the schools is to my mind related more to legal derivations, rather than the inclusion or exclusion of rationalism in one's legal methodology.

76. al-Shīrāzī, *al-Lumaʿ*, 62.

77. In later Shāfiʿī *fiqh* terminology, *aṣaḥ* came to mean the soundest of two (or more) valid opinions, whereas *ṣaḥīḥ* meant there was only one valid opinion, the other possible opinion being an error. It is unclear to me whether or not this is the intended implication of al-Shīrāzī's usage of these terms, but considering that throughout *al-Lumaʿ* he cites various opinions, often representing an intra-Shāfiʿī school disagreement, I am tempted to argue that these terms (*aṣaḥ*, *ṣaḥīḥ*) were intended in the above-mentioned technical sense.

78. See al-Shīrāzī, *al-Lumaʿ*, 357, for an example of al-Shīrāzī presenting various views wherein Mālik, Abū Ḥanīfa, and some Shāfiʿīs agree with the Muʿtazalīs. Regarding *ijtihād*, he discusses the question of whether or not all *mujtahid*s are correct regardless of differing outcomes. In the realm of *uṣūl al-dīn*, whose rulings are *ʿaqlī* (rational) rather than *sharʿī* (legal), he states that the correct opinion is that there is only one truth with regard to the major theological issues, such as the creation of human actions, or the inhabitants of heaven seeing Allah. He rejects as incorrect (*fasād*) the opinion that all the *mujtahid*s are correct in these types of issues. However, with regard to there being only one truth versus all *mujtahid*s being correct in *legal* matters which do not fall under the category of *ijmāʿ*, he accepts two varying views, the first that there is only one truth and all else is false (*bāṭil*)—this being attributed to al-Shāfiʿī, the second being that all the *mujtahid*s are correct regardless of their differing outcomes. The latter opinion is attributed to Mālik, Abū Ḥanīfa, the Muʿtazalīs, and al-Ashʿarī himself.

79. *Matn Abī Shujāʿ*, 573.

80. Haim Gerber, *Islamic Law and Culture, 1600–1840* (Leiden and Boston: Brill, 1999), 82.

81. Other scholars critical of certain aspects of various popular forms of Sufism include Ibn al-Jawzī, Ibn Qudāmah, and the Qāḍīzādeli movement

in seventeenth-century Istanbul. While each of these unique and varying perspectives on Sufism would further broaden the scope of this discussion, they have regrettably been omitted in the interest of brevity and clarity. Like Ibn Taymiyya's thought, the aforementioned omitted scholars provide weight to the argument that what many Orientalists and contemporary Muslim opponents of Sufism had mistakenly read as blanket condemnations of Sufism, were in fact specific critiques by scholars that embraced significant aspects of Sufism, Ibn al-Jawzī and Ibn Qudāmah via their abridgement and emendation of al-Ghazālī's "Revival of the Religious Sciences," and Qāḍīzādeli's indebtedness to al-Birgilī's (d. 981/1573) Sufi writings.

82. Michael Winter, *Society and Religion in Early Ottoman Egypt: Studies in the Writing of 'Abd al-Wahhab al-Sha'rānī* (New Brunswick, NJ: Transaction, 2007), 58. N. Hanif, *Biographical Encyclopaedia of Sufis: Africa and Europe* (New Delhi: Sarup & Sons, 2002), 171. Except where otherwise noted, much of al-Shaʿrānī's biographical information is drawn from Hanif's work.

83. Duncan B. MacDonald, *Development of Muslim Theology, Jurisprudence and Constitutional Theory: 1863–1943* (New York: Charles Scribner's, 1903), 280–81.

84. Hanif, *Biographical Encyclopaedia of Sufis*, 170.

85. Winter, *Society and Religion*, 46.

86. Ibid., 164.

87. Knysh, *Ibn Arabi in the Later Islamic Tradition*, 313.

88. Whether or not this criticism extended to all orders that used the *khalwa*, or just the Khalwatiyya of his time, needs to be further explored.

89. al-Maqrīzī, *al-Khiṭaṭ al-Maqriziyya*, 4:441–42.

90. al-Bājūrī, *Hādhihi Ḥāshiya Ibrāhīm al-Bājūrī ʿalā matn al-shamāʾil al-Muḥammadiyya li-al-Muḥammad b. ʿĪsā al-Tirmidhī* (Egypt: Maṭbaʿat al-Saʿda, 1925), 52. I am indebted to Khaled El-Rouayheb for bringing this reference to my attention.

91. George Makdisi, "Ibn Taymiyya: A Sufi of the Qadiriya Order," *American Journal of Arabic Studies* 1 (1973): 118–29.

92. That is to say, if the chain of narration (*isnād*) for the text on which Makdisi bases his claims has certain weaknesses, or if, because there is only one chain of narration, which does not produce certain knowledge (according to many scholars of *uṣūl al-fiqh*), then his (Ibn Taymiyya's) other texts prove a strong support for and connection to the great Sufis of the past.

93. Diego R. Sarrio "Spiritual anti-elitism: Ibn Taymiyya's doctrine of sainthood (walāya)." *Islam and Christian-Muslim Relations* 22, no. 3 (2011), 276–77.

94. See Ibn Taymiyya's chapter on Sufism in *Majmuʿat al-fatāwā* (Mansura: Dār al-Wafāʾ, 2005), vols. 10 and 11.

95. "Problematic utterances" is a useful word for *shaṭḥ*, though Massignon's more ornate term "theopathic locutions" is also used.

96. Ibn Taymiyya, *Majmuʿat al-fatāwā*, 10:129–32.

97. This is because one of the conditions for being legally responsible (*taklīf*) is being of sound intellect. Thus, "the pen is lifted" from one who is

mad or not in possession of his intellect at a given moment. Ibn Taymiyya, *Majmuʿat al-fatāwā*, 2:240.

98. Ibid. Massignon, however, felt that there was in fact a difference between the two, namely that al-Ḥallāj advocated *waḥdat al-shuhūd* (oneness of witnessing) and that Ibn al-ʿArabī advocated *waḥdat al-wujūd*.

99. Although I do not know whether or not he claimed to have experienced *fanāʾ*.

100. That is, if in fact early *madrasa*s focused solely on subjects like *fiqh* or *ḥadīth*; some have argued that this is not the case.

101. Such as his claim that the universe was pre-eternally existent as an ever abiding created thing, *makhluqan dāʾimān*.

102. George Makdisi, "Ibn Taymiyya." Online: <http://www.muslimphilosophy.com/it/itya.htm> [May 2, 2007].

103. Aaron Spevack, "Jalāl al-Dīn al-Suyūṭī" in *Essays in Arabic Literary Biography, 1350–1850*, ed. Joseph E. Lowry and Devin J. Stewart (Wiesbaden: Harrassowitz, 2009).

104. Sartain expressed some reservation as to whether there was enough proof of al-Suyūṭī's actual affiliation with the Shādhilīs, however, given that one of al-Suyūṭī's teachers was a Shādhilī, as was one of his own students and biographers, coupled with the preference for Shādhilī teachings that he expresses in his writings, the claim of the Shādhilīs that he was among their ranks is certainly tenable. Sartain, *Jalāl al-Dīn al-Suyūṭī*, 1:35–36.

105. See Spevack, "Jalāl al-Dīn al-Suyūṭī" for a sample list of these. For the full list, see Muḥammad b. Ibrāhīm al-Shaybānī and Aḥmad al-Khāzindār (eds), *Dalīl al-makhṭūṭāt al-Suyūṭī* (Kuwait: Manshurāt Markaz Makhṭūṭāt, 1995).

106. One capable of deriving legal rulings directly from the Qurʾān and *Ḥadīth* using the methodology of his school's founder.

107. Al-Suyūṭī remained Ashʿarī in his theological views, as discussed in more detail in Chapter 2; more research is needed to determine if al-Suyūṭī had only *manṭiq*-based *kalām* in mind, and not al-Ashʿarī's *kalām* that did not use *manṭiq*.

108. Al-Suyūṭī's use of the possessive pronoun "our" indicates his affiliation with these scholars, in keeping with the usual technical usage of "we," "us," "our." Jalāl al-Dīn al-Suyūṭī, *al-Ḥāwī li-l-fatāwī* (Beirut: Dār al-Kutub al-ʿIlmiyya, 1983), 2:202.

109. *Tuḥfat al-murīd*, 67.

110. al-Suyūṭī, *Taʾyīd al-ḥaqīqat al-ʿaliyya wa tashyīd al-ṭarīqat al-shādhiliyya*, ed. ʿAbdallāh al-Ghumārī l-Ḥasanī (Cairo [?]: al-Maṭbaʿat al-Islāmiyya, 1934).

111. The Day of Judgment or Resurrection follows an initial destruction of the universe, as described in the Qurʾān and *Ḥadīth*. Mountains become like discarded wool, the cosmos collapses, and all created things are eradicated, except for the few which are exempted, as discussed in what follows.

112. The throne and the footstool are enormous created objects at the farthest reaches of the cosmos. The throne in particular represents the "edge" of the cosmos and is considered a symbol of Allah's power. It is also a subject

of heated debate among the various theological schools and sects regarding Allah's being without a place and not being contained by the six directions.

113. The tailbone, according to some, is the seed, so to speak, from which people will be resurrected on the Day of Judgment.

114. The preserved tablet is a large cosmic object on which the destined future is written. The pen was commanded to write on the preserved tablet all events that would come to pass.

115. al-Bājūrī, *al-Musalsalāt*, 3–5.

116. The term "orthodoxy" does not have an appropriate Arabic equivalent. I use the term "orthodox" in the context of debates over the soundness of a scholar's beliefs and the matter of whether or not these beliefs conform with agreed-upon tenets of the Ahl al-Sunna. As discussed below, I do not believe it is the place of the Western academy to declare one group or individual orthodox and another heretical.

117. Knysh, *Ibn Arabi in the Later Islamic Tradition*, 206.

118. For al-Subkī's reversal of his original criticism of Ibn al-ʿArabī, after the meanings of Ibn al-ʿArabī's words were explained and clarified to him (al-Subkī), see Muḥammad Rajab Ḥilmī, *Burhān al-azhar fī manāqib al-Shaykh al-Akbar* (Egypt: Maṭbaʿat al-Saʿāda, 1908/09[?]), 32–33.

119. Albert Hourani, *A History of the Arab Peoples* (Cambridge, MA: Harvard University Press, 1991), 181.

120. Knysh, *Ibn Arabi in the Later Islamic Tradition*, 213.

121. al-Suyūṭī, *al-Ḥāwī li-l-fatāwī*, 2:234.

122. al-Suyūṭī, *Sharḥ maqamāt*, ed. Maḥmūd al-Durūbī (Beirut: Muʾassasat al-Risāla, 1989), 2:917–18. I am indebted to G. F. Haddad for his assistance in helping me locate this particular edition. His articles online about al-Suyūṭī have been indispensable in my own studies and writings on al-Suyūṭī.

123. Ibn Taymiyya, *Ibn Taymiyya Against the Greek Logicians*, trans. Wael Hallaq (Oxford: Clarendon Press and New York: Oxford University Press, 1993), li.

124. Jonathan P. Berkey, "Culture and Society During the Late Middle Ages," in the *Cambridge History of Egypt*, vol. 1: *Islamic Egypt*, ed. Carl F. Petry (Cambridge, UK: Cambridge University Press, 1998), 402.

125. Ibid.

126. Michael Chamberlain, "The Crusader Era and the Ayyubid Dynasty," in the *Cambridge History of Egypt*, vol. 1: *Islamic Egypt*, ed. Carl F. Petry (Cambridge, UK: Cambridge University Press, 1998), 232.

127. Elmer H. Douglas, "Al-Shādhilī, A North African Ṣufī, According to Ibn al-Ṣabbāgh," *Muslim World* 38, no. 4 (October 1948), 271. Also see Douglas, *The Mystical Teachings of al-Shadhili: Including his Life, Prayers, Letters, and Followers: A Translation from the Arabic of Ibn al-Sabbagh's Durrat al-asrār wa tuḥfat al-abrār* (Albany: State University of New York Press, 1993).

128. I understand the rendering of a right over oneself to mean that one recognizes the validity and authority of these great past masters.

129. Qurʾān 3:191.

130. al-Suyūṭī, *al-Ḥāwī li-l-fatāwī*, 234.

131. Al-Suyūṭī's treatise proving the validity and even necessity of *ijtihād* after the time of the four imams.

132. See Ibn Taymiyya's *fatwā* on *samāʿ*, which he opposed as an impermissible innovation that occurred after the end of the third century of Islam. Ibn Taymiyya, *Majmuʿat al-fatāwā*, 11:35.

133. Had it been merely a grammatical issue, al-Bājūrī's citing al-Suyūṭī would not indicate his acceptance of al-Suyūṭī's overall orthodoxy, as the Muʿtazalī grammarian and exegete al-Zamakhsharī is often cited in the Qurʾānic exegetical literature.

134. Makdisi concurs in several of his works, including "Muslim Institutions of Learning in Eleventh-Century Baghdad," *BSOAS* 24, no. 1 (1961): 1–56.

Chapter 4

1. Snouck Hurgronje, "E Sachau."

2. Wael Hallaq, "Was the Gate of Ijtihad Closed?" *IJMES* 16 (1984): 3–41.

3. The notion of the end of *ijtihād* has been a commonly held belief in Western studies of Islamic law until recently. It is still commonly held among some Muslims as well. See David Smock, "Ijtihad: Reinterpreting Islamic Principles for the Twenty-first Century," online: <http://www.usip.org/pub/specialreport/sr125.html#> [Jan. 13, 2008]. Smock mentions some prominent Muslim voices in America and their views on the end of *ijtihād*, and the need for its revival. They too neglect the levels of *ijtihād* that Hallaq discusses, and as I discuss below in relation to al-Bājūrī.

4. Snouck Hurgronje, "E. Sachau," 386.

5. al-Bājūrī, *Matn Abī Shujāʿ*, 32–35.

6. Ibid., 35.

7. Hallaq, "Ijtihad," 22.

8. Ibid.

9. Snouck Hurgronje, "E. Sachau," 387.

10. Cuno and Spevack, "al-Bājūrī" [original quote from: Christiaan Snouck Hurgronje, "Muhammedanisches Recht nach schafi itischer Lehre von Eduard Sachau," *ZDMG* 53 (1899), 117.]

11. Sartain, *Jalāl al-Dīn al-Suyūṭī*, 65.

12. Hallaq, "Ijtihad," 17.

13. Sartain, *Jalāl al-Dīn al-Suyūṭī*, 64.

14. al-Bājūrī, *Matn Abī Shujāʿ*, 35. The *ḥadīth*, narrated in the collection of Abū Dāwūd, states that at the advent of each century, Allah sends someone to renew the religion.

15. See Hallaq, "Ijtihād," 25, for an excellent comparison of at least three different uses of the term "*mujtahid muṭlaq*" by Ibn Taymiyya, al-Suyūṭī, and al-Ghazālī.

16. al-Bājūrī, *Matn Abī Shujāʿ*, 34.

17. *Tuḥfat al-murīd*, 247.

18. al-Bājūrī, *Matn Abī Shujāʿ*, 35.

19. Sartain, *Jalāl al-Dīn al-Suyūṭī*, 64.

20. Wahba al-Zuhayli, *al-Fiqh al-Islāmī wa adilatuhu* (Damascus: Dār al-Fikr, 1983), 1:47–48.

21. Hallaq, "Ijtihad," 15.

22. *Tarjīḥ* means weighing the various opinions of higher ranking *mujtahids* on particular issues, and giving preference to one over the others.

23. al-Zuhaylī, *al-Fiqh al-Islāmī*, 1:47–48. Quoted in ʿImād al-Dīn Abī Hijla, *al-Najjūm al-lāmiʿa fī thaqāfat al-Muslim al-jāmīʿa* (Amman: Dār al-Rāzī, 1999), 408.

24. al-Bājūrī, *Matn Abī Shujāʿ*, 616–17.

25. Ibid., 617.

26. Ibid.

27. Due to al-Suyūṭī's statement, it might be necessary to interpret the scholars mentioned by al-Bājūrī as denying *taqlīd* beyond their *taqlīd* of al-Shāfiʿī's methods.

28. *Tuḥfat al-murīd*, 76. The literal statement is "Taking (*al-akhdh*) the sayings (*al-qawl*) of another without knowing its proofs." However, al-Bājūrī then further defines his terms, *al-akhdh* means *al-iʿtiqād*, and *al-qawl* means sayings, actions, and tacit approval.

29. Ibid., 250.

30. al-Bājūrī, *Matn Abī Shujāʿ*, 36.

31. Another possibility is that they were not *muqallids* at all, but did not find a need to produce a method that differed from their Imam's. There is, in reality, some ambiguity in the discussion of some of the immediate followers of the four Imams; were they at the same level as their teachers but chose not to produce new methods, or were they at the level of *mujtahid al-madhhab*?

32. al-Bājūrī, *Matn Abī Shujāʿ*, 616–17.

33. *Tuḥfat al-murīd*, 250–51. Al-Bājūrī uses the passive past tense *qīla* (it was said) in all three cases, thus, perhaps, indicating that no *muʿtammad* or dominant opinion had been arrived at.

34. While al-Bājūrī does not mention this point (i.e., the specification of the dowry amount), it is presumably what is meant, as al-Kalbī relates a consensus that the dowry payment itself is a necessary condition of marriage. See al-Kalbī, *al-Qawānīn al-fiqhiyya*, 174.

35. Ibid., 169.

36. I am indebted to Shaykh Faraz Rabbani for the clarification of the Ḥanafī position on the guardian and specification of the dowry.

37. *Tuḥfat al-murīd*, 250–51.

38. *Tuḥfat al-murīd*, 343.

39. Ibid.

40. El-Rouayheb, "Opening the Gate," 270.

41. In the Mālikī school, *fatwā*s and the judgments of *qāḍī*s can be drawn from at least five sources, considered to be *muʿtammad* (relied upon)

"1. *al-muttafaq ʿalay* (the agreed upon ruling); 2. *al-rājiḥ* (the preferred ruling); 3. *al-mashhūr* (the well-known ruling); 4. *al-musāwī* (the ruling which is equal to another ruling); and 5. *mā jarā bihi al-ʿamal* (the existing *ʿamal*)." See Muḥammad Riyāḍ, *Uṣūl al-fatwā wa-l-qaḍāʾ fī l-madhhab al-Mālikī* (Casablanca: Maṭbaʿat al-Najāḥ al-Jadīda, 1996), 471.

42. Gerber, *Islamic Law and Culture*, 38–43.

43. Ibid., 8–9.

44. Lutz Wiederhold, "Legal Doctrines in Conflict: The Relevance of Madhhab Boundaries to Legal Reasoning in the Light of an Unpublished Treatise on Taqlīd and Ijtihād," *Islamic Law and Society* 3, no. 2 (1996), 235n2.

45. Ibid.

46. Sartain, *Jalāl al-Dīn al-Suyūṭī*, 94.

47. Peter Gran, Review of *Ṭuruq and Ṭuruq-linked Institutions in Nineteenth-Century Egypt: A Historical Study in Organizational Dimensions of Islamic Mysticism* by F. de Jong, *IJMES* 11, no. 4 (July 1980), 550.

48. *Tuḥfat al-murīd*, 328–39.

49. Muḥammad Amīn al-Kurdī, *Tanwīr al-qulūb fī muʿāmalat ʿallām al-ghuyūb* (Aleppo: Dār al-Qalam al-ʿArabī, 1991), 465cf.

50. *Tuḥfat al-murīd*, 340.

51. Ibid.

52. Ibid.

53. Ibid.

54. "I am the slave of the Koran while I still have life. / I am the dust on the path of Muḥammad, the chosen one. / If anyone interprets my words in any other way, I deplore that person, and I deplore his words." From a poem by Jalāl al-Dīn Rumi. See Shems Friedlander, *The Whirling Dervishes* (Albany: State University of New York Press, 1992), xx.

55. *Tuḥfat al-murīd*, 248.

56. Ibid., 248–49.

57. Ibid., 40.

58. The word *ʿarifīn* is the plural of *ʿārif*, literally, "knower of God."

59. *Tuḥfat al-murīd*, 40.

60. Ahmad Atif Ahmad, "Structural Interrelations of Theory and Practice in Islamic Law: A Study of takhrij al-furuʿ ʿala al-uṣūl Literature" (PhD diss., Harvard, 2005), 64.

61. That is to say, there could be *wājib* aspects of Sufism, *mandūb* aspects, and *mubāḥ* aspects. Presumably one could also imagine that some aspects could be *wājib*, *mandūb*, or *mubāḥ* for one person, but *makrūh* or *ḥarām* for another, as can be the case in many other aspects of *fiqh*.

62. *Tuḥfat al-murīd*, 334.

63. *Tuḥfat al-murīd*, 56.

64. Al-Bājūrī mentions that ʿUmar approved of praying *tarāwīḥ* in a group, rather than at home, by saying "What a good *bidʿa* this is." However, some scholars mention that this was in fact done by the Prophet in his

time, but ʿUmar was not yet aware of it. Thus, it was not a *bidʿa* per se, but ʿUmar's acceptance of it, thinking it was a *bidʿa,* indicates that there can be good innovations. Nonetheless, al-Bājūrī appears to be of the opinion that *tarāwīḥ* in a group is an innovation.

65. *Tuḥfat al-murīd,* 393. See Schacht, *Introduction to Islamic Law,* 76, for more on *maks* (pl. *makūs*), which he defines as "market dues."

66. *Tuḥfat al-murīd,* 159.

67. Ibid.

68. Ibid., 105.

69. Ibid.

70. Ibid.

71. Ibid.

72. Louis Massignon, *Hallaj: Mystic and Martyr,* trans. Herbert Mason (Princeton, NJ: Princeton University Press, 1994), 266–70.

73. Louis Massignon, *The Passion of al-Hallaj: Mystic and Martyr of Islam,* trans. Herbert Mason, 3 vols. (Princeton, NJ: Princeton University Press, 1982), 1:75–79.

74. Massignon, *Passion of al-Hallaj,* 2:52–53.

75. Ibid., 2:47.

76. Ibid.

77. In addition to being apparently unaware of the issues that Massignon raises regarding the authenticity of many commonly cited reports about al-Ḥallāj, al-Bājūrī does not appear to be overly concerned with the various understandings of *waḥdat al-wujūd* as *waḥdat al-shuhūd* (oneness of witnessing), which is the proper interpretation of al-Ḥallāj's thought according to Massignon, Mason, and others.

78. See Knysh, *Ibn Arabi in the Later Islamic Tradition,* for details of those who condemned Ibn al-ʿArabī on similar grounds.

79. Gesink, "Chaos on the Earth."

80. See Massignon's works for more views for and against al-Ḥallāj.

81. Shaykh al-Shāghūrī's teachings on *waḥdat al-wujūd* were taken from "Shaykh ʿAbdurrahman Interpreted," recordings of the shaykh and commentary by his student Nuh Keller, and distributed until recently by www.tariqatapes.com. Ibn Taymiyya also recognizes a similar bifurcation, but insists that Ibn al-ʿArabī was of the pantheist category.

82. Tuḥfat al-murīd, 156.

83. Ibid., 157.

84. Ibn al-Jawzi, *Attributes of God,* trans., Bin Hamid ʿAlī, 8. I am indebted to Professor Bin Hamid ʿAlī's summary of the relationship of the *ẓāhir* meaning to the root meaning in the language, which was the inspiration for my reflection on the relationship between Ibn Taymiyyah's use of the term *ẓāhir* and the Ashʿarī conception of *ẓāhir.*

85. *Tuḥfat al-murīd,* 156. "Mā afāda maʿnā lā yaḥtamilu ghayrihi"; I am indebted to Shaykh Faraz Rabbani for helping me to understand the nuanced definitions and meanings of this passage.

86. "[The meaning of *naṣṣ* in al-Laqānī's poem is not] that which opposes the *ẓāhir*, i.e., that which conveys a complete, self-contained meaning that does not imply other than it [i.e., *naṣṣ* in its technical sense]." *Tuḥfat al-murīd*, 156.

87. al-Bājūrī, *Matn Abī Shujāʿ*, 616–17.

88. Ibn al-Jawzī, *Attributes of God*, trans., Bin Hamid ʿAlī, 6.

89. Ibid.

90. Ibid., 18. Ibn Taymiyya's exact words, as translated by Bin Hamid ʿAlī, are "that of it which precedes to the healthy mind of he who understands that language."

91. Ibid.

92. Ibid.

93. *Tuḥfat al-murīd*, 156.

94. The *ṣifāt al-maʿānī* are power, will, knowledge, life, hearing, seeing, speech.

95. *Tuḥfat al-murīd*, 159. Qurʾān 48:10.

96. *Tuḥfat al-murīd*, 157.

97. Ibid., 156. He declares the weaker opinion to be that they are those who lived in the first three centuries of Islam.

98. Ibid., 157–59.

99. This word can be translated as establishing, sitting, cooking something until it is well done, etc. I have thus left it untranslated, in keeping with the discussion on *tafwīḍ*.

100. Ibn Kathīr, *Tafsīr al-Qurʾān al-ʿaẓīm* (Cairo: Maktabat Awlād al-Shaykh li-l-Turāth and Muʾassassat al-Qurṭuba, 2000), 6:320.

101. I have read that Ibn Kathīr also affirmed Ibn Taymiyya's contextual definition of *ẓāhir*, but have not been able to locate this source.

102. Literally, the "howness."

103. See R. M. Frank, "Elements in the Development of the Teaching of Ashʿarī," *Le Muséon* 104 (1991): 141–190. The most important aspect of Frank's discussion is his demonstration that the issue of *kayfiyyah* pertains to corporeal features, and therefor the addition of "without modality" is intended to disassociate corporeality from one's affirmation of one of Allah's attributes. Also cited in Binyamin Abrahamov, "The Bi-lā Kayfa Doctrine and Its Foundations in Islamic Theology," *Arabica: The Journal of Arabic and Islamic Studies* 42, no. 3 (1995): 365–379.

104. This is an answer to those who try to interpret the *tafwīḍ* of other Atharī scholars to be *tafwīḍ al-kayfiyya* rather than *tafwīḍ al-maʿnā*. For there is no intelligible meaning of a *yad* that is unlike any corporeal *yad*, such that any additional attributes (*kayfiyya*) can be superadded to it.

105. See Frank, *Being and their Attributes*.

106. This could be gleaned from al-Nawawī's opinion that one is not required to delve into this subject, ". . . it is not required of people that they plunge into that [discussions of the meaning of the verses pertaining to attributes]." However, he does admit—after mentioning harsh opinions against

kalām—that *kalām* becomes a necessity if it is the only way to remove doubts from one's mind. al-Nawawī, *al-Majmūʿ sharḥ al-muhadhdhab,* 42.

107. Thus they will have to address the issue of whether or not words have original root–linguistic meanings, followed by later derivations of metaphorical usages.

108. Portions of this section on logic served as the basis for a significantly more detailed study of jurists' views on logic between the twelfth and fifteenth centuries. See Spevack "Apples and Oranges."

109. The *Oxford English Dictionary* defines realism as follows "1. Philos. a. The scholastic doctrine of the objective or absolute existence of universals, of which Thomas Aquinas was the chief exponent."

110. Oliver Leaman's review of *Ibn Taymiyya Against the Greek Logicians* (trans. Hallaq) brings to light the fundamental conflict between Ibn Taymiyya's nominalism and the Greek philosophers' realism.

111. As mentioned in chapter 4, and further discussed in my article ("Apples and Oranges"), Ibn Taymiyya's claims regarding hidden heretical ideas within the method itself may have been removed from the *manṭiq* of the later logicians, as al-Bājūrī mentions.

112. *Tuḥfat al-murīd,* 316–17. The following discussion of nominalism and realism reflects some clarifications added to the paperback edition of the present work, and differs slightly from the original hardcover edition.

113. Ibid., 316, line 122 of the poem.

114. Ibn Khaldūn, *The Muqaddimah: An Introduction to History,* trans. Franz Rosenthal (New York: Pantheon Books, 1958), 3:137–147.

115. Aloys Sprenger's translation of al-Kātibī's *Shamsiyya* can be found in Muḥammad Aʿlá b. ʿAlī Tahānawī, *A Dictionary of the Technical Terms Used in the Sciences of the Musalmans,* ed. Mohammad Wajih, Abd al-Haqq, and Gholam Kadir (Calcutta: Asiatic Society of Bengal, 1862), 11.

116. El-Rouayheb, "Opening the Gate," 265. I am not sure what the relationship is between this text and that of Porphyry.

117. al-Bājūrī, *Ḥāshiya al-Bājūrī ʿalā al-sullam fī ʿilm al-manṭiq* (Cairo: Maktaba wa Maṭbaʿa Muḥammad ʿAlī Ṣabīḥ wa Awlādihi, 1966), 30.

118. Ibid.

119. Ibid.

120. Ibid.

121. See Spevack, "Apples and Oranges," where I discuss the implications of this issue in greater detail.

122. Ibid.

123. Al-Bājūrī does not mention them by name here, but based on Ibn Khaldūn's history of logic, these are presumably who are meant, as they are the logicians who wrote before the Arab logicians developed the science to the point that the earlier scholars were no longer mentioned. Ibn Khaldūn, *Muqaddimah,* 3:137–147.

124. Ibid.

125. Sartain, *Jalāl al-Dīn al-Suyūṭī,* 28–32.

126. See Sartain and el-Rouayheb for more on al-Suyūṭī's claims in relation to those around him, including his own teachers.

127. See Spevack, "Apples and Oranges," where I offer examples of monolithic treatment of subjects wherein the logicians in fact differed.

128. al-Bājūrī, *Ḥāshiya al-Bājūrī ʿalā al-sullam*, 32.

129. al-Ghazālī, *Deliverance from Error: An Annotated Translation of al-Munqidh min al-Dalāl and Other Relevant Works of al-Ghazālī*, trans. Richard Joseph McCarthy (Louisville, KY: Fons Vitae, 1980), 65.

130. al-Bājūrī, *Ḥāshiya al-Bājūrī ʿalā al-sullam*, 32–33.

131. The *Mudawwana* is the second most relied upon book in the Mālikī *madhhab*, after Mālik's *Muwaṭṭaʾ*. See Riyāḍ, *Uṣūl al-fatwā*, 494.

132. Ibid., 490–98. Each of these three possible scenarios (strongest proofs, Ibn Qāsim's opinion, and the greatest number of opiners) are a bit more detailed and nuanced in their actual definitions. See Riyāḍ, *Uṣūl al-fatwā*, 493–503 for more detail on the Mālikī conception of *mashhūr*.

133. The issue of the permissibility of *manṭiq* among Māturīdī scholars is not addressed here.

134. al-Bājūrī, *Ḥāshiya al-Bājūrī ʿalā al-sullam*, 31–32.

135. *Tuḥfat al-murīd*, 76–79. Al-Bājūrī's *Risāla fī ʿilm al-tawḥīd* is a good example of general proofs.

136. al-Bājūrī, *Ḥāshiya al-Bājūrī* (commentary on *Umm al-barāhīn*). See p. 14 (after *qawlihi: al-Wujūd*).

137. Wisnovsky, *Avicenna*, 110.

138. Ibid., 128.

139. al-Bājūrī, *Ḥāshiya al-Bājūrī* (commentary on *Umm al-barāhīn*), 37.

140. "If it came into existence on its own, that would lead to a union of equivalence and preponderance." Ibn ʿĀshir, *al-Murshid al-muʿīn*, 3.

141. In addition to al-Bājūrī's reference to a *mīzān* (scale) (*Ḥāshiya al-Bājūrī* [commentary on *Umm al-barāhīn*], 38), Watt also mentions that this refers to a scale (see *Islamic Creeds*, 96), as do commentaries on *al-Murshid al-muʿīn*.

142. *Ḥāshiya al-Bājūrī* (commentary on *Umm al-barāhīn*), 38.

143. The definition of contingent attributes (*aʿrāḍ*) can vary between the sciences or theological sects. In its current usuage, it is, at base, an attribute or property that may come and go, such as warmth, coolness, redness, whiteness, or the likes.

144. See below for the discussion of the proof for Allah's attribute of *baqāʾ*.

145. See William Lane Craig, *Kalām Cosmological Argument* (New York: Barnes and Noble, 1979) for details on other versions of this point, specifically al-Ghazālī's discussion about the number of rotations of celestial bodies being different in number—due to their differing speed of rotations—while simultaneously being equal (i.e., infinite).

146. Presumably the flood in Noah's time.

147. *Tuḥfat al-murīd*, 105.

148. He does, however, address the issue of a multitude of creators by referring to an infinite regress of causality, but this is after proving that the

universe had a beginning by referring to the absurdity of an infinite number of finite things.

149. See Wolfson, *Philosophy of the Kalam*, 663–719, for different conceptions of *kasb*. By al-Bājūrī's time, and prior, the theory completely denied any causality for anything other than Allah.

150. "It is by no means clear that God provides a natural terminator to the regresses"; see Richard Dawkins, *The God Delusion* (Boston: Houghton Mifflin, 2006), 78.

151. This contradicts the Ashʿarī maxim that "whatever undergoes change is in time, and thus created." The proofs are long, but, in short, if an infinite thing undergoes change it would lead to an infinite number of changes in state, which would then lead to two timelines of simultaneously equal and varying lengths.

152. I hope to be able to address the Ashʿarī perspective on these popular philosophical or pseudo-philosophical discussions in the future.

153. Al-Sanūsī, al-Laqānī, al-Taftazānī, and others.

154. I.e., whatever begins needs a cause. Proven in 1a above.

155. I.e., if something beginninglessly eternal comes to an end, it would lead to an infinite regress into the past.

156. Despite its potential roots in pre-Avicennian *kalām*, the explicit statement of Allah's being the necessarily existent by later *mutakallimūn* can be viewed as the source of the ordering of al-Sanūsī's proofs, in that once you have proven Allah to be necessarily existent, all else follows, that is, the impossibility of His nonexistence (the opposite of necessity of existence) entails His beginningless and endless eternality, and so on. However, al-Sanūsī's proofs appear to go beyond this, at least providing detail for each step of the process, perhaps indicating a development in al-Sanūsī not found in Ibn Sīnā. For more on the development of the tenet of necessity of existence, see Robert Wisnovsky, "One Aspect of the Avicennian Turn in Sunnî Theology," *Arabic Sciences and Philosophy* 14, no. 1 (March 2004), 81cf.

157. Ibn Taymiyya, *al-Jawāb al-ṣaḥīḥ li man baddala dīn al-masīḥ*, ed. ʿAlī b. Ḥasan b. Naṣir, ʿAbd al-ʿAzīz b. Ibrāhīm al-ʿAskar, Jamrān b. Muḥammad al-Ḥamadān (Riyadh: Dār al-ʿAṣama, 1999).

158. Ibn Taymiyya, *Answering Those Who Changed the Religion of Jesus Christ* (N.p.: Umm al-Qura, n.d.), 199. This is a partial translation of Ibn Taymiyya's, *al-Jawāb al-ṣaḥīḥ*, with slight modifications.

159. Ibid., 195.

160. Ibn Taymiyya, *Ibn Taymiyya Against the Greek Logicians*, trans. Hallaq, 155.

161. Conditions a, b, and c, above for defining *kalām*.

162. Binyamin Abrahamov, *Islamic Theology: Traditionalism and Rationalism* (Edinburgh: Edinburgh University Press, 1998), 14.

163. al-Bukhārī, *Ṣaḥīḥ al-Bukhārī* (chapter on) "Tafsīr," Sūrat al-Qiṣaṣ.

164. Ibn Kathīr, *Tafsīr al-Qurʾān*, 492.

165. Muḥammad b. Mufliḥ al-Maqdīsī, *al-Ādāb al-sharʿiyya wa-l-minaḥ al-marʿiyya* (Mecca: Maktabat Niẓār Muṣṭafā l-Bāz, 1996), 1:265–266. Ibn

Mufliḥ's treatment of the views of the scholars regarding *kalām* offers a unique glimpse into the varying definitions and views on *kalām* within Atharī circles. See 259–67.

166. Richard J. McCarthy, *The Theology of al-Ash'ari* (Beirut: Imprimerie Catholique, 1953), 134.

Chapter 5

1. The possible reasons for which were discussed in the introduction to this work.

2. Majid Fakhry, *History of Islamic Philosophy* (New York: Columbia University Press, 2004), 333.

3. See J. N. D. Anderson, *Islamic Law in Africa* (London: F. Cass, 1970), 103.

4. See Suzanne Pinckney Stetkevych, "From Text to Talisman: Al-Būṣīrī's *Qasīdat al-Burdah* (*Mantle Ode*) and the Supplicatory Ode," *Journal of Arabic Literature* 37, no. 2 (2006): 145–89.

5. Abbas Amanat, "The Harmony of Natural Law and Shari'a in Islamist Theology," in *Shari'a: Islamic Law in the Contemporary Context*, ed. Abbas Amanat and Frank Griffel (Stanford, CA: Stanford University Press, 2007), 38–61.

6. Presumably a reference to the influence of Karl A. Wittfogel's book *Oriental Despotism*.

7. Sachau, *Muhammedanisches Recht nach schafītischer Lehre*.

8. Snouck Hurgronje, in *Verspreide Geschriften*.

9. Th. W. Juynboll, "Bādjūrī (or Baydjūrī), Ibrāhīm b. Muḥammad," *EI*^{2}.

10. Ibid.

11. See Cuno and Spevak, "al-Bājūrī."

12. Martin van Bruinessen, "Kitab Kuning: Books in Arabic Script Used in the Pesantren Milieu," *Bijdragen tot de Tāl-, Land- en Volkenkunde* 146 (1990): 226–69, online: <http://www.let.uu.nl/Martin.vanBruinessen/personal/publications/kitab_kuning.htm> [Dec. 3, 2007].

13. Muḥammad Bin Abdur Rahman Ebrahim, *Shamā'il Tirmidhi: With Commentary Khass'il Nabawi sallallhu ʿalayhi wasallam* (Noida, India: Islamic Books Service, 2002).

14. Moulavi M. H. Babu Sahib, *The Tenets of Islam: Being a Translation and Extensive Commentary on Kitāb jawharat al-tawḥīd* (Singapore: Islamic Religious Council Centre of Singapore, 2000).

15. Abd al-Raziq, "Arabic Literature," 762. Abd al-Raziq leaves out the "r" in Abyārī.

16. Sachau, *Muhammedanisches Recht nach schafiitischer Lehre*, xxii.

17. A video of the *ijāza*-granting ceremony can be found online: <http://alimamalallama.com/section.php?id=74&cat_id=2&mm_id=608#the_player>.

18. I am indebted to Kallas's student Shaykh Faraz Rabbani for narrating this statement.

19. Gran, "Quest," 68.

20. As mentioned previously, after a certain point, Sufi and *taṣawwūf* became blanket terms for the practitioners and the methods that dealt with spiritual purification, shunning worldliness, and achieving some sort of unitive experience.

21. This is also the impression of al-Bājūrī that Sachau gleaned from his *fiqh* works; he adds "he corrects many a mistake, gives a sharper form to many a rule, and adds a lot of facts worth knowing, be it from his own or from other sources." Sachau, *Muhammedanisches Recht nach schafiitischer Lehre*, xxii.

Bibliography

ʿAbd al-Raḥīm. "Bājūrī, Shaykh Ibrahim, al-," *Coptic Encyclopedia*. Edited by Aziz Suryal Atiya. Macmillan, 1991. Online: <http://ccdl.libraries.claremont.edu/cdm4/item_viewer.php?CISOROOT=/cce&CISOPTR=298>.

ʿAbd al-Raḥmān b. ʿAbd al-Laṭīf b. ʿAbdullah Āl al-Shaykh, *Mashāhir al-ʿulamā' najd wa ghayrihā*. Riyadh: Dār al-Yamāmah lil-Baḥth wa-al-Tarjamah wa-al-Nashr, 1974.

Abd al-Raziq, M. H. "Arabic Literature Since the Beginning of the Nineteenth Century." *BSOAS* 2, no. 4 (1923): 755–62.

Abī Hijla, ʿImād al-Dīn. *al-Najjūm al-lāmiʿa fī thaqāfat al-Muslim al-jāmīʿa*. Amman: Dār al-Rāzi, 1999.

Abrahamov, Binyamin. *Islamic Theology: Traditionalism and Rationalism*. Edinburgh: Edinburgh University Press, 1998.

Abū Shāma. *Kitāb al-rawḍatayn fī akhbār al-dawlatayn*. 2 vols in 1. Cairo: Matbaʿat Wādī l-Nīl, 1287/1870–71.

Ahmad, Ahmad Atif. "Structural Interrelations of Theory and Practice in Islamic Law: A Study of takhrij al-furuʿ ʿala al-uṣūl Literature." PhD diss., Harvard, 2005.

Algar, Hamid. "The Naqshbandī Order: A Preliminary Survey of its History and Significance." *Studia Islamica* 44 (1976): 123–52.

Alwani, Tahir al-. *Source Methodology in Islamic Jurisprudence: Usul al-fiqh al-Islami*. Translated by Yusuf Talal DeLorenzo and A. S. al-Shaykh-Ali. Herndon, VA: International Institute of Islamic Thought, 1994.

Amanat, Abbas. "The Harmony of Natural Law and Shari'a in Islamist Theology," in *Shari'a: Islamic Law in the Contemporary Context*,

Anderson, J. N. D. *Islamic Law in Africa*. London: F. Cass, 1970.

Ansari, Muhammad Abdul Haq. *Sufism and Shari'a: A Study of Shaykh Ahmad Sirhindī's Effort to Reform Sufism*. Leicester, UK: Islamic Foundation, 1986.

Anṣārī, Zakariyya al-. *Ghāyat al-wuṣūl fī sharḥ lubb al-uṣūl*. Egypt: Dār al-Kutub al-ʿArabiyya, n.d.

Bājūrī, Ibrāhīm al-. *Durar al-ḥisān*. Online: <http://makhtota.ksu.edu.sa/makhtota/339/5> [May 30, 2012].

———. *Hādhihi ḥāshiya al-ʿallāma al-Shaykh Ibrāhīm al-Bājūrī ʿalā risālat al-ustādh al-Shaykh Muḥammad al-Faḍālī fī Lā ilāha illa-Llāh*. Cairo: Maṭbaʿat ʿUthmān ʿAbd al-Rāziq, 1301/1884.

———. Hādhihi ḥāshiya Ibrāhīm al-Bājūrī ʿalā matn al-shamāʾil al-Muḥammadiyya li-al-Muḥammad b. ʿĪsā al-Tirmidhī. Egypt: Maṭbaʿat al-Saʿda, 1925.

———. *Ḥāshiya al-Bājūrī*. Handwritten copy. Harvard Widener Library. Catalog number 2274.823.568.1861. (A commentary on al-Sanūsī's *Umm al-barāhīn*.)

———. *Ḥāshiya al-Bājūrī ʿalā al-sullam fī ʿilm al-manṭiq*. Cairo: Maktaba wa Maṭbaʿa Muḥammad ʿAlī Ṣabīḥ wa Awlādihi, 1966. (A commentary on al-Akhḍarī.)

———. *Ḥāshiya Ibrāhīm al-Bājūrī l-musammā bi-l-mawahib al-laduniyya ʿalā l-shamāʾil al-Muḥammadiyya*. Egypt: al-Maṭbaʿa al-Baḥiyya, 1883.

———. *Ḥāshiya al-Shaykh Ibrāhīm al-Bayjūrī ʿalā Sharḥ al-ʿAlāma Ibn al-Qāsim al-Ghazzī ʿalā Matn al-Shaykh Abī Shujāʿ*. Beirut: Dār al-Kutub al-ʿIlmiyya, 1999.

———. *Ḥāshiya Ibrāhīm al-Bājūrī al-musammāt bi-Taḥqīq al-maqām ʿalā Kifāyat al-ʿawāmm fī ʿilm al-kalām li-Muḥammad al-Faḍālī*. Būlāq: al-Maṭbaʿa al-Azhariyya, 1329/1906.

———. *al-Musalsalat*. Cairo: Dār al-Kutub al-Miṣriyya. Catalog no. 252. *Muṣṭalaḥ ḥadīth*.

———. *Risāla fī ʿilm al-tawḥīd*. See Shirbīnī, Muḥammad al-Nashshār.

———. *Tuḥfat al-murīd*. Beirut: Dār al-Kutub al-ʿIlmiyya, 1995.

———. *Tuḥfat al-murīd ʿalā jawharat al-tawḥīd*. Critical edition by ʿAlī Muḥammad Jumʿa. Cairo: Dār al-Salām, 2006.

Barmāwī, Ibrāhīm b. Muḥammad al-. Ḥāshiya Ibrāhīm al-Barmāwī al-Shāfiʿī ʿalā Sharḥ al-Ghāya li-Ibn Qāsim Ghazzī. Cairo: al-Maṭbaʿa al-ʿĀmira, 1287/1870.

Bāṣabrayn, ʿAlī b. Aḥmad. *Ithmid al-ʿaynayn fī baʿḍ ikhtilāf al-shaykhayn*. Beirut: Dār al-Fikr al-Muʿāṣir; Damascus: Dār al-Fikr, 1996.

Bā Sūdān, ʿAbdallāh b. Aḥmad. *Zaytūnat al-ilqāḥ: Sharḥ manẓūmat Ḍawʾ al-miṣbāḥ fī aḥkām al-nikāḥ*. Jedda: Dār al-Minhāj, 2002.

Bayṭār, ʿAbd al-Razzaq al-. *Ḥilyat al-bashar fī tārīkh al-qarn al-thālith ʿashar*. Damascus, 1961–63.

Bayṭār, ʿAbd al-Razzāq, and Muḥammad Bahjat Bayṭār. *Ḥilyat al-bashar fī tārīkh al-qarn al-thālith ʿashar*. Beirut: Majmaʿ al-Lugha al-ʿArabiyya, 1993; repr. of 1961.

Bencheneb, H. "al-Sanūsī, Abū ʿAbd Allāh Muḥammad b. Yūsuf b. ʿUmar b. Shuʿayb." *EI*[2]. Online: <http://www.encislam.brill.nl/subscriber/entry?entry=islam_COM-1001> [October 20, 2007].

Berkey, Jonathan P. "Culture and Society During the Late Middle Ages," in the *Cambridge History of Egypt*, Vol. 1: *Islamic Egypt*. Edited by Carl F. Petry. Cambridge, UK: Cambridge University Press, 1998.

Brockopp, Jonathan E. "Early Islamic Jurisprudence in Egypt: Two Scholars and their Mukhtasars." *IJMES* 30, no. 2 (May 1998): 167–82.

Bukhārī, Muḥammad b. Ismāʿīl al-. *Ṣaḥīḥ al-Bukhārī*. Critical edition by Jawād ʿAfānah. Amman: n.p., 2003.

Būṭī, Muḥammad Saʿīd al-. *al-Lāmadhhabiyya: Akhṭar bidʿa tuhaddidu al-sharīʿa al-Islāmiyya*. Damascus: Maktabat al-Fārābī, 1985.

Chamberlain, Michael. "The Crusader Era and the Ayyubid Dynasty," in *Cambridge History of Egypt*, Vol. 1: *Islamic Egypt*. Edited by Carl F. Petry. Cambridge, UK: Cambridge University Press, 1998.

Chaumont, Eric. "Encore au sujet de l'Ash'arisme d'Abu Ishaq Ash-Shirazi." *Studia Islamica* 74 (1991): 167–77.

———. "al-Shirazi, al-Sheikh al-Imam Abu Ishaq Ibrahim b. 'Ali b. Yusuf al-Firuzabadi." *EI*². Online: <http://www.encislam.brill.nl> [March 19, 2007].

Chittick, William C. *Faith and Practice of Islam: Three Thirteenth-Century Sufi Texts*. Albany: State University of New York Press, 1992.

Commins, David Dean. The Wahhabi mission and Saudi Arabia, London: I. B. Tauris, 2006.

Coulson, Noel J. *A History of Islamic Law*. Edinburgh: Edinburgh University Press, 1971.

Craig, William Lane. *Kalām Cosmological Argument*. New York: Barnes and Noble, 1979.

Cuno, Kenneth M., and Aaron Spevack. "al-Bājūrī, Ibrāhīm b. Muḥammad." *EI*³.

Dawkins, Richard. *The God Delusion*. Boston: Houghton Mifflin, 2006.

Delanoue, Gilbert. *Moralistes et politiques musulmans dans l'Egypte du XIXe siècle (1798–1882)*. 2 vols. Cairo: Institut français d'archéologie orientale du Caire, 1982.

Douglas, Elmer H. "Al-Shādhilī, A North African Ṣūfī, According to Ibn al-Ṣabbāgh." *Muslim World* 38, no. 4 (October 1948): 257–79.

———. *The Mystical Teachings of al-Shadhili: Including his Life, Prayers, Letters, and Followers: A Translation from the Arabic of Ibn al-Sabbagh's Durrat al-asrār wa tuḥfat al-abrār*. Albany: State University of New York Press, 1993.

Ebrahim, Muhammad Bin Abdur Rahman. *Shamā'il Tirmidhi: With Commentary Khass'il Nabawi sallallhu ʿalayhi wasallam*. Noida, India: Islamic Books Service, 2002.

Fahey, R. S. *Enigmatic Saint: Ahmad ibn Idris and the Idrisi Tradition*. Evanston, IL: Northwestern University Press, 1990.

Fakhry, Majid. *A History of Islamic Philosophy*. New York: Columbia University Press, 2004.

Fletcher, Madeleine. "The Almohad Tawhid: Theology which Relies on Logic." *Numen* 38, Fasc. 1. (June 1991): 110–27.

Frank, R. M. *Being and their Attributes: The Teaching of the Basrian School of Mu'tazila in the Classical Period*. Albany: State University of New York Press, 1978.

Friedlander, Shems. *The Whirling Dervishes*. Albany: State University of New York Press, 1992.

Fuḍālī, Muḥammad al-. "The Sufficiency of the Commonality in the Science of Scholastic Theology," in *Development of Muslim Theology, Jurisprudence, and Constitutional Theory*, edited by Duncan B. MacDonald. Lahore: Premier Book House, 1960.

Gerber, Haim. *Islamic Law and Culture, 1600–1840*. Leiden and Boston: Brill, 1999.

Gesink, Indira Falk. " 'Chaos on the Earth': Subjective Truths versus Communal Unity in Islamic Law and the Rise of Militant Islam." *American Historical Review* 108, no. 3 (June 2003). Online: <http://www.historycooperative.org/journals/ahr/108.3/gesink.html#REF15> [January 13, 2008].

———. Islamic Reform and Conservatism: Al-Azhar and the Evolution of Modern Sunni Islam. London: Tauris Academic Studies, 2010.

Ghazālī, Abū Ḥāmid al-. *Deliverance from Error: An Annotated Translation of al-Munqidh min al-Dalāl and Other Relevant Works of al-Ghazālī*. Translated by Richard Joseph McCarthy. Louisville, KY: Fons Vitae, 1980.

Goldschmidt, Arthur. *Biographical Dictionary of Modern Egypt*. Boulder, CO: Lynne Rienner Publishers, 2000.

Gran, Peter. *Islamic Roots of Capitalism: Egypt, 1760–1840*. Foreword by Afaf Lutfi al-Sayyid Marsot. Austin: University of Texas Press, 1979.

———. "Quest for a Historical Interpretation of the Life of Shaykh al-Azhar Ibrahim al-Bajuri (1784–1860)—an Agenda Article," in *Islāh am taḥdith Miṣr fī ʿasr Muḥammad ʿAlī*. Cairo: al-Majlis al-Aʿla, 1999.

———. "Rediscovering al-Attar." *Al-Ahram Weekly Online*, no. 770. 24–30 November 2005. Online: <http://weekly.ahram.org.eg/2005/770/cu4.htm> [May 30, 2012].

———. Review of *Ṭuruq and Ṭuruq-linked Institutions in Nineteenth-century Egypt: A Historical Study in Organizational Dimensions of Islamic Mysticism* by F. de Jong. *IJMES* 11, no. 4 (July 1980): 549–50.

Hallaq, Wael. *A History of Islamic Legal Theories: An Introduction to Sunnī uṣūl al-fiqh*. New York: Cambridge University Press, 1997.

———. "Was the Gate of Ijtihad Closed?" *IJMES* 16 (1984): 3–41.

Hanif, N. Biographical Encyclopedia of Sufis: Africa and Europe. New Delhi: Sarup and Sons, 2002.

Heer, Nicholas, ed. *Islamic Law and Jurisprudence*. Seattle: University of Washington Press, 1990.

Ḥibshī, Abdullah Muḥammad al-. Jāmiʿ al-shurūḥ wa-l-ḥawāshī: muʿjam shāmil li-asmāʾ al-kutub al-mashrūḥa fī l-turāth al-islāmii wa-bayān shurūḥiha. 3 vols. Abu Dhabi: Abu Dhabi Authority for Culture and Heritage Cultural Foundation, 2004.

Ḥilmī, Muḥammad Rajab. *Burhān al-azhar fī manāqib al-Shaykh al-Akbar*. Egypt: Maṭbaʿat al-Saʿāda, 1908/1909[?].

Hourani, Albert. *A History of the Arab Peoples*. Cambridge, MA: Harvard University Press, 1991.

Ibn ʿĀshir. *al-Murshid al-muʿīn*. Casablanca: Dār al-Furqān li-l-Nashr al-Ḥadīth, 2002.

Ibn Ḥajar al-Haytamī. *al-Fatāwā al-ḥadithiyya*. Egypt: Muṣṭafā l-Bābī l-Ḥalabī, 1970.

Ibn al-Jawzī, ʿAbd al-Raḥmān. *The Attributes of God: Ibn al-Jawzī's dafʿshuba al-tashbih bi-akaff al-tanzih*. Translated and introduced by Abdullah bin Hamid Ali. Bristol, UK: Amal Press, 2006.

Ibn Kathīr. *Tafsīr al-Qurʾān al-ʿaẓīm*. 15 vols. Cairo: Maktabat Awlād al-Shaykh li-l-Turāth and Muʾassasat Qurṭaba, 2000.

Ibn Khaldun. *The Muqaddimah: An Introduction to History*. Translated from the Arabic by Franz Rosenthal. 3 vols. New York: Pantheon Books, 1958.

Ibn Khallikān. *Wafayāt al-aʿyān wa-anbāʾ abnāʾ al-zamān*. Beirut: Dār Ṣādir, 1994.

Ibn al-Ṣalāḥ. *Ṭabaqāt al-fuqahāʾ al-Shāfiʿiyya*. Vol. 1. Beirut: Dār al-Bashāʾir al-Islāmiyya, 1992.

Ibn Ṭāhir al-Baghdādī, ʿAbd al-Qāhir. *Moslem Schisms and Sects (al-fark bain and firak) Being the History of the Various Philosophic Systems Developed in Islam*. Translated from the Arabic with introduction and notes by Abraham S. Halkin. 2 vols. Tel Aviv: Palestine Publishing, 1935.

Ibn Taymiyya, Aḥmad b. ʿAbd al-Halīm. *Ibn Taymiyya Against the Greek Logicians*. Translated and introduced by Wael Hallaq. Oxford: Clarendon Press and New York: Oxford University Press, 1993.

———. *al-Jawāb al-Ṣaḥīḥ li man baddala dīn al-masīḥ*. Edited by ʿAlī b. Ḥasan b. Naṣir, ʿAbd al-ʿAzīz b. Ibrāhīm al-ʿAskar, Jamrān b. Muḥammad al-Ḥamadān. 7 vols. Riyadh: Dār al-ʿAṣama, 1999. Translated to English as *Answering Those Who Changed the Religion of Jesus Christ*. N.p.: Umm al-Qura, n.d.

———. *Majmuʿat al-fatāwā*. 32 vols. Mansura: Dār al-Wafāʾ, 2005.

———. *Qāʿida jalīla fī l-tawaṣṣul wa-l-wasīla*. ʿAjmān: Maktabat al-Furqān, 2001.

Ibrahim, Mohammed Zakyi. "Communication Models in the Holy Qur'an: God-Human Interaction." PhD diss., McGill University, Montreal, 1997.

Idris, H. R. "Ibn Abi Zayd al-Kayrawani, Abū Muḥammad ʿAbd Allah b. Abī Zayd ʿAbd al-Raḥmān." *EI*[2]. Online: <http://www.encislam.brill.nl/subscriber//entry?entry=islam_SIM-3061> [September 13, 2007].

Jabartī, ʿAbd al-Raḥmān al-. 'Ajā'ib al-āthār fī al-tarājim wa-al-akhbār. Cairo: Dār al-Kutub al-Miriyya, 1998, 25.

Jackson, Sherman A. "Islam(s) East and West: Clash of Imaginations?" (Lecture delivered at Harvard Divinity School, March 2007). Online: <http://www.hds.harvard.edu/cswr/resources/lectures/sjackson.html> [January 13, 2008].

———. *Islamic Law and the State: The Constitutional Jurisprudence of Shihāb al-Dīn al-Qarāfi*. Leiden and New York: E. J. Brill, 1996.

Jong, F. de. Ṭuruq and Ṭuruq-linked Institutions in Nineteenth-Century Egypt: A Historical Study in Organizational Dimensions of Islamic Mysticism. Leiden: Brill, 1978.

Juynboll, Th. W. "Bādjūrī (or Baydjūrī), Ibrāhīm b. Muḥammad." *EI*^{2}. Online: <http://www.encislam.brill.nl/subscriber/entry?entry=islam_SIM-1014> [August 16, 2007].

Kalbī, Muḥammad b. Aḥmad Ibn Juzay al-. *al-Qawānīn al-fiqhiyya*. ʿAyn Malīla, Algeria: Dār al-Hudā, 2000.

Keller, Nuh. "The Place of Tasawwuf in Traditional Islam." Online: <http://www.masud.co.uk/ISLAM/nuh/sufitlk.htm> [January 13, 2008].

———, trans. *Reliance of the Traveller*. Translated from the Arabic *ʿUmdat al-sālik wa ʿuddat al-nāsik*. Evanston, IL: Sunna Books 1991; 1994.

———. *Sea Without Shore: A Manual of the Sufi Path*. Amman: Sunna Books, 2011.

Kenny, Joseph P. "Muslim theology as presented by M. b. Yusuf as-Sanusi: especially in his al-Aqida al-Wusta." PhD diss., Edinburgh University, 1970.

Khan, Geoffrey. "Early Arabic Grammatical Theory: Heterogeneity and Standardization." Review of *Early Arabic Grammatical Theory: Heterogeneity and Standardization* by Jonathan Owens. *BSOAS* 55, no. 3 (1992): 546–47.

Knysh, Alexander D. *Ibn Arabi in the Later Islamic Tradition: The Making of a Polemical Image in Medieval Islam*. Albany: State University of New York Press, 1999.

Kurdī, Muḥammad Amīn al-. *Tanwīr al-qulūb fī muʿāmalat ʿallām al-ghuyūb*. Aleppo: Dār al-Qalam al-ʿArabī, 1991.

Laoust, H. "Ibn Taymiyya, Taqī al-Dīn Aḥmad Ibn Taymiyya." *EI*^{2}. Online: <http://www.encislam.brill.nl/subscriber/entry?entry=islam_SIM-3388> [January 18, 2008]

Leaman, Oliver. Review of *Ibn Taymiyyah Against the Greek Logicians* by Wael B. Hallaq. *BSOAS* 58, no. 1. (1995): 123–24.

Leiser, Gary. "Hanbalism in Egypt before the Mamluks." *Studia Islamica* 54 (1981): 155–58.

Macdonald, Duncan B. *Development of Muslim Theology, Jurisprudence and Constitutional Theory: 1863–1943*. New York: Charles Scribner's, 1903.

Madelung, W. "al-Taftazānī." EI.^{2}

Maḥāmilī, Aḥmad b. Muḥammad al-. al-Lubbāb fī fiqh al-Shafiʿī. Medina: Dār al-Bukhārī, 1416/1996.

Makdisi, George. "Ashʿarī and the Ashʿarites in Islamic Religious History." [1] *Studia Islamica* 17 (1962): 37–80 and [2] *Studia Islamica* 18 (1963): 19–39.

———. "Ibn Taymiyah." Online: <http://www.muslimphilosophy.com/it/itya.htm> [May 2, 2007].

———. "Ibn Taymiyya: A Sufi of the Qadiriya Order." *American Journal of Arabic Studies* 1 (1973): 118–29.

———. "Muslim Institutions of Learning in Eleventh-Century Baghdad." *BSOAS* 24, no. 1 (1961): 1–56.

———. *The Rise of Humanism in Classical Islam and the Christian West*. Edinburgh: Edinburgh University Press, 1990.

Maqdīsī, Muḥammad b. Mufliḥ al-. *al-Ādāb al-shar'iyya wa-l-minaḥ al-mar'iyya*. Vol. 1. Mecca: Maktabat Nizār Muṣṭafā l-Bāz, 1996.

Maqrīzī, Aḥmad b. 'Alī. *al-Mawā'iẓ wa-l-i'tibār fī dhikr al-khiṭaṭ wa-l-āthār*. 6 vols. London: Mu'assasat al-Furqān li-l-Turāth al-Islāmī, 2002.

———. *al-Mawā'iẓ wa-l-i'tibār fī dhikr al-khiṭaṭ wa-l-āthār*. London: Mu'assasat al-Furqān li-l-Turāth al-Islāmī, 2002.

Massignon, Louis. *Hallaj: Mystic and Martyr*. Translated, edited, and abridged by Herbert Mason. Princeton, NJ: Princeton University Press, 1994.

———. *The Passion of al-Hallaj: Mystic and Martyr of Islam*. Translated from the French with a biographical foreword by Herbert Mason. 3 vols. Princeton, NJ: Princeton University Press, 1982.

Mayer, Ann. "The Shari'a: A Methodology or a Body of Substantive Rules?" in *Islamic Law and Jurisprudence*, edited by Nicholas Heer. Seattle: University of Washington Press, 1990.

McCarthy, Richard J. *The Theology of al-Ash'ari*. Beirut: Imprimerie Catholique, 1953.

Melchert, Christopher. *The Formation of the Sunni Schools of Law, 9th–10th Centuries C.E.* Leiden and New York: Brill, 1997.

Metcalf, Barbara Daly. Islam in South Asia in Practice. Princeton, NJ: Princeton University Press, 2009.

Miṣrī, Aḥmad b. al-Naqīb al-. 'Umdat al-sālik wa 'uddat al-nāsik. Edited by Ṣāliḥ Mu'adhdhin and Muḥammad al-Ṣabbāgh. Damascus: Maktabat al-Ghazālī, 1405/1985.

Mitchell, Timothy. Colonising Egypt. New York: Cambridge University Press, 1988.

Motzki, Harald. *The Origins of Islamic Jurisprudence: Meccan Fiqh before the Classical Schools*. Translated from the German by Marion H. Katz. Leiden: Brill, 2002.

Mubārak, 'Alī. *al-Khiṭaṭ al-Tawfīqiyya al-jadīda li-Miṣr al-Qāhira wa-muduniha wa-bilādiha al-qadīma wa-shahīra*. 15 vols. Cairo: Maṭba'at Dār al-Kutub, 1969.

Nasr, Seyyed Hussein. "Fakhr al-Din al-Razi," in A History of Muslim Philosophy, edited by M. M. Sharif Wiesbaden: Harrassowitz, 1963.

Nawawī, Abī Zakariyā Muḥyī l-Dīn b. Sharaf al-. *al-Majmū' sharḥ al-muhadhdhab*. 18 vols. Cairo: Maṭba'at al-'Āṣimah, 1966–69. See Haddad's translation of al-Nawawī's statement to this effect online: <http://www.livingislam.org/n/tawil_e.html> [November 29, 2007].

———. *al-Maqasid: Nawawi's Manual of Islam*. Translation and notes by Nuh Ha Mim Keller. Beltsville, MD: Amana Publications, 2002.

Newman, Daniel. *An Imam in Paris: al-Tahtawi's Visit to France (1826–31)*. London: Saqi Books, 2009.

Nguyen, Martin. "The Confluence and Construction of Traditions: al-Qushayrī (d. 465/1072) and the Intersection of Qur'ānic Exegesis, Theology, and Sufism." PhD diss., Harvard University, 2009.

Qayrawānī, ʿAbdallāh b. ʿAbd al-Raḥmān b. Abī Zayd al-. *Kitāb al-jāmiʿ fī l-sunan wa-l-ādāb wa-l-māghāzī wa-l-tārīkh*. Beirut: Muʾassassat al-Risāla and Tunis: al-Maktabat al-ʿAtīqa, 1982.

Quwaysinī, Ḥasan b. Darwīsh. *Sharḥ naẓm al-Sullam al-munawraq fī l-manṭiq li-ʿAbd al-Raḥmān al-Akhḍarī*. al-Dār al-Bayḍāʾ: Dār al-Rashād al-Ḥadītha, 2006.

Reinhart, A. Kevin. "Kitāb al-Luma' fī uṣūl al-fiqh: le Livre des Rais illuminant les fondements de la compréhension de la loi: Traité de théorie légale musulmane." Review by Eric Chaumont. *BSOAS* 64, no. 3 (2001): 405–06.

Riyāḍ, Muḥammad. *Uṣūl al-fatwā wa-l-qaḍāʾ fī l-madhhab al-Mālikī*. Casablanca: Maṭbaʿat al-Najāḥ al-Jadīda, 1996.

Rouayheb, Khaled el-. "Opening the Gate of Verification: The Forgotten Arab-Islamic Florescence of the Seventeenth Century." *IJMES* 38, no. 2 (May 2006): 263–81.

———. "Sunnī Muslim Scholars on the Status of Logic." Islamic Law and Society 11, no. 2 (2004): 213–32. Online: <http://www.jstor.org/stable/3399304>.

Sabūnī, Abū ʿUthmān Ismāʿīl b. ʿAbd al-Raḥmān al-. *The Creed of the Pious Predecessors*. Translated anonymously. Edited by Badr Abdullah ibn al-Badr. Brixton, UK: Masjid Ibn Taymiyya, 1999.

Sachau, Eduard. *Muhammedanisches Recht nach schafiitischer Lehre*. Stuttgart: W. Spemann, 1897.

Sahib, Moulavi M. H. Babu. *The Tenets of Islam: Being a Translation and Extensive Commentary on Kitāb jawharat al-tawḥīd*. Singapore: Islamic Religious Council Centre of Singapore, 2000.

Sanūsī, al-. *Muqaddima Ḥashiya al-Bājūrī ʿalā Matn al-Sanūsī*, or *Umm al-barāhīn*. (Publication information unavailable.) Handwritten copy from Princeton University Library. Call Number 2274.823.568.1861.

———. *Umm al-barāhīn*. With commentary of Muḥammad al-Miṣrī. Private manuscript library in Mali. Online: <http://www.loc.gov/exhibits/mali/mali-exhibit.html> [January 13, 2008].

Sarrio, Diego R. "Spiritual Anti-Elitism: Ibn Taymiyya's Doctrine of Sainthood (Walāya)." *Islam and Christian-Muslim Relations* 22, no. 3 (2011): 276–77.

Sartain, E. M. *Jalāl al-Dīn al-Suyūṭī: Biography and Background*. 2 vols. Cambridge and New York: Cambridge University Press, 1975.

Ṣāwī, Aḥmad b. Muḥammad al-. *Ḥāshiya al-Ṣāwī ʿalā Jawharat al-tawḥīd fī ʿilm al-kalām*. Beirut: Dār al-Kutub al-ʿIlmiyya, 2010.

———. Kitāb Sharḥ al-Ṣāwī ʿalā Jawharat al-tawḥīd. Beirut: Dār Ibn Kathīr, 1997.

Schacht, Joseph. *An Introduction to Islamic Law*. Oxford: Clarendon Press, 1982.

Shaghouri, ʿAbdurrahman. "Shaykh ʿAbdurrahman Interpreted." Private recording and commentary by his student Nuh Keller.

Shamsy, Ahmed el-, "The First Shāfiʿī: The Traditionalist Legal Thought of Abū Yaʿqūb al-Buwayṭī." *Islamic Law and Society* 14, no. 3 (2007).

———. "From Tradition to Law: The Origins and Early Development of the Shāfiʿī School of Law in Ninth-Century Egypt." PhD diss., Harvard University, 2009.

Shaṭṭī, Ḥasan al-. *Mukhtaṣar lawāmiʿ al-anwār al-bahiyya, li-sharḥ al-durra l-muḍiyya fī ʿiqad al-firqa al-marḍiyya*. [Abridgment of al-Safarīnī's work]. Damascus: Ṭubiʿa fī Maṭbaʿat al-Taraqqī, 1931.

Shaybānī, Muḥammad b. Ibrāhīm al- and Aḥmad al-Khāzindār, eds. *Dalīl makhṭūṭāt al-Suyūṭī*. Kuwait: Manshūrāt Markaz al-Makhṭūṭāt, 1995.

Shīrāzī, Abū Isḥāq Ibrāhīm b. ʿAlī b. Yūsuf Fīrūzābādī al-. *al-Ishāra ilā madhhab ahl al-ḥaqq*. Cairo: al-Majlis al-Aʿlā li-l-Shuʿūn al-Islāmiyya, Markaz al-Sīra wa-l-Sunna, 1999.

———. Kitāb al-Maʿūna fī l-jadl. Kuwait: Jamʿīyat Iḥyāʾ al-Turāth al-Islāmī, Markaz al-Makhṭūṭāt wa-l-Turāth, 1987.

———. *al-Lumaʿ fī l-uṣūl al-fiqh*. (Printed with *Takhrīj aḥādīth al-lumaʿ fī l-uṣūl al-fiqh*.) Critical edition and commentary on the *ḥadīth*s found in *al-Lumaʿ* by ʿAbdallāh al-Ghumārī. N.p.: ʿAlām al-Kutub, n.d.

———. *al-Muhadhdhab fī fiqh al-Imām al-Shāfi'ī*. Edited by Muḥammad al-Zuḥaylī. Damascus: Dār al-Qalam; Beirut: al-Dār al-Shāmiyya, 1992–96.

Shirbīnī, Muḥammad al-Nashshār. *Ḥāshiya al-tuḥfa al-saniyya ʿalā l-risālat al-Bājūriyya; wa bi-hāmishihā minḥat al-barāyā bi mā fī l-basmala min al-mazāyā*. Egypt: Maṭbaʿat Muḥammad Muṣṭafā, 1318 [1900].

Smock, David. "Ijtihad: Reinterpreting Islamic Principles for the Twenty-first Century." Online: <http://www.usip.org/pubs/specialreports/sr125.html#work> [January 13, 2008].

Snouck Hurgronje, C. "E Sachau: Muhammedanisches Recht nach schafiitischer Lehre," in *Verspreide Geschriften van C. Snouck Hurgronje*. Vol. 2. Bonn und Leipzig: Kurt Schroeder, 1923–27.

———. "Muhammedanisches Recht nach schafi itischer Lehre von Eduard Sachau." ZDMG 53 (1899).

Spevack, Aaron. "Apples and Oranges: The Logic of the Early and Later Logicians." *Islamic Law and Society* 17, no. 2 (2010).

———. "Jalal al-Din al-Suyuti," in *Essays in Arabic Literary Biography, 1350–1850*, edited by Joseph E. Lowry and Devin J. Stewart. Wiesbaden: Harrassowitz, 2009.

Stetkevych, Suzanne Pinckney. "From Text to Talisman: al-Būṣīrī's *Qasīdat al-Burdah* (*Mantle Ode*) and the Supplicatory Ode." *Journal of Arabic Literature* 37, no. 2 (2006): 145–89.

Subkī, Tāj al-Dīn ʿAbd al-Wahhāb b. ʿAlī, al-. *Ṭabaqāt al-Shafiʿiyya al-kubrā*. Edited by Muṣṭafā ʿAbd al-Qādir Aḥmad ʿAṭā. 6 vols. Beirut: Manshūrāt Muḥammad ʿAlī Bayḍūn, Dār al-Kutub al-ʿIlmiyya, 1999.

Suyūṭī, Jalāl al-Dīn al-. al-Ḥāwī li-l-fatāwī. Beirut: Dār al-Kutub al-ʿIlmiyya, 1983.

———. Ḥusn al-muḥāḍara fī tārīkh Miṣr wa-l-Qāhira. Edited by Muḥammad Abū l-Faḍl Ibrāhīm. Cairo: ʿĪsā al-Bābī l-Ḥalabī, 1967–68.

———. *Sharḥ Maqamāt*. Vol. 2. Edited by Maḥmūd al-Durūbī. Beirut: Muʾassasat al-Risāla, 1989.

———. *Taʾyīd al-ḥaqīqa al-ʿaliyya wa tashyīd al-ṭarīqa al-shādhiliyya*. Critical edition by ʿAbdallāh b. Muḥammad b. al-Ṣiddīq al-Ghumārī l-Ḥasanī. Cairo[?]: al-Maṭbaʿat al-Islāmiyya, 1934.

Swartz, Merlin. "A Seventh-Century Sunni Creed: The Aqida Wasitiya." *Humaniora Islamica* 1 (1973).

Taftazānī, Masʿūd b. ʿUmar al-. *al-Talwīḥ ilā kashf ḥaqāʾiq al-tanqīḥ*. Beirut: Sharikat al-Arqām Ibn Abī l-Arqam, 1998.

Taftāzānī, Saʿd al-Dīn al-. *A Commentary on the Creed of Islam Saʿd al-Dīn al-Taftāzānī on the Creed of Najm al-Dīn al-Nasafī*. Translated by Earl Edgar Elder. New York: Colombia University Press, 1950.

Tahānawī, Muḥammad Aʿlá b. ʿAlī. *A Dictionary of the Technical Terms Used in the Sciences of the Musalmans*. Edited by Mohammad Wajih, Abd al-Haqq, and Gholam Kadir. 2 vols. Calcutta: Asiatic Society of Bengal, 1862.

Ṭaḥḥān, Maḥmūd al-. *Taysīr muṣṭlaḥ al-ḥadīth*. Riyadh: Maktabat al-Maʿārif, n.d.

Tibawi, A. L. "Origin and Character of al-Madrasah." *BSOAS* 25, no. 1/3 (1962): 225–38.

Tobgui, Carl Sharif el-. "Reason, Revelation, and the Reconstitution of Rationality: Taqi al-Din Ibn Taymiyya's Darʿ Taʿārud al-ʿaql wa'l naql, or, 'The Refutation of the Contradiction of Reason and Revelation.'" PhD diss., McGill University, 2012.

Toledano, Ehud R. State and Society in mid-Nineteenth Century Egypt. New York: Cambridge University Press, 1990.

Trimingham, J. Spencer. *The Sufi Orders in Islam*. New York and Oxford: Oxford University Press, 1998.

van Bruinessen, Martin. "Kitab Kuning: Books in Arabic Script Used in the Pesantren Milieu." *Bijdragen tot de Taal-, Land- en Volkenkunde* 146 (1990): 226–69. Online: <http://www.let.uu.nl/Martin.vanBruinessen/personal/publications/kitab_kuning.htm> [December 3, 2007].

Von Schlegell, Barbara R. *Principles of Sufism by al-Qushayri*. Introduction by Hamid Algar. Berkeley, CA: Mizan Press, 1990.

Watt, Montgomery. *Islamic Creeds*. Edinburgh: Edinburgh University Press, 1994.

Wiederhold, Lutz. "Legal Doctrines in Conflict: The Relevance of Madhhab Boundaries to Legal Reasoning in the Light of an Unpublished Treatise on Taqlīd and Ijtihād." *Islamic Law and Society* 3, no. 2 (1996): 234–304.

Wisnovsky, Robert. "Avicenna and the Avicennian Tradition," in The Cambridge Companion to Arabic Philosophy, edited by Peter Adamson and Richard C. Taylor, 92–136. New York: Cambridge University Press, 2005.

———. "One Aspect of the Avicennian Turn in Sunnî Theology." *Arabic Sciences and Philosophy* 14, no. 1 (March 2004), 65–100.

Winter, Michael. *Egyptian Society under Ottoman Rule, 1517–1798*. London and New York, Routledge, 1992.

———. Society and Religion in Early Ottoman Egypt: Studies in the Writing of 'Abd al-Wahhab al-Sha'rānī. New Brunswick, NJ: Transaction, 2007.

Wolfson, Harry Austryn. *The Philosophy of the Kalam*. Cambridge, MA: Harvard University Press, 1976.

Yusuf, Hamza. *The Content of Character: Ethical Sayings of the Prophet Muhammad*. San Francisco: Sandala, 2005.

Zuhayli, Wahba al-. *al-Fiqh al-Islāmī wa adilatuhu*. Vol. 1. Damascus: Dār al-Fikr, 1983.

Index

Made in the USA
Middletown, DE
23 April 2021

38317236R00132